TREASURES FROM PAUL

Philippians

by
KEN CHANT

TREASURES FROM PAUL
Philippians
Ken Chant

Copyright © 2012 by Ken Chant

ISBN 978-1-61529-057-4

Vision Publishing

1672 Main St. E 109

Ramona, CA 92065

1-800-9-VISION

www.booksbyvision.com

All rights reserved worldwide

No part of the book may be reproduced in any manner whatsoever without written permission of the author except in brief quotations embodied in critical articles of reviews.

A NOTE ON GENDER

It is unfortunate that the English language does not contain an adequate generic pronoun (especially in the singular number) that includes without bias both male and female. So *"he, him, his, man, mankind,"* with their plurals, must often do the work for both sexes. Accordingly, wherever it is appropriate to do so in the following pages, please include the feminine gender in the masculine, and vice versa.

FOOTNOTES

A work once fully referenced will thereafter be noted either by "ibid" (the same) or "op. cit." (the work previously cited).

SCRIPTURE TRANSLATIONS

All scripture translations in these pages are my own, unless otherwise noted.

Table of Contents

PREFACE ON WRITERS AND PILGRIMS 5
INTRODUCTION THE JOYFUL LETTER 13
ONE THE SLAVES OF CHRIST 17
TWO THE PRICELESS GRACE OF GOD 25
THREE NEVER ASHAMED 31
FOUR BEGUN – AND FINISHED! 43
FIVE WHEN BAD THINGS HAPPEN TO GOOD PEOPLE 57
SIX WHISPERING HOPE 73
SEVEN MADE IN THE IMAGE OF GOD 87
EIGHT THE MYSTERY OF THE ATONEMENT 103
NINE THE FIVE "SOLAS" 115
TEN ADVANCING IN CHRIST 139
ELEVEN YOU DON'T KNOW ME 163
TWELVE ESCAPING THE PAST 173
THIRTEEN KENOSIS 183
FOURTEEN ASCLEPIUS AND HIS ILK 201
FIFTEEN REJOICE IN THE LORD 215
SIXTEEN THE KISS OF PEACE 225
SEVENTEEN ANXIOUS ABOUT NOTHING 241
EIGHTEEN SELF-SUFFICIENT 255
NINETEEN STRONG IN CHRIST 265

ABBREVIATIONS

Abbreviations commonly used for the books of the Bible are

Genesis	Ge	Habakkuk	Hb
Exodus	Ex	Zephaniah	Zp
Leviticus	Le	Haggai	Hg
Numbers	Nu	Zechariah	Zc
Deuteronomy	De	Malachi	Mal
Joshua	Js		
Judges	Jg		
Ruth	Ru	Matthew	Mt
1 Samuel	1 Sa	Mark	Mk
2 Samuel	2 Sa	Luke	Lu
1 Kings	1 Kg	John	Jn
2 Kings	2 Kg	Acts	Ac
1 Chronicles	1 Ch	Romans	Ro
2 Chronicles	2 Ch	1 Corinthians	1 Co
Ezra	Ezr	2 Corinthians	2 Co
Nehemiah	Ne	Galatians	Ga
Esther	Es	Ephesians	Ep
Job	Jb	Philippians	Ph
Psalm	Ps	Colossians	Cl
Proverbs	Pr	1 Thessalonians	1 Th
Ecclesiastes	Ec	2 Thessalonians	2 Th
Song of Songs	Ca *	1 Timothy	1 Ti
Isaiah	Is	2 Timothy	2 Ti
Jeremiah	Je	Titus	Tit
Lamentations	La	Philemon	Phm
Ezekiel	Ez	Hebrews	He
Daniel	Da	James	Ja
Hosea	Ho	1 Peter	1 Pe
Joel	Jl	2 Peter	2 Pe
Amos	Am	1 John	1 Jn
Obadiah	Ob	2 John	2 Jn
Jonah	Jo	3 John	3 Jn
Micah	Mi	Jude	Ju
Nahum	Na	Revelation	Re

Ca is an abbreviation of *Canticles*, a derivative of the Latin name of the *Song of Solomon*, which is sometimes also called the *Song of Songs*.

PREFACE

ON WRITERS AND PILGRIMS

"Human success," says Sirach (10:5), "comes from the hand of the Lord, but upon writers he confers special honour!" I feel in some measure the truth of those words, for it cannot be other than a high privilege to write about the dazzling themes that are embedded in Paul's *Letter to the Philippians*!

IMPROVING A MASTERPIECE?

Yet I ask myself, can a man increase the brightness of the sun by lighting a candle? Can a clumsy hand do other than disfigure the beauty of a masterpiece? Is it absurd to expect a bucket of gravel to increase the grandeur of a mountain, or a paper petal to enhance the beauty of a perfect rose? Dare I try? The task seems impossible. But perhaps the finger of God will touch my stuttering words and transform them into something more than they are? Perhaps I will be like David, made able to run faster than I can run, and to leap higher (Ps 18:29). Or perhaps it will be with me as it was for the old rabbi –

> As for me, I was like a canal branching out from a river to become a watercourse for a pleasure-garden. I said, "I will water my garden and soak its flower-beds." But then my canal became a river and my river a sea! Again, I will make good teaching shine like the dawn, causing its light to be seen from far away. And again, I will pour out doctrine like prophecy and bequeath it to future generations. And let me assure you that my labour has not been for myself alone but for all those who crave wisdom (Sir 24:30-34).

Sirach first sees himself as a little channel running off a great river, whose purpose is to water a lovely garden. Yet because his ideas are not his own, but come from scripture, and because he clings to sound doctrine, his words are suddenly touched by divine inspiration. He labours, not for his own pleasure but to bring knowledge to people who seek wisdom; therefore his words are fired by a spirit of prophecy. Lo! His small canal becomes a river and his river an ocean! Like the dawn, his teaching will drive back darkness, turning night into full day, and bring radiant light to many generations.

Well, I cannot make such a bold claim for this rivulet of mine, and I do not for a moment suppose that it will reach the extraordinary longevity *Sirach* [1] has attained. But I can hope! And for some readers at least, this babbling brook of human thought may become a stream of divine revelation, and the stream an ocean of transforming truth.

Yet I empathise with the cry of the great Samuel Johnson, who in 1750 launched a new journal, *The Rambler*. He was its main contributor, and aware of the enormity of the task he had laid upon himself, he prayed –

> Almighty God, the giver of all good things, without whose help all labour is ineffectual, and without whose grace all wisdom is folly; grant, I beseech thee, that in this undertaking thy Holy Spirit may not be withheld from me, but that I may promote thy glory, and the salvation of myself and others: grant this, O Lord, for the sake of thy son JESUS CHRIST. Amen. [2]

---

1) Which was first written in Hebrew by Sirach, *circa* 185 B.C., and some fifty years later translated into Greek by his grandson (see his *Prologue* to the translation).

2) Boswell's Life of Samuel Johnson, *Aetat. 41*.

AN INFALLIBLE WORK?

My task is not as onerous as Johnson's, yet I repeat his prayer with all fervency, knowing that I must be even more dependent than he upon the Lord. (3) And if my cry is heeded, and these pages promote the glory of Christ and assist even a few readers to attain a fuller salvation, then my toil will be well requited.

Still, prayer does not preclude the possibilities of human error. Johnson's most famous work was his *Dictionary of the English Language*, published in 1755. Although not the first English dictionary, it was superior to all its predecessors, and remained in use for nearly 180 years. (4) Johnson undergirded his dictionary too with prayer, yet his pleas did not eliminate error. Thus Boswell wrote –

> A few of Johnson's definitions must be admitted to be erroneous. ... (But) it is enough to observe, that his *Preface* announces that he was aware there might be many such in so immense a work; nor was he at all disconcerted when an instance was pointed out to him. A lady once asked him how he came to define *Pastern* (5) as the *knee* of a horse? Instead of making an elaborate defence, as she expected, he at once answered, "Ignorance, madam, pure ignorance." (6)

I too must plead a measure of ignorance, and I crave your pardon for any mistakes you may find herein, either in doctrine or in fact. I make no claim to infallibility. I hope

---

3) It is, after all, a small thing to edit a magazine (I have myself over the years been editor of several different journals); but to touch scripture? – that should make any writer tremble!
4) It was finally replaced in 1928 by the massive *Oxford English Dictionary*.
5) "Pastern" is the part of a horse's hoof where a shackle is fastened. It is well below the knee.
6) Op. cit. *Aetat. 46.*

only that the Lord has helped me to write a book that will offer some measure of spiritual enrichment to its readers.

I must also honestly admit – although I strive to be objective and to adhere to scripture – that these pages probably display some personal prejudice. No one can altogether avoid partiality. However, I doubt that any passage shows the bias Johnson built into some of his definitions. As Boswell says –

> Talking to me upon this subject when we were at Ashbourne in 1777, he (Johnson) mentioned a still stronger instance of the predominance of his private feelings in the composition of this work, than any now to be found in it. "You know, Sir, Lord Gower forsook the old Jacobite interest. When I came to the word *Renegado*, [7] after telling that it meant 'one who deserts to the enemy, a revolter,' I added, 'Sometimes we say a GOWER.' Thus it went to the press; but the printer had more wit than I, and struck it out." [8]

WITHOUT PREJUDICE?

Nonetheless, whether or not I am more objective, or less prejudiced, than Dr Johnson, the unhappy fact remains that a truly objective writer has never yet existed. We are all compounded of a multitude of diverse social and cultural influences that are constantly moulding us into what we are. Hence we each look through a set of eyes that differs in some

---

7) An archaic spelling of "renegade".

8) Op. Cit. Some other quaint examples of Johnson's prejudice are – Pension. "An allowance made to any one without an equivalent. In England it is generally understood to mean pay given to a state hireling for treason to his country." Oats. "A grain which in England is generally given to horses, but in Scotland supports the people." Excise. "A hateful tax levied upon commodities, and adjudged not by the common judges of property, but wretches hired by those to whom excise is paid."

measure from all others. No two people ever see anything exactly the same way, nor are they impacted by words to an equal degree. Words themselves carry a compound of sensations, memories, images, that vary for every person. An entirely detached writer, therefore, lacking all partisanship, free of any personal prejudice, simply cannot be found, nor ever will be in this life.

So here is a reality that we must all humbly acknowledge – arguments that one person finds compelling may not be so persuasive to another. Ideas that stir me deeply may leave another unmoved. "Surely," cries one, "this matter is blindingly obvious!" "Hardly," retorts another, "I don't see it that way at all!" Things that are plain to me may be obscure to others – indeed, because of who they are and the way life has shaped them, they may be *unable* to see them. Or, they may see them in a different colour, or find in them a different value.

One of the startling discoveries of modern science is that human perception of even something so basic as colour is highly subjective. That is, how people see colour, what colours they see, and how many, are strongly influenced by culture. We see what we have been trained to see by our parents and by the society in which we were raised. Colour recognition is learned, and in different cultures people learn it differently. If we humans are incapable of seeing even bright colours in the same way, it is hardly surprising if we cannot agree on vastly more profound issues!

So no two people will ever get exactly the same meaning out of a book, even the Bible, or be impacted by it in exactly the same way. In the end, the most any interpreter of scripture can truthfully say is, "This is how I understand the words of the Bible." And how each interpreter sees scripture is shaped to a greater or lesser measure by who they are – that is, by presumptions and prejudices of which they may not even be aware. So while the *Bible* certainly speaks with complete authority, *my* book, with equal certainty, does not, nor does any other. You, dear reader, must judge for yourself whether or not *my* reading of scripture captures its truth and meaning for *you*. Dogmatism belongs only to a small number of biblical ideas; for the rest, there is room for a wide diversity of opinion, interpretation, and shades of meaning.

NO OBJECTIVE TRUTH?

I do not mean that there is *no* objective truth. Some things, of course, must be true for every rational person [9] – that day and night follow each other; that we are presently alive yet must die; that food, drink, and rest are essential for life; that no new-born baby can speak fluently; and a thousand other facts. In scripture, too, certain truths are so clearly stated, and so manifestly fixed by God, that no room remains for dissent. But there are not many such. Large areas of Christian belief and practice are open to diverse understanding and application. And the more abstract the ideas under discussion, the more likely there will be dissent among Bible readers.

The Bible is a book, and like any other it must be read intelligently, understood reasonably, and applied fairly and practically. That pathway will be trod by its readers in many different ways. It is a path I have tried to follow in my own way, and to stick to closely. But I have probably wandered unaware off the track here and there!

The same Dr Samuel Johnson, in 1749 wrote a tragic play *Irene*, which survived only nine performances; about which Boswell writes –

---

[9] Unless, of course, one is a solipsist who insists that nothing is actually knowable, except that the self exists. Everything else, for all we know or can prove, may simply (so they say) be a delusion! In other words, I can be reasonably sure that *I* exist, since here I am thinking about myself; but I cannot be sure that you do, for you may be only an invention of my mind! For a Christian, of course, who accepts the witness of scripture, all such solipsistic propositions are nonsense.

When asked how he felt upon the ill success of his tragedy, he replied, "Like the Monument;" meaning that he continued firm and unmoved as that column. And let it be remembered, as an admonition to the *genus irritabile* [10] of dramatic writers, that this great man, instead of peevishly complaining of the bad taste of the town, submitted to its decision without a murmur. He had, indeed, upon all occasions, a great deference for the general opinion: "A man (said he) who writes a book, thinks himself wiser or wittier than the rest of mankind; he supposes that he can instruct or amuse them, and the public to whom he appeals, must, after all, be the judges of his pretensions." [11]

With those sentiments I fully agree. That is, every writer is guilty of the arrogance of supposing that he is "wiser and wittier than the rest of mankind", especially if we presume to be teachers rather than mere entertainers. Yet we are rescued from pride if we willingly accede to our readers' judgment without a murmur. Thus I am happy to show due deference to your opinion, and freely allow your right to determine for yourself whether I have written truly or not.

TELL ME IF I'M A THIEF!

Well-read readers may find in these pages echoes of more writings than I have actually cited. I apologise in advance for that lack of scrupulous acknowledgment. Some of what you will find here is based on memories, sometimes unconscious, of stuff that I have read or heard in books, magazines, articles, and sermons across many years, and that I never annotated. I now have no idea where those ideas came from. Wherever possible, of course, I have noted my sources, but if

---

10) The company of writers who are over-sensitive, taking offence too quickly, unable to bear any criticism of their works.
11) Op. cit. Aetat. 40.

you find unacknowledged passages that you think should be noted, and can provide details, please tell me.

So now, dear reader, I leave this work in your hands, hoping you will find that it has indeed lived up to its "pretensions" of revealing some of the marvellous treasures buried in Paul's letter. If you do find spiritual wealth here, then let us rejoice together, for that has been my prayer and my goal. If you do not, then let the fault be mine. Yet my prayer remains the same, that you will press forward with joy in your pilgrimage to the Celestial City, walking more firmly on the gospel path, always advancing toward *"the goal, and striving to win the prize that belongs to our heavenly calling in Christ Jesus."* (Ph 3:14)

INTRODUCTION

THE JOYFUL LETTER

If one word could be used to summarise Paul's *Letter to the Philippians*, it would be *"joy"*; and if there is one verse that encapsules the theme of the letter it would be *"rejoice in the Lord always, and again I say,* **'Rejoice!'**" (4:4; 1:4, 25; 2:2, 29; 4:1)

That the letter should be so redolent of laughter is astonishing, given Paul's painful first contact with the city. The dramatic story is told in *Acts 16:12-40,* how Paul and Silas arrived in Philippi, preached there, were arrested for causing a public nuisance, and brutally flogged. They were then thrown into a cell, where their legs, chained into stocks, were agonisingly stretched to the point of dislocation. There, at midnight, despite their lacerated backs and tortured limbs, they sang hymns and praised God. The Lord responded by causing an earthquake to smash open the stocks and to release the prisoners from their chains.

Observing these extraordinary events, the chief jailer and his family converted to Christ and were baptised that same night, while the magistrates, learning to their horror that Paul was a Roman citizen whom they had illegally flogged, came to him and Silas, humbly apologised, and begged them to leave the city.

I remain uncertain what my reactions would have been to such an amazing sequence of misery and miracle! Would I remember mostly the pain and so look on the city with loathing thereafter? Or would my recollections be dominated by the marvellous earthquake, the delight of a family's embrace of Christ, the satisfaction of receiving an abject apology from the city authorities, and the loving welcome of Lydia and her family? I would hope the latter! But in any case, that is what Paul did. He chose to remember the miracle of the earthquake, the love of the new Christians, the joy of a successfully planted church, and the pleasure he had found in two later visits to the city prior to writing his letter to them. And so his letter laughs!

Paul had an obvious love for the church at Philippi (1:8; 4:1). Alone among the churches to whom he wrote, he had no criticism of that church for false doctrine, or for divisions, ungodly deeds, and the like. True, there were some individuals whom he felt obliged to rebuke (1:15; 3:2, 18; 4:2), but he had no criticism to offer, only affection, which he expressed to the church as a whole. His letter was written in part to assure them of his love and his care for them, and also to deal with a handful of other matters of interest, without any special overriding theme, except perhaps gratitude. Paul was grateful for a generous gift that he had received from them, and for which he thanked them heartily. The gift was carried to him by Epaphroditus, whom Paul was particularly glad to see again (4:10, 14-18), especially because he (Epaphroditus) had only recently recovered from a serious illness (2:25-27).

While *Philippians* is more of a friendly *letter* than a *treatise* on dogma, it adds at least two elements to our understanding of the gospel, in the form of a passionate *emphasis*, and an important *dogma* –

1. **_The Emphasis_** – No matter what he is writing about, or to whom, Paul cannot resist drawing continual attention to Christ, and to the need for every believer to live a Christ-centred life. No less than 40 times in this short letter Paul mentions the Lord Jesus Christ, involving Christ in every aspect of Christian life, witness, and service. Indeed, for Paul *"to live is Christ"* (1:21), and he could not endure the thought of life without Christ. [12]

---

12) These ideas I have gleaned from several commentaries.

2. **_The Dogma_** – The greatest statement about Christ that Paul makes in this letter relates to a Greek word that he applies to the Lord only here (2:7), and nowhere else in the NT. The passage has given birth to a body of doctrine known as *Kenotic Theory* – which means only that it deals with the mystery of how Jesus, though *"he was truly God, did not try to cling to his equality with God but instead emptied himself* (Greek – ekenosen) *and took on the form of a slave."* A later chapter of this book will deal with this wonderful and mysterious *kenosis* of Christ.

And now, two final comments before we begin our search for treasure. The studies that follow make no pretence of providing a full commentary on Paul's letter to the *Philippians*. If you want detailed information about background, when and why the letter was written, or verse by verse exposition, then you should turn to the internet, or to any good Bible dictionary, encyclopaedia, or commentary.

What you will find here is *treasure* – that is, nuggets dug out of diverse passages from the letter. The meditations draw on other parts of scripture also, and are always directed toward successful Christian life, to the enrichment of your mind and spirit, and to the enhancement of your service of Christ and the church.

I should add that several key passages from *Philippians* are missing from this book, because I have already dealt with them in one or more of my other *Vision Publishing* books. And in reverse, there are some passages dealt with in other books that I have nonetheless included here – they seemed too important to omit. Where that has happened, you will find mention of it in a footnote.

May you indeed be richer for reading these pages.

ONE

THE SLAVES OF CHRIST

> From Paul and Timothy, slaves of Christ Jesus,
> to the overseers, deacons, and all the saints in
> Christ Jesus who are at Philippi. *(Ph 1:1)*

Do we have every privilege, or none? Are we ranked higher than the archangel, [13] or should we call ourselves the offal of the earth? Are we rich or poor? Weak or strong? Are we princes or paupers, or neither, or both?

In fact, we are at the one time both the mightiest and the least, possessing everything and owning nothing. How can this be?

Scripture portrays us in two shapes. We are described as reigning with Christ in the heavenlies, blessed already with every imaginable blessing, royal priests who possess <u>free access to the throne of God, people who can speak against the powers of darkness</u> with the authority of the King himself.

But we are also described as people who are called to endure hardship in the service of Christ, to be ready to suffer for the cause of righteousness, to be stripped of everything we possess, and to offer our lives on the altar of discipleship. Thus Paul calls himself and Timothy the *"slaves"* of Christ, implying that this appellation should be welcomed gladly by every Christian.

---

13) If you wonder why I have used the singular instead of the plural, it is because, contrary to popular opinion, only one being is named in scripture as an archangel, and that is Michael. Neither Gabriel nor any other being is titled an archangel.

The Greek word is *doulos*, which may be translated as "servant"; but it comes from a root that means to bind up or chain, so that its more usual sense is "slave". What does that mean?

A DEMAND FOR RADICAL HUMILITY
A SLAP ON THE FACE

Do you remember how Jesus taught that we should turn the other cheek if someone strikes us on the face? (Lu 6:29) Have you ever imagined that happening to you? Someone slaps your cheek, and at once, without retaliating, you present your other cheek for a blow! Did Jesus really expect us to behave so meekly? I suppose circumstances might alter the case. If the blow is struck as an insult to Christ, or just because you are a Christian, probably you should do exactly as Jesus says! But if it is a buffet given in mere anger, you are probably entitled to defend yourself, but not to strike back angrily. Or, if allowing violence when it is in your power to stop it will only encourage more and worse brutality, then prudence would say that you should do so. Or, if the blow is part of an assault that involves or hurts other people, then you are entitled to use as much force as necessary to prevent it. And so on. There should be reason and balance in all things. But acting merely out of spite, or taking personal revenge for some hurt, is always forbidden by Christ.

However, there is a deeper meaning in this matter of *turning* the other cheek. You can strike someone on *both* sides of the face only by using the back of your hand for the second blow. Visualise a person standing in front of you and slapping your left cheek with the flat of his right hand. Then he swings his arm back to smite your right cheek also. He cannot turn his hand over, except with difficulty, so he will likely hit you with the back of his hand.

In the 1963 epic film *Cleopatra*, Richard Burton plays Mark Anthony, and Elizabeth Taylor plays the Queen. In one scene they quarrel violently and Cleopatra slaps the Roman as hard as she can on his left cheek. He remains unmoved. She slaps him again. He still fails to react. So then she backhands him on his right cheek, and at once, deeply insulted, he retaliates furiously and knocks her to the ground. Then, as now, any slap on the face was deemed an outrage; but a back-handed blow was (and is) doubly so! Hence Jesus was not talking so much about *non-retaliation* as he was about *humility*. He was asserting that Christian men and women should be able to accept indignities without responding violently. Can we indeed practice such humility? Are we equal to such forbearance? Does God really expect it?

Humility was not admired by the ancients, for it was associated with a cowering slave. Meekness was reckoned weakness. Thus anything that bore the appearance of timidity was scorned as ignoble, mean, unworthy of any self-respecting person. Nor are attitudes today much different. But Jesus came to lift a different standard, and to set a different example. The world says: "Might is right!"; but the gospel says, "The meek are truly mighty!" the world says, "Demand your rights!", but the gospel says, "Do not curse those who treat you harshly, but pray for them and bless them!"

And we might add that the state of the world after twenty centuries of following its own rules of self-assertion and retaliation hardly weakens the precept of Christ!

Jesus came, not to rule, but to serve; and he bids us follow his example.

LIKE A LITTLE CHILD

Jesus was the first founder of a worldwide religion (and perhaps he is still the only one) to present a little child as an example (Mt 18:1-5). Even today that remains a revolutionary notion; but in Bible days it was scornfully improbable. People then did not admire children, nor see them as unspoiled innocents, natural, loving, and beautiful. Those are modern concepts. Even our Christian forefathers up to a couple of centuries ago usually did not praise children, nor think they had sweet virtues that adults should copy. Quite the contrary. The life of a child was cheap. Children were deemed weak and helpless, lacking status, standing little higher than beggars or slaves. [14] Even middle-class and upper-class children, who had a much easier life, were still seen as little more than small adults – as you can easily prove by looking, say, at 19th century pictures of children. Many of them show grown-up faces on childish bodies. The artists were incapable of seeing them as they truly were, not miniature adults but a separate kind of creature; not grownups in small bodies, but persons in their own right with characteristics that belong only to the young.

That is what Jesus meant when he said that we must *"become humble like a little child"*. It was not a picture of charming innocence, of gentleness and virtue. Rather, he had in mind children as they then were – lowly and vulnerable commodities who were valued primarily for the services they could render the adult world. Thus we too are to adopt an attitude of humility, reckoning ourselves to be in debt to all, and especially to God. We are his slaves.

HUMILITY IS NOT SERVILITY

But childlike vulnerability, and a general policy of non-retaliation, are only part of the character of Christian humility. Never suppose that humility means supine passivity, or helpless servility –

---

14) Some of this was a product of the general cheapness of life in those times; some of it was self-protection from the pain of the appalling incidence of child mortality. For example, one of the chief founders of the modern novel, Samuel Richardson (1689-1761), early lost all six children and his wife from his first marriage; and of the six children of his second marriage, only four girls survived. Or, think of Queen Anne of Great *Britain* (died 1714). She had 17 children, all of whom were either miscarried, stillborn or died within two years. Such relentless sorrow was common until less than 200 years ago.

THE HUMBLE KNOW WHEN TO BE ANGRY

Was any man ever more truly humble than Jesus, who did not grasp at equality with God, but *"made himself nothing"* and *"took upon himself the very form of a slave"* (Ph 2:6-7). Yet he was able to take up a whip and drive the money-changers out of the Temple of God (Jn 2:15; also Mt 23:13,27,33; etc.) So there is a time when even the humblest person in the church may rightly blaze with fury, and act violently, if nothing less will serve to achieve a righteous end. Yet Jesus never used anger in his own defence, but only to uphold the honour of God or to protect the weak (Mk 3:5; Lu 13:15).

THE HUMBLE KNOW WHEN NOT TO BE ANGRY

They would rather *be* wronged than *do* wrong. Have you ever truly faced up to the meaning of Paul's words about allowing yourself to be cheated –

> *To have lawsuits at all with one another shows that you are already defeated. Why not rather suffer wrong? Why not rather be defrauded? But you yourselves wrong and defraud – even your own brothers! (1 Co 6:6-8)*

Modern mores are based on demanding one's "rights". How sternly opposite is Paul's injunction, *"Why not rather suffer wrong? Why not rather be defrauded?"* Every modern notion of "justice" is offended! Surely I'm entitled to protect my assets, to preserve my prosperity? Sometimes, yes. But there are other times when demanding your rights may produce more defeat than victory, cause more loss than gain, bring more hurt than joy. Then it is better by far to suffer loss cheerfully, and to give up your goods for the glory of God (He 10:34).

However, if taking action to defend yourself or your property does not violate the royal law of love, which should govern our lives, then you may be entitled to prevent fraud. Or, if failing to act may be seen as encouraging wickedness, or will result in putting control of your life into the hands of cheats and robbers, then you should probably do what you must to thwart them. But once again, never do so in spitefulness, nor vindictively, nor to find pleasure in revenge.

Always weigh up the end result before acting. Will going to court cause more harm than it will do real good? Then abandon the action. Will defending your rights cheat your brother of his? Choose to be defrauded instead! Can protecting worldly wealth justify imperilling a brother's soul, or even worse, your own? Then cast it all aside, and count it but dung! (Ph 3:8-9)

I will not pretend that these choices are easy. Sometimes the issues are deeply complex, so that it is difficult to decide whether action or non-action is best. The questions arise: should I be vulnerable or aggressive, passive or stern, vigorous or gentle? How can I resolve this paradox of practising violence and gentleness at the same time, of being both passive and forceful, vulnerable in some circumstances but an inferno of fury in others –as Jesus was?

Seek out the love of God and resolve to do what will best reflect that love. Let the peace of God also be an umpire in your soul, allowing the Spirit of peace to guide you (Ph 4:7). Ask the Lord for wisdom, who is always willing to show you the path to follow (Ja 1:5-6). Be like Jesus who knew both how to flog and to be flogged! His guiding principles were twofold – _his love for God_ (so he whipped the money-changers out of the temple); and _his love for people_ (so he yielded his own back to the lash for their redemption).

In the end, the only really strong people in the world are those who know how to embrace true Christ-like humility.

A DEMAND FOR RADICAL OBEDIENCE

Six times in the gospel of *Matthew* Jesus retorts, *"... but I say to you ..."* –

- ***Matthew 5:22*** – ***But I say to you*** that everyone who is angry with his brother will be liable to judgment; whoever insults his brother will be liable to the council; and whoever says, 'You fool!' will be liable to the hell of fire.
- ***Matthew 5:28*** – ***But I say to you*** that everyone who looks at a woman with lustful intent has already committed adultery with her in his heart.
- ***Matthew 5:32*** – ***But I say to you*** that everyone who divorces his wife, except on the ground of sexual immorality, makes her commit adultery, and whoever marries a divorced woman commits adultery.
- ***Matthew 5:34*** – ***But I say to you***, do not take an oath at all, either by heaven, for it is the throne of God, or by the earth, for it is his footstool.
- ***Matthew 5:39*** – ***But I say to you***, do not resist the one who is evil. But if anyone slaps you on the right cheek, turn to him the other also.
- ***Matthew 5:44*** – ***But I say to you***, love your enemies and pray for those who persecute you. [15]

Christ sets *his* word against a cluster of popular ideas that reflect a lower standard than he wanted his disciples to achieve. He insists that we should never be content with less than the highest and the best. Not mediocrity but excellence should be our goal every day. Our example is found in Christ alone (1 Pe 2:21). The only approval we truly desire is his. Our deepest yearning is that we might one day hear him say, *"Well done, good and faithful servant!"* (Mt 25:21, 23)

Are you the prisoner of Christ and under his lordship?

I would be pleased if I could reach the nobility of Babylas, who was bishop of Antioch in the early part of the 3rd

---

15) The above passages all come from the *English Standard Version* (ESV).

century. He was noted for his godliness and courage. When the emperor Philip the Arabian (16) came to an Easter service in 244, Babylas bravely barred his entrance to the church. Philip had gained the throne by murdering his predecessor, the emperor Gordian, and Babylas insisted that he must undergo a time of penance for the crime. Only then would he be allowed into the church. Some six years later, after Philip himself had been deposed and his throne taken by Decius, Babylas was imprisoned and cruelly martyred by the new emperor. Just before he died, the bishop left instructions that nothing should be buried with his naked body except the chains he had worn during his imprisonment and torture. They were the symbol of his loyalty to God and his love for the church. (17) He wanted no other trophy to present to the Lord on the day of his glory.

Such "chains" as Babylas wore were all that the early church possessed, yet they turned the world upside down! Our programmes, even our miracles, are worthless unless we too display such "chains" – bonds of loyalty, love, courage, obedience and faithfulness. On the day of resurrection they will be the highest proof that we were indeed the slaves of Christ.

---

16) Some historians think that he, not Constantine 60 years later, was the first Christian emperor.

17) Some of the details about the life and death of Babylas are uncertain, but his request to be buried naked with his chains is true.

TWO

THE PRICELESS GRACE OF GOD

> *It is right for me to feel this way about you all, because I hold you in my heart, for you are all partakers with me of **grace**, both in my imprisonment and in the defence and confirmation of the gospel. . . . The **grace** of the Lord Jesus Christ be with your spirit. (Ph 1:27; 4:23)*

Sometimes in Christian life it seems that we just can't get airborne. We feel like we are trudging through sticky mud and can hardly lift our feet to take a single step. One of the sweetest remedies for that dilemma is to renew your sense of the grace of God. Paul understood its importance. He prayed most earnestly that the Lord would impart grace to the Philippians, and that they would never stop partaking of that divine grace.

I want to explore this glorious theme under three headings –

1. The Richest Gift
2. The Kindest Action
3. The Greatest Response

THE RICHEST GIFT

One of the great ideas restored to the church by the 16th century Protestant Reformation was *"Sola Gratia"*. This means that salvation comes to us by <u>Grace Alone</u>. It is the doctrine that salvation is unmerited. That is, we cannot make any salvific claim upon God based upon birth, rank, wealth, achievement, ethnic identity, or anything at all apart from the *free gift* of righteousness conveyed to us by Christ.

Indeed the gospel insists that all human beings have failed both morally and spiritually and are utterly cut off from God unless he graciously intervenes to rescue them –

> *The wages of sin is death, but the gift of God is eternal life, which cannot be gained by human desire and striving, but only by God's mercy. . . . . For by grace you have been saved through faith, as a gift from God, and never by any effort of yours. Yes, God has saved us, not because of any good thing we have managed to do, but only because of his unfailing grace! (Ro 6.23; 9:16; Ep 2:8-9; Tit 3:5)*

Unhappily, because of our fallen nature, we tend to have an unwarranted confidence in human ability, and a hunger to build our own righteousness, so that we find it immensely hard to surrender to grace alone. Yet we *must* avoid emulating those who are determined to build their own righteousness and reject the gift of God –

> *Since they decline to know the righteousness that comes from God, they keep on running around, trying to establish their own, refusing to submit to God's righteousness! (Ro 10:3)*

We should join with Paul in scornfully rejecting all such nonsense. He is adamant –

> *For Christ's sake I have endured the loss of everything, and I reckon it all trash, so long as I may gain Christ, and be found in him. I cast off all righteousness of my own that comes from keeping some law, and hold only to the righteousness that comes through faith in Christ, yes, the righteousness God himself gives that depends upon faith alone. (Ph 3:8-9)*

How strongly he emphasises his dependence upon the righteousness of Christ <u>alone</u>, that comes by grace <u>alone</u>, through faith _alone_, as the gift of God _alone_. All other righteousness, along with all other possessions, he calls trash when they are placed beside the glory of Christ. [18]

By contrast, think about the ancient hermits and stylites (pillar saints), notably the three most renowned, Simeon Stylites, Daniel the Stylite, and the astonishing 7th century ascetic, St Alypius, who lived on top of a stone column outside the Greek city of Paphlagonia for 67 years, suffering unimaginable privations and pains. He and his fellow monks supposed that their sufferings, perched on their stone columns, would give them a special right to salvation and a higher throne in heaven. But could you seriously suppose that sitting on top of a high pillar, for no matter how long, could add so much as one atom to the grace that the Father is willing to give us freely in Christ? No! Those hermits, monks, and ascetics of old were sadly deluded. Not all their lashings and fastings, nor the thorns they laced through their inner garments, nor the nauseating herbs they mixed with their food, nor any nor all of the torments they imposed upon themselves could bring them as close to the throne of God as a simple murmur of the name of Jesus can do for any believer. [19]

So once again, salvation cannot be in any sense a human work, but must be brought to us supernaturally by the Holy Spirit, who unites us with Christ. Thus by grace alone we are carried from endless death to eternal life, becoming the very children of the Father.

THE KINDEST ACTION

It is easy to think about the grace of God only in the abstract, as a nice piece of doctrine. But because we are dealing with God, [20] his grace is never passive, nor ever merely a

---

18) In *Chapter Nine* below, I will take up again the theme of *Sola Gratia*.
19) The theme of this paragraph, too, will be continued in *Chapter Nine* below.
20) "My Father never stops working" (Jn 5:17).

potential, nor just a dogma to argue about, but it is ever active, working on behalf of each believer. This is because, just as God _is_ love, and therefore he is always loving, so, because he _is_ also grace, therefore he is always gracious – that is, he cannot do other than act in harmony with grace.

So the grace of God is always powerfully active, and it touches us in three ways –

UNFAILING LOVE

If God loved us while we were his enemies how much more will he continue to love us now! – *"Even when we were dead in our sins, and because of his great love for us and his limitless mercy, God has made us alive in Christ!"* (Ep 2:4)

So I cannot say that yesterday God loathed me, today he loves me, but tomorrow he may loathe me again! His love is constant, sure, dependable, both to save us and keep us saved!

UNFAILING KINDNESS

> *"God sends rain not only upon the righteous but also upon the unrighteous, and he compels the sun to rise upon the evil as well as the good"* (Mt 5:45).

About which a renowned British judge and peer, Baron Charles Bowen (died 1894), speaking from vast judicial experience, once said –

> The rain it raineth on the just,
> And also on the unjust fella;
> But chiefly on the just, because
> The unjust steals the just's umbrella. [21]

---

[21] The only source I have been able to find for this piece of doggerel, is its citation in Walter Sichel's 1923 book, The Sands of Time. Sichel himself was an English lawyer.

Likewise, when we behave well, and when we behave badly, the Father still drenches us with grace, for the chief meaning of "grace" is kindness bestowed on the undeserving. (22)

UNFAILING EMPOWERMENT

The Father is not content merely to be kind to those in prison, he also wishes to liberate them! So the divine grace brings not merely *pardon* but also *freedom* –

> Rock of Ages, cleft for me,
> Let me hide myself in thee;
> Let the water and the blood
> From thy riven side which flowed,
> Be of sin the <u>double cure</u>;
> Cleanse me from its <u>guilt</u> and <u>power</u>. (23)

So then, because of his grace, Christ first breaks the chains of our servitude then by grace endows us with all that is necessary both to serve him and to live abundantly.

THE GREATEST RESPONSE

Paul once asked, *"Shall we then continue in sin so that grace may abound?"* (Ro 6:1)

In a sense, the proposition is *true* – that is, the more we sin, the more grace will abound! We should never allow that human sin is stronger than divine grace! God's grace is *always* immeasurably greater than my sin, as the ocean is greater than a street puddle, as a forest fire is greater than a dry stick. But in *practice* two things prevent us from so deliberately abusing the grace of God –

1. It is impossible truly to embrace the kindness of God while wilfully mocking that kindness.

---

22) I will have more to say about the mysteries of divine providence, and the problem of pain, in *Chapter Five* below.

23) A.M. Toplady (1775).

2. It is impossible truly to sustain faith in Christ while wilfully choosing the way of sin.

So then, let us both renounce sin but also declare that, even if we should happen to sin, so long as we cling to Christ, whether with serene trust or desperate hope, the grace of God will continue to be our salvation, shield, sustenance, and our security for eternal life.

THREE

NEVER ASHAMED

This royal throne of kings, this scept'red isle,
This earth of majesty, this seat of Mars,
This other Eden, demi-paradise,
This fortress built by Nature for herself
Against infection and the hand of war,
This happy breed of men, this little world,
This precious stone set in the silver sea,
Which serves it in the office of a wall,
Or as a moat defensive to a house,
Against the envy of less happier lands;
This blessed plot, this earth, this realm, this England,
This nurse, this teeming womb of royal kings . . .
England, bound in with the triumphant sea,
Whose rocky shore beats back the envious siege
Of wat'ry Neptune, is now <u>bound in with shame</u> . . . [24]

Just as England should have been a happy and blessed land, basking in the favour of God, but instead was fastened in chains of shame, so are many Christians today. But Paul would have none of it –

> *"I hold to an eager expectation and hope that I will never have anything to be ashamed of. On the contrary and very boldly, I will continue to trust, now and always, that whether I live or*

---

[24] William Shakespeare, Richard II *(2.i.40)*, part of the death-bed speech of the king's uncle, John of Gaunt, the Duke of Lancaster. The realm lay in shame because of the decadence and venality of the royal court, which was bringing ruin upon a previously prosperous land. Richard was murdered in February 1400, probably by starvation, in Pontefract Castle in Yorkshire. It was a horrific end to a reign that had begun well until the young king came under the influence of corrupt counsellors.

> *die, Christ will be exalted in my body!" (Ph 1:20)*

Now this takes us to one of the commonest and most crippling problems facing the church – thousands of ashamed saints, disabled by their shame!

WHAT DOES "SHAME" MEAN?

Rabbi Sirach long ago described two kinds of shame –

> Keep on the alert for every opportune moment, and never be ashamed to be yourself. Remember, there is a shame that brings sin, as well as one that brings high honour. (4:20-21)

So there are things that you should be ashamed to do, and things that you would be ashamed for not doing! *Sinful* shame makes you timid about serving God or making a bold stand for Christ and for righteousness. *Honourable* shame keeps you from doing wrong and compels you to do what is right.

Bad shame stops you from being truly yourself. Good shame makes you reach for the highest and the best. The former shame, the kind that cripples, the kind that wraps chains around its victims, is the shame I am dealing with here. But notice first that this "shame" differs from "guilt" – Christian people know how to rid themselves of guilt (by repentance and trust in the blood of Jesus); but all too often, shame lingers on, suffocating spiritual life, preventing the shame-fastened person from serving God with any vigour or confidence.

Now guilt is best handled by the grace of God; but shame is something we have to deal with ourselves.

That is why Paul, in our text, said that he was determined never to do, or be, or have, anything that would make him ashamed of himself.

Let us look at the two kinds of shame, the good and the bad –

POSITIVE SHAME

There is a healthy kind of shame that we must all maintain, which Sirach delightfully describes in one of his admonitions to his young disciples –

> There are times when shame should be thrown off, when it should not be allowed to rule over you. But there are other times when you should indeed be thoroughly ashamed. You should be ashamed of being found guilty of immorality, of telling lies, of committing a crime, or of doing something that offends the congregation. Be ashamed of behaving dishonestly with a partner or friend, or of stealing from people where you live. Be ashamed of denying the truth of God and his covenant. Be ashamed of putting your elbow on the table at mealtimes, of being nasty in giving or receiving, of rudely ignoring someone's greeting, or of lusting after a prostitute. Be ashamed of hardening your heart against a relative, of cheating someone out of his rightful share, or of desiring another man's wife. Be ashamed of meddling with any girl in your neighbour's household, and stay away from her bed. Be ashamed of speaking abusively to other people, or of bestowing cold charity and belittling people. Be ashamed of repeating what you have heard and of betraying a secret. Then you will be known as a person with a proper sense of shame and everyone will speak well of you. (Sir 41:16-22)

Well, popularity may not be the noblest reason for behaving honourably, but it certainly beats behaving dishonourably! Mostly, of course, we should have a positive shame about doing the sorts of things Sirach lists, because they are against the royal law of love. And many other aspects of daily conduct, and of ethical, moral, and pleasant behaviour could be added to Sirach's list – things that self-respect alone, if no higher motive, should keep us from doing.

Sirach includes in his list a need to display good manners, including keeping your elbows off the table! My parents dinned that rule into me without any knowledge of its antiquity! [25] But is it really important? Hardly! Then why mention it? Why mix such a minor issue with weighty matters like truth, justice, and purity? I think the old rabbi gathered together a number of items, some of great value, some insignificant, simply to present a picture of a gracious lifestyle, pleasing in every way to both man and God. A courteous lifestyle, well mannered, godly, upright, showing appropriate behaviour in every situation, of which no one should ever be ashamed. Even the apostle includes courtesy as a mark of godly character (1 Pe 3:8). And Moses added a solemn warning of divine indignation against any young person who refuses to stand when an elderly person enters a room! (Le 19:32)

If nothing else will move us toward such a life, says scripture, then at least allow shame to do so, because we should be ashamed to live any other way.

NEGATIVE SHAME

Against that positive and useful shame, there is a negative and destructive shame, which we must banish if we hope to live with true freedom in Christ. On this, too, Sirach offers some excellent counsel –

> My son, do not hesitate to accept whatever credit is due to you. Always think worthily about yourself, according to your true value. Who will commend a man who is ashamed of himself, or honour a man who dishonours himself? Too much shame can sometimes kill a

---

25)   *Circa* **185 B.C.**

man! So there are times when you should push shame away, or you will find yourself doing wrong. (Sirach 10:28-29; 20:22; 41:16; 42:1)

Paul echoed those sentiments when he encouraged Christian people to *"think soberly"* about themselves – not supposing themselves to be more than they are, nor less than they are, but to look at themselves openly and honestly (Ro 12:3). [26] You are not all bad. You are not all good. Commend yourself in Christ for what is good, and take action against what is bad. But know this – no one will think any better of you than you do of yourself! If you think you are rotten, it cannot be surprising if other people share your opinion! There is death – if not physical, then spiritual – in allowing the wrong sort of shame to possess your spirit. It is a sin. But why is this so?

WHY IS THIS SHAME HARMFUL?
SHAME DESTROYS PERSONAL CONFIDENCE

Unrestrained shame leads to a sense of incompetence, of unfitness for the task, a gloomy apprehension of failure; or worse, a tendency to cause one's own failure out of a sense of getting one's just deserts. Interestingly, the familiar term "shamefaced" is actually a corruption of an older English word, "shamefast" – that is, "held fast by shame." And if shame holds you fast then you will not be able to hold fast to the good things the Lord wants to pour into your life.

Here is a general rule of life – people are seldom able to receive or to retain what they feel they do not deserve. Hence a survey taken in Australia of twenty-one lottery-millionaires found that only *one* of them had actually benefitted from his winnings. The others had suffered in various ways – family dissolution, financial chaos, loss of friends, destruction of their place in life, even illness. They had all either quickly squandered their new-found wealth, been cheated out of it,

---

26) I take up this theme again in *Chapter Ten*, below.

or had unwisely given it away. One couple, even before they had actually received their prize, managed to overspend it and were heavily in debt! How could such folly occur? Probably because none of them, except one man, was able to believe that the good fortune was deserved, and so they found ways to rid themselves of it.

The same can happen in church life. A pastor may pray, fast, toil for growth in his congregation, only to find, when the increase comes, that he can't tolerate it. Unable to persuade himself that he merits such blessing, he finds ways to whittle the congregation down until it has returned to its former small size. [27]

Likewise, Christian people who are prisoners of shame will probably find themselves unable to believe for, or to expect that God will give them any great thing. And if he does, they will probably try to find some way to cast it aside or nullify it.

SHAME DESTROYS SOCIAL ASSURANCE

Where shame holds sway there will be insecurity. The "shamefast" feel threatened by life and society; they cannot believe that they merit the support and help of their neighbours. Do they walk into the church before a service and see groups of people chatting away? The shamefast just *know* that *they* are the topic of conversation, and that *bad* things are being said about them! They cannot feel worthy to mix with the saints in the church, because surely they are too sinful, too unclean, too lowly to deserve good friends and an open welcome. Consequently, their shame becomes the cause of a quite sinful focus upon themselves, and the ruin of the true bond of love and mutual respect that should bind together the people of God.

---

27) I do not in the least mean that every smaller church comes under this indictment. There are many reasons why some congregations grow numerically while others don't. But in some cases, a shamefast pastor is one of them.

SHAME DESTROYS SPIRITUAL AUTHORITY

How well the devil plays on this factor, striving to block all attempts to deal with the problem; for if he can lock a believer into feelings of shame, then he will effectively paralyse that believer's spiritual life and service for Christ. No one in the grip of shame will be able to speak with real authority against any of the works of darkness. Faith to heal the sick in Jesus' name will be vitiated (Mk 16:18). If they try to move a mountain, paralysis will seize the voice of the shamefast (11:23-24). The exercise of spiritual authority depends upon an environment of personal assurance and confidence in Christ, of having the right to speak boldly in Jesus' name, and of faith that stands serene in the grace of God.

SHAME DESTROYS HEAVENLY EXPECTATIONS

For an ashamed believer, expecting a miracle will be impossible. The shamefast will be unable to anticipate anything from God except wrath. They dare not expect God to do anything great and wonderful, for (they say within themselves) has not God's trust been betrayed?

Oh! they know that the Lord has certainly forgiven their sin; but how can an undeserving and unworthy person (they say again to themselves) ever hope for restoration to the highest levels of divine favour? So the shamefast cripple themselves spiritually, and may rightly be found at fault by God for allowing such wrongful shame to hold sway over them.

HOW CAN THIS SHAME BE OVERCOME?

The first and most necessary step is to recognise the problem – that step by itself will take the shamefast at least halfway to victory! A problem understood is often a problem reduced in size and made manageable. Are you shamefast? Then honestly admit it, and begin to find God's solution. Surely you can see that the Father finds no pleasure in your condition? Instead, he wishes you to emerge from it into a new life of freedom and joy in Christ.

So then, what is the solution? How can you break the stifling grip of shame over your life? How can you turn enervating shame into vibrant confidence? Simply –

LOOK TO THE CROSS

This is something, of course, that every person, not just the shamefast, must do, for everyone has an inescapable need of divine pardon. We may all echo McBeth's lament, after he had plunged the dagger into Duncan's heart –

> What hands are here? Ha, they pluck out mine eyes!
> Will all great Neptune's ocean wash this blood
> Clean from my hand? No, this my hand will rather
> The multitudinous seas incarnadine,
> Making the green one red. [28]

How easily we may feel that our sin, like that of the Scottish regicide, is great enough to incarnadine the vast ocean. And indeed, in a sense it is true, for there is a deep mystery lurking within sin that strips it of boundaries and makes it measureless. Yet the mystery of Christ is greater, and his grace past the measure of all the oceans in all the galaxies of our universe. Your sin can no more discolour that grace, nor restrain its effectiveness, than a bottle of red ink can stain even a small sea or turn aside its flowing waves. Cast your shame into the ocean of divine grace and it will be swiftly absorbed and soon vanish.

The Greek author Arrian of Nicomedia describes an extraordinary event in the life of Alexander the Great –

> (Alexander) thought this was a suitable opportunity to settle the debts of the army, and ordered a list of individual debts to be drawn up, with a promise to pay them. At first, few put down their names; they feared Alexander

---

28)   Shakespeare, McBeth, *Act two, sc. 2.*

was testing them to find out who thought the soldier's pay insufficient and who was living above his means. When it was reported that the majority would not put their names down, but concealed any bonds they had, he condemned the soldiers' lack of trust. A king should not say anything but the truth to his subjects, and they must not imagine their king to be saying anything but the truth to them.

So he had tables set up in the camp with gold on them, and men charged with the distribution of money to anyone who could show a bond, and he ordered the debts to be settled but without now drawing up a list of names. In this way they were convinced that Alexander was speaking the truth, and their pleasure at not being individually identified was even greater than their satisfaction at seeing their debts paid off. It is said that up to 20,000 talents were distributed to the army on that occasion. [29]

Now that is a fine parable of the relationship that many Christians have with their Commander. They cannot bring themselves to trust his promise of complete remission of their sins. Or, like the soldiers of Alexander, they are too ashamed to admit how foolish they have been, or how irresponsible to incur debts they could neither pay nor escape.

Alexander was rightly angry about their reluctance to believe what he had promised. Was he not a king? How could they imagine that he would ever speak less than the truth to them? Nonetheless, he graciously reinforced his word by

---

29) Anabasis of Alexander, Sec. 7.4.4-5.6; tr. by M. M. Austin. "Anabasis" means a military march, or advance, into an invaded territory. Arrian died *circa* 160 A.D.

setting up in front of them tables loaded with gold coins from his personal treasury. Then his clerks urged the soldiers to present their bills to be paid in full. So they came, at first in a trickle, which quickly became a flood of eager men, whose debts were all paid in full without question.

How much more to be trusted is the word of the King of kings! No matter how ashamed you are, cast it aside! Be chained down by guilt no longer, but present your debt and it will be entirely remitted, not by silver and gold that perish, *"but by the precious blood of Christ"* (1 Pe 1:18-19) that will retain its efficacy for ever!

Indeed, Christ endured measureless *shame* just so that *we* could escape it – see *Hebrews 12:2*; and *1 Peter 2:6*.

So then, let the shamefast face their shame and cast it off at the foot of the cross of Christ. And let us all allow the blood of Jesus to be our only and altogether sufficient covering, ridding us of every debt we might ever have owed to the broken law of God.

LOOK TO THE PROMISE

What marvellous things are spoken in scripture of each believer – that in Christ we have become the very righteousness of God; that we are more than conquerors; that we have been strengthened in our inner self with the might of God himself; that we are enthroned with Christ in heavenly places and are blessed with every spiritual blessing; that eternal life is our possession and Paradise our destiny – and on, and on! The challenge is before us to believe God's promises, all of them, heartily, and out of that faith to develop a positive self-image and joyful self-esteem.

LOOK TO THE SPIRIT

What a boon we have in Holy Spirit baptism! Can we be so bad if the Holy Spirit is pleased to dwell in us? (1 Co 3:16; 6:19) So be filled with, and rise up in the Holy Spirit, allowing him to fashion in you a new boldness, an innate confidence, and a head held high. Let him take the dullness from your eye, the heaviness from your heart, the reluctance from your spirit! You will then find yourself in harmony with scripture as you *"no longer hang your head in shame, but look straight ahead with honest confidence",* always expecting the very best from the Father as he fulfils his promises in your life (Pr 4:25, GNB).

CONCLUSION

We all have many things to be ashamed of, in thought, word, and deed, and no doubt you have sincerely repented of them and found in Christ the pardon of God, perfect peace, and the removal of all guilt. But have you handled the ongoing problem of shame? For some, release from that crippling manacle will come in a moment of prayer; others may need a longer time. But in any case, this day, right now, is the time to start! Believe the good news of the gospel! Trust in the promise of God! Walk in the Spirit! Put the past behind you and press on toward the prize that God has set aside for you in Christ! (Ph 3:13-14)

I speak to myself, as well as to you dear reader. How heartily I pray and trust that when I reach the end of my pilgrimage, which for me cannot now be too far away, I will honestly be able to cry with Paul (in the words of our text) –

> *"I hold to an eager expectation and hope that I will never have anything to be ashamed of. On the contrary and very boldly, I will continue to trust, now and always, that whether I live or die, Christ will be exalted in my body!" (Ph 1:20)*

FOUR

BEGUN – AND FINISHED!

> God has granted you this remarkable privilege – for the glory of Christ you have been called not only to <u>believe</u> in him but also to <u>suffer</u> for him ... And of this I am very sure, that God has not only begun a good work in you, he will also bring it to completion on the day when Jesus comes *(1:29; 1:6)*.

In the year 304 three Greek maidens, Agape, Chionia, and Irene were martyred for Christ during the persecution ordered by the emperor Decius –

> When violence broke out in their district, they at first fled to the mountains, where they spent their days in prayer. But they were discovered and brought back to the city to face the magistrate. When they refused to offer a sacrifice to the divinity of Caesar they were condemned to die. The two older maidens (*Agape* and *Chionia*) were taken out and burnt to death, perishing bravely for Jesus. The youngest, *Irene*, because of her singular beauty, was stripped naked and sent to a military brothel, there to have only one loaf of bread a day, and to be used by the soldiers until she died. But loveliness and holiness radiated from her so ethereally that no man dared to touch her. Word of this reached the magistrate. In blazing anger he hauled her out of the brothel, castigated the timidity of the soldiers, and then commanded that she too should be burnt to death. The flames took her life but could not consume the same dauntless faith her friends

had shown. She died singing the praises of her Saviour and God. (30)

What gives ordinary people such constancy in the face of awful pain, such purity in the face of overwhelming temptation, such love in the face of unspeakable cruelty, such faith in God, despite a midnight of horror? Paul gives the answer in our text and in *Philippians 3:7-11* – it is the explosive confidence that comes from knowing that Jesus has conquered death, and that in him all who believe have come to everlasting life and a magnificent crown in Paradise!

If you truly know that Christ is alive from the dead, that in him you too have defeated death, and that life and immortality are therefore irrevocably yours (2 Ti 1:9-10), then you too will –

NEVER AGAIN THINK YOURSELF INSIGNIFICANT

More than seven thousand million people are presently living on our planet. No one who has ever lived, not even Jesus, is known to the majority of them; indeed, the names of even the most renowned men and women are known to only a minority of the earth's inhabitants. Think also about the tens of thousands of people who perish in floods, pestilences, earthquakes and war; yet Providence seems indifferent to their fate, as if they held no more value than a falling leaf. Then measure yourself against the vastness of the known universe, which has more than 150 billion galaxies, many of them much larger than our own Milky Way, containing in total thousands of billions of stars like our sun.

It is easy to feel overwhelmed, insignificant, irrelevant! –

> There was a water drop, it joined the sea,

---

30) Based on The Oxford Dictionary of Saints, ed. D. H. Farmer; Oxford University Press, 1987; *in loc*; plus other sources.

A speck of dust, it was fused with the earth;
What of your entering and leaving this world?
A fly appeared, and disappeared.

How long are we to be prisoners of workaday reason?
What difference does it make if we're here a hundred
years or one day?
Pour wine into the bowl before we too are turned
Into wine-bowls in the potter's shop.

Oh, what a long time we shall not be,
yet the world will endure,
And neither name nor sign of us will exist!
Before this, we were not, and there was no deficiency;
After this, when we are not, it will be the same as it was
before.

I once bought a pot from a potter,
Which told everything when it said,
"I was an emperor and had a golden goblet,
Now I'm any drunkards wine pot!" (31)

Thus the words of a world-weary 12th century Persian poet. But anyone who contemplates the human condition apart from Christ must come to the same conclusions. We are born, we live, we die, and in the immense span of time and space we have no more significance than a tiny insect flying unobserved into and out of a very large room.

But how stunningly Christ changes all that! When he rose from the dead, *each person* who *believes* in him also *arose* with him to endless glory, undying renown, and indestructible identity (Ro 8:18-19, 23). Let me illustrate in a shadowy way what this means, by using two anecdotes from

---

31) The Ruba'iyat of Omar Khayyam (12th century Persian mathematician, philosopher, poet); tr. by Peter Avery & John Heath-Stubbs; Penguin Classics, 1983; Quatrains 41, 51, 208, 227. "Ruba'iyat" simply means "quatrains", that is, stanzas of four lines.

Dryden's translation of Plutarch's *Life of Alexander the Great* –

> It is related that the first time Alexander sat on the royal throne of Persia under the canopy of gold, Demaratus the Corinthian, who was much attached to him and had been one of his father's friends, wept, in an old man's manner, and deplored the misfortune of those Greeks whom death had deprived of the satisfaction of seeing Alexander seated on the throne of Darius.

Unlike those unhappy Greeks, death cannot deprive us either of the limitless joy of seeing Christ enthroned in glory, or of our destiny to share with him the throne and all the splendours of the Father's kingdom for ever!

> Another time, as one of the common soldiers was driving a mule laden with some of the king's treasure, the beast grew tired, and the soldier took the treasure on his own back, and began to march with it, till Alexander, seeing the man so overcharged asked what was the matter; and when he was informed, just as he was ready to lay down his burden for weariness, "Do not faint now," said he to him, "but finish the journey, and carry what you have there to your own tent for yourself!"

That soldier suddenly found strength he didn't know he possessed! Where the fear of failure and of death failed, the promise of such a dazzling prize succeeded grandly. He picked up the sacks of gold that a mule could hardly carry, slung them over his shoulder, forgot all about his previous exhaustion, staggered down the road to his tent, and found himself rich beyond his craziest hopes!

In a superbly greater way our King too offers to give us the treasure that is rightly his. We but need to continue faithful to the end and it will be ours forever! How can such a splendid hope fail to energise every part of the believer's life, imparting inexhaustible confidence, courage, tenacity and joy?

Thus faith surmounts the evidence of our senses, and the seeming triumph of the grave over human life, and enables gentle maidens and strong men alike to laugh at torture and to endure without faltering the most horrific anguish. Knowing Christ, and the power of his resurrection, and the glorious prize to come in Paradise, nothing can quench their zeal nor stifle their praise, until they stand before their King and hear his benediction, *"Well done, good and faithful servant!"* (Mt 25:21, 23)

Yet some modern poets still echo the cynical Persian, and ascribe to life scant value –

> It will be all the same in a hundred years;
> What a spell-word to conjure up
> smiles and tears!
> How oft do I muse, 'mid
> the thoughtless and gay.
> On the marvellous truth that
> those words convey!
> And can it be so? Must the valiant and free
> Hold their tenure of life on this frail decree?
> Are the trophies they've reared
> and the glories they've won
> Only castles of frostwork confronting the sun?
> And must all that's joyous and brilliant to view
> As a midsummer dream be as perishing, too? . .
> .
> For Time, as he speeds on invisible wings,
> Disenamels and withers earth's costliest things.
> And the knight's white plume,
> and the shepherd's crook;
> And the minstrel's pipe and the scholar's book;
> And the Emperor's crown,
> and his Cossacks' spears,
> Will be dust alike in a hundred years. . . .

> To what end is this conflict of hopes and fears,
> If 'tis all the same in a hundred years? . . .

Thus far the poet sinks in dreary hopelessness; and indeed, without Christ, what else can be said? If Jesus did not conquer death, then the best any of us can hope for is to go peacefully to our graves, to perish, to be remembered for a few years, and then to be utterly forgotten, as if we had never been. Nowadays one cannot even inscribe *R.I.P.* on a tombstone, because in many city cemeteries all graves are dug up after a couple of decades, and used again!

Think about yourself. Do you know anything about your grandparents? Perhaps a little. How about your great-grandparents? Do you even know their names? And suppose you actually can trace your genealogy back a few centuries, what then? On my father's side I can name my ancestors back to about 1500, and on my mother's, back to about 1200. But they are only names. I know nothing about them, except that they were born, lived, had children, and died. And as for all my earlier forebears, across many millennia, about them I know absolutely nothing, nor does anyone else! They have been totally forgotten, along with all their laughter and tears, their struggles, their triumphs and defeats, and their noblest achievements. They are all as if they had never been, gone and forgotten like an ephemeral mist. And their fate will be mine too, if time continues.

So, without Christ, death is the end, and we are all but dust blowing around the surface of an indifferent planet, which itself must one day perish, along with the galaxy of which it is an infinitesimal part. But then I remember that *"by many infallible proofs"* (Ac 1:3, KJV) Jesus proved to his disciples that he had conquered death, and that in him they too would live and never die (Jn 5:24-26; 11:25-26). And at once the song changes –

> *Ah, 'tis not the same in a hundred years,*
> *How clear soever that motto appears.*
> *For know ye not that beyond the grave,*

Far, far beyond where the cedars wave
On the Syrian mountains, and where the stars
Come glittering forth in their golden cars,
There bloometh a land of perennial bliss,
Where we smile to think of the tears in this?
And the pilgrim reaching that radiant shore
Hath the thought of death in his heart no more,
But layeth his staff and sandals down
For the victor's wreath and the angel's crown. . . .
Then be glad, my heart, and forget thy tears;
*For 'tis **not** the same in a hundred years!* (32)

NEVER AGAIN THINK YOUR WORK UNIMPORTANT

How humdrum, how mundane, how futile our daily round often seems. We get up, go to work, come home, go to bed, only so that we can get up, go to work – and on, and on, day after day. Every day millions of people ask, "Why am I doing this? What purpose can it possibly have? What is the use of all this toil and trouble?" And often the answer comes –

> The old professor was staring at the ceiling with dull eyes. "Every man knows in his heart," he said, "that nothing is worth doing." (33)

Indeed, we all face two burdensome problems –

THE BURDEN OF ENDLESS ROUTINE

A note was found pinned to the jacket of an 18th century British aristocrat who had committed suicide in London – "All this buttoning and unbuttoning!" Perhaps, given the extraordinary number of buttons that clothing bore in those days, he had good reason to bring it all to an end. But have

---

32) From the poem *In a Hundred Years*, which is among a collection of recitations that are part of a book on public speaking – The Art of Expression, by Grace A. Burt; pub. by Heath & Co., Boston, USA, 1905; pg. 142-143. The author and the date of the poem are not given.

33) G. K. Chesterton, The Man Who Was Thursday.

you not felt, even in our time, the frustration of continually peeling off layers of garments, only to replace them with more layers?

The same idea was expressed by an American poet and humourist, Benjamin King –

THE PESSIMIST

Nothing to do but work,
Nothing to eat but food,
Nothing to wear but clothes
To keep one from going nude.

Nothing to breathe but air
Quick as a flash tis gone;
Nowhere to fall but off,
Nowhere to stand but on.

Nothing to comb but hair,
Nowhere to sleep but in bed,
Nothing to weep but tears,
Nothing to bury but dead.

Nothing losing but songs,
Ah, well, alas! alack!
Nowhere to go but out,
Nowhere to come but back.

Nothing to see but sights,
Nothing to quench but thirst,
Nothing to have but what we've got
Thus through life we are cursed. . . . [34]

---

34) Benjamin King (1857-94), *The Pessimist.* From Ben King's Verse, ed. by Nixon Waterman; pub. by The Press Club of Chicago, Chicago USA, 1894; pg. 126.

But the futility of an endless and seemingly pointless routine is not the worst of our problems, for there is also –

THE BURDEN OF FUTILE LABOUR

Are any of us renowned in our deeds; do any of us do work that cannot be replaced? I suppose a few of my readers will be able to claim a modicum of fame; yet I doubt that any of us will be able to achieve renown that will endure for even a century, let alone a millennium. As Adam Lindsay Gordon wrote in his poem *Cui Bono* (st. 4) –

> *'Tis a weary round to which we are bound,*
> *The same thing over and over again;*
> *Much toil and trouble and a glittering bubble*
> *That rises and bursts, is the best we gain.*

How then can we find value in our work? Simply, contemplate the life of Jesus –

- he died a felon, unknown outside of Judea, a peasant who had made no contribution to politics, culture, art, literature, commerce, or indeed anything, except to stir up a religious controversy among the despised Jews
- by any worldly measure his life was a failure; yet what majesty is now his!

But his present fame rests upon his resurrection and ascension, which impelled his disciples to record his triumphs. If he had not conquered the grave his name would have perished with him and been soon forgotten. Yet his resurrection did not depend upon any great thing he had done, but rather upon *who* he was – a man without sin, who had been fully obedient to the Father's will.

We are prone to measure people by what they *do*; but God measures us by what we *are*. The Father cares about *you* far more than he cares about your achievements. What we *do* is important only because it reflects what we *are* – which was demonstrated in the life, death, and resurrection of Jesus. The *Man* who did the miracles was of vastly greater value than any of his mighty works, not excepting his resurrection. The empty tomb primarily demonstrated that he was truly holy, hence the Spirit with great power showed that he was the Son of God when he raised himself from the dead! (Ro 1:4)

For us the wonderful consequence is this – whatever we do in the light and life of Jesus' resurrection takes on a transcendent worth. Even the most ordinary tasks gain redemptive value, working salvation in us more fully, earning each believer a crown of righteousness, building a golden stairway to the stars (2 Ti 4:8).

> (Sherlock Holmes turned to Dr Watson, and said with great and solemn sorrow), "What is the meaning of it, Watson? What object is served by this circle of misery and violence and fear? It must tend to some end, or else our universe is ruled by chance, which is unthinkable. But what end? There is the great standing perennial problem to which human reason is as far from an answer as ever." (35)

True, human reason never has been able to penetrate the mystery of why we are here and where did we come from. Evolutionary theory may say something about processes, but it cannot say anything about origins. Nor can any other human field of human learning and thought. But faith *knows* – indeed,

> *faith that knows Christ also knows the power that his resurrection from the dead has released! (Ph 3:10),*

and in that knowledge, and in that experience, we find both the reason for our existence and its ultimate purpose. So we

---

35) The final words of The Adventure of the Cardboard Box, by Sir Arthur Conan Doyle; first published in the *Strand Magazine* in 1892.

rejoice. We may not have all the answers (1 Co 13:12), but we know who we are in Christ, and what our goal is, and our final destiny, and we are content.

NEVER AGAIN THINK THE GRAVE IS AN ENEMY

Empedocles (circa 450 B.C.) was a physician, poet, and philosopher who had a vast influence in shaping Greek thought. His ideas continue to have an impact in our time. Indeed, his intellectual powers and accomplishments were so great he began to think himself a god, or at least to reckon that his fellows should call him one. When he was about 60 years old, he climbed to the top of Mt Etna, in Sicily, and cast himself into its volcanic crater. He supposed that the molten lava would utterly consume him, and that people would think he had been translated up to heaven, there to take his place among the gods on the Olympian heights. Unhappily for his apotheosis, the volcano thwarted his purpose. An updraft caught one of his sandals and threw it onto the mountain's side, where it was found a day or two later by his friends. (36)

We are all like that. Try as we might to avoid the issue, we find ourselves constantly confronted by the "sandals" of our mortality! Every day some reminder of the grave presents itself – the setting sun; the passing of another birthday; the onset of sickness; the demise of a loved one; the incipient death of sleep; walking through a cemetery.

Yet we deeply feel that death cannot be the end. So across the ages people have cried for proof of immortality, which finally came to us in the gospel! (2 Ti 1:10) Christ has given us the hope that the sages of the past longed for in vain. Hence Paul says that we can now share gladly with the saints *"in suffering for the gospel by the power of God, who saved us*

---

36) The story is told in Lives and Opinions of Eminent Philosophers, viii. 67, 69, 70, 71, by Diogenes Laërtius, circa 250 B.C.

and called us to a holy calling, not because of our works but because of his own purpose and grace, which he gave us in Christ Jesus before the ages began" (vs. 8-9)

And again he says, *"God has granted you this remarkable privilege – for the glory of Christ you have been called not only to <u>believe</u> in him but also to <u>suffer</u> for him"* (Ph 1:29). With such splendour enshrouding them, and such hope throbbing within them, Agape, Chionia, and Irene were able to sing while the flames consumed their mortal bodies. And across the centuries a multitude of martyrs – men, women, young people, even children – equally assured of conquering death in Christ, have added their own anthems of joyous praise.

You have been called to *believe* in Christ. Do you now agree with Paul that we have also been given the privilege of *suffering* with Christ and for him in the service of the gospel? If so, then you can be confident, with Paul, that the Father, who has begun such a good work in you, will now go on to bring it to completion! (Ph 1:6)

CONCLUSION

In the year 1571, on October 7th, a great naval battle, known as the *Battle of Lepanto*, was fought near Greece between Christians and Turks. Had the Turks won, the Mediterranean would have become a Muslim lake, and Europe a province of the Ottoman Empire. There were 300 ships on each side, the greatest armada of galleys ever assembled to that time. The Christian fleet was commanded by Don John of Austria, only 25, but a brilliant leader. The Turkish fleet was led by the military commander and statesman, grand admiral Ali Pasha.

On the evening before the battle, the two admirals called their fleets to prayer. Don John knelt on his main deck, in full view of his sailors and marines, and with uplifted hands called upon the God of Heaven to give victory to his trusting servants.

Ali Pasha, too, prayed to Allah. But his real confidence was in two sacred emblems. One was the Ottoman standard, a huge green banner upon which the name of Allah had been embroidered 29,000 times, along with many texts from the Holy Qu'ran. No fleet that carried it had ever been defeated in battle. The other was a little crystal ball that the Pasha wore on a gold chain around his neck. Embedded in the crystal was the right canine molar of the prophet Mahomet. "By the Tooth of the Prophet," boasted Ali, "the Christian infidels will be crushed and ground into helpless submission!"

Within 24 hours the Turkish fleet had been annihilated, and Ali Pasha was dead.

A Christian soldier cut off his head and took the Prophet's Tooth as a souvenir. The sacred banner was also captured; 25,000 Turkish troops and seamen were killed; and 15,000 Christian slaves were released from the oars of the Turkish galleys. (37)

You may laugh at Ali Pasha putting his trust in a banner and a tooth; but are we any wiser? In what is *your* trust placed – money; learning; good works? Some other earthly object or achievement? Rather, let our boast be only and ever Jesus Christ, and him crucified, risen, and ascended, God's guarantee that *your* life has infinite value, that your *work* is irreplaceable, and that the coming grave is nothing more than an open door to Paradise!

---

37) Based 0n the account given in Great Sea Battles, by Oliver Warner; *Lepanto*; Hamlyn Publishing Group Ltd, London U.K., 1972; pg. 15-23. I do not mean to imply that those who pray to God will never lose a war, while those who pray to Allah will never win one. History shows many examples to the contrary. Prayer is only one of the factors that can influence the outcome of battles. But there is no denying that the *Battle of Lepanto* was a vastly important victory for the survival of a "Christian" Europe. One is inclined to think, however, that God, who perhaps gave the Christian fleet victory on that occasion, might not do so again unless the people truly turn back to him. It was a lesson Israel had to learn in its day (1 Sa 7:2-4).

FIVE

WHEN BAD THINGS HAPPEN TO GOOD PEOPLE

> Ladybird, ladybird,
> Fly away home,
> Your house is on fire
> And your children all gone.
> All except one,
> And that's little Anne,
> And she has crept under
> The frying pan.

The origins of that ancient nursery rhyme are lost in antiquity, but it certainly goes back several hundred years. It has always had a spiritual significance. In the Middle Ages, ladybirds were called *Our Lady's Bird*, referring to the Virgin Mary, perhaps because the insect's seven spots reminded people of the *Seven Sorrows of the Virgin*. [38] For this reason the superstition developed that ill luck would follow anyone who harmed one. [39] It was also thought that good luck would follow if a ladybird landed on your hand and then flew away while you recited the rhyme and gently breathed upon it.

Even as a child, although I knew nothing about those superstitions, I sensed the spiritual mystery that was somehow enshrined in the poem. I used to put the little

---

[38] In German it is called a "Marienkafer" – "Mary's Beetle". *The Seven Sorrows* in Roman Catholic devotions are – Simeon's Prophecy; the Flight into Egypt; the Boy Jesus Lost for Three Days; the Via Dolorosa; Jesus' Death on the Cross; Mary Receiving His Body into Her Arms; the Burial of His Body in the Tomb.

[39] J. B. Redmond, Superstitions of Nature.

beetle on my finger, blow on it softly, recite the lines, and then watch in wonder as the seeming earth-bound insect suddenly produced gossamer wings and flew away. But I was also troubled by a sense of injustice and cruelty – why should such pain fall upon such a delicate and entrancingly lovely creature? Why such a harsh and pitiless fate? What had *she* done to deserve that her home and children should be destroyed?

Thus we come to our text for this chapter, which continues the theme of the sufferings of Paul, and of the church. The apostle was in prison (Ph 1:7,12-14), for no crime except that of preaching Christ – and why should *that* be a crime? Well, of course, in any reasonable society it would not be. But so great is the rebellion of the human race against God, that simply being a Christian has often been reason enough to enrage onlookers and to merit a violent death. Yet Paul had no complaint. He simply stated the fact. He was not surprised by it. He did not demand from God some good reason for his sufferings. He shook no fist at heaven nor railed against fate. On the contrary, he found in his pain good cause for joy, and set an example of what all Christians should expect –

> *God has graciously granted you the privilege not only of believing in Christ, but also of suffering for him. That is why you are enduring the same struggle that you know I have had, and now hear that I still have. ... Your faith and your service are like a sacrifice being offered to the Lord, and it may happen that I will have to yield my own life as part of that sacrifice. But if so, I rejoice, and I share my joy with you. In the same way, you should be glad, and share your joy with me. (Ph 1:29-30; 2:17-18)*

A HARD QUESTION

We cannot escape pain. Indeed, Paul makes the astonishing claim that God has graciously granted us the *privilege* of suffering for him! As if we should thank him for it, which we should, but not many are able to do so! Yet Paul could speak with authority. Had he not been flogged, tortured in prison stocks (in Philippi), and did he not there sing so lustily that an earthquake broke him loose? The Philippians knew what Paul had suffered in their town; they knew that he was still suffering (in prison in Rome); they knew that he had rejoiced despite the torturing lash and stocks; they knew that he was still rejoicing; and now they held in their hands his joyful letter, in which he tells them that such pain would be God's gift to them too. He expected them to convey to him their joy in suffering just as he had done for them.

Yet surely there is a puzzling tension between the reality of suffering, and the equally forceful reality of the many promises of peace, triumph, and abundance in Christ. How can we reconcile those two conflicting ideas?

I want to explore here, not the significance of suffering persecution as a Christian, though that is a deep mystery, but rather the even deeper mystery of pain in general, especially when it strikes down people who are virtuous, kind, and godly.

We all face this problem: *why do bad things happen to good people*? Worshippers are brutally murdered in the very house of God; an apostle lies rotting in prison; Christian women are raped; innocent victims are torn apart in some ghastly torture chamber; believers go bankrupt; thieves steal from a church; godly families are destroyed in a car wreck; wracking sickness robs a groaning saint of life. On and on goes the litany of pain. We cry – "How can the Lord ignore the grinding torment and misery that engulfs the earth?"

This mystery first touched my life when my little sister Christine died. Not long after, when I was 14, my Mother was taken by cancer. Then, despite all our prayers, Alison and I had to lay our second child, our son Gavin, in the grave. And over the years we have had to pass through several other dark valleys, both personal and professional.

Is there any purpose in such suffering? Is pain a punishment for sin? How should we respond to hurt and injustice? Against a background of sorrow, two questions are commonly asked –

- is there some purpose in human sorrow?
- were the victims being punished for sin?

No doubt there are occasions when either or both of those factors are at work. Our problem is that we can seldom say with any certainty whether there is anything more than simple misfortune involved in life's disasters. For that reason, Jesus refused to allow that there was any necessary connection between certain things that are often connected in the popular mind – that is,

- there is no inevitable connection between personal sin and tragedy; and
- there is no inevitable connection between personal virtue and prosperity

In other words, the wicked may prosper, and the virtuous may suffer loss. Thus, Christians are sometimes protected supernaturally – like the girl whose attacker ran away and did not rape her, because he saw two "tall men" (actually angels) suddenly standing either side of her. But (as many examples in scripture show) there is no guarantee of such protection. Thus I know a godly woman who was twice raped in her own home while her husband, who was a policeman, was at work. Happily, she held on to her faith, her husband gave her all his love and support, and together they rebuilt their life and happiness.

Likewise, Daniel tells us about three young men who expected God to rescue them; but if he chose not to do so, they still would not bow before nor serve the emperor's golden idol (Da 3:17,18).

So let us simply admit that

SUFFERING IS A FACT OF LIFE

In 1842 Longfellow wrote a poem, *The Rainy Day*, in which he coined the familiar saying –

> Into each life some rain must fall,
> Some days must be dark and dreary.

We can no more hold back sorrow than we can banish black clouds, thunder, lightning, and rain – even in the midst of summer. Nor do the elements consider our virtue; they act impartially and indifferently upon godly and ungodly alike

> Like us, the lightning-fires
> Love to have scope and play;
> The stream, like us, desires
> An unimpeded way;
> Like us, the Libyan wind delights to roam at large.
>
> Streams will not curb their pride
> The just man not to entomb,
> Nor lightnings go aside
> To give his virtues room;
> Nor is that wind less rough which blows a good man's barge.
>
> Nature, with equal mind,
> Sees all her sons at play;
> Sees man control the wind,
> The wind sweep man away;
> Allows the proudly-riding and the foundering bark.
>
> And, lastly, though of ours
> No weakness spoil our lot,
> Though the non-human powers

Of Nature harm us not,
The ill deeds of other men make often our life dark. (40)

So, whether from the indifferent forces of nature, or the malice of enemies, and even if we ourselves have neither weakness nor fault to merit pain, still suffering will come upon us. Therefore we must say that there is no <u>necessary</u> connection between personal virtue and prosperity, nor between personal sin and tragedy: good things, and bad things, happen alike to good people and bad people –

> *When times are good, you should be cheerful; when times are bad, think what it means. God makes them both to keep us from knowing what will happen next. I have seen everything during this senseless life of mine. I have seen good citizens die for doing the right thing, and I have seen criminals live to a ripe old age. ... Here is something else I have learned: the fastest runners and the greatest heroes don't always win races and battles. Wisdom, intelligence, and skill don't always make you healthy, rich, or popular. We each have our share of bad luck. None of us knows when we might fall victim to a sudden disaster and find ourselves like fish in a net or birds in a trap. (Ec 7:14-15; 9:11-12)*

At heart we all know the truth of the Preacher's words. Yet we find them unsettling – we prefer constancy and conformity – we dislike an unpredictable Deity. Something in us abhors grey shadows. We crave a brightly coloured scene, where all is clear, and nothing remains uncertain. Consequently, how dismayed we are when some unexpected event wrecks our neatly crafted structures! We can't

---

40)   From the poem *Empedecles on Etna*, by Matthew Arnold (1822-1888).

understand why things often don't work out the way we think they should. But like it or not, life frequently fails to follow the path we expect.

MYSTERIES OF PROVIDENCE

Yet here is the greater irony: we are more often trapped by our own facile judgments than by any act of God. A large part of the mystery of life would disappear – or at least our questions would vanish – if we would only stop trying to force the Lord to live by our rules! Instead, we are frequently like the pastor who came home from a vacation –

> After being met at the airport by a friend who was also a backslidden parishioner, the pastor asked if there were any news. His friend reported that a terrible fire had just swept through the neighbourhood, and his house was among the smoking ruins. He had lost everything he owned in the blaze.
>
> "Aha!" cried the preacher. "I warned you that calamity would strike if you didn't repent!"
>
> "Fair enough," the fallen saint admitted with rueful humility; "but there is some more bad news. The fire also reduced *your* house to a pile of ashes!"
>
> The horrified minister hastily revised his opinion. "The ways of God," he lamented, "are indeed beyond understanding!"

He learned that divine providence seldom conforms to our prejudice!

Jesus taught the same lesson –

> *I tell you to love your enemies and pray for anyone who mistreats you. You will then be acting just like your Father in heaven, for he makes the sun rise on good and bad people alike; and he sends rain alike upon people who*

> *do right and those who do wrong. (Mt 5:44-45)*

But that passage shows also that the reverse of our first question is true – that is, good things happen to bad people, just as bad things happen to good people. Indeed, Jesus' words enclose a mystery that is greater than the mystery of pain: *why is there laughter and happiness in the world?* – we have no more merited happiness than we have deserved suffering. Someone has well said that when the mystery of joy has been explained then one can demand explanation for the mystery of pain. Why does God give us tears? Why does God give us laughter? We probably deserve the former more than we merit the latter. But both are given to us – and indeed, there still remains in the world more joy than sorrow, more sunshine than bleakness, more love than hate, more song than lamentation, and more life than death.

In the end, apart from declaring that ultimately all sorrow is a result of the poison of sin and of the depredations of Satan, the Bible offers no explanation of why in a particular instance a wicked person prospers while a righteous person is crushed; nor why the reverse may equally happen.

We must simply accept that suffering is a part of life, and it may fall indiscriminately upon anyone, whether deserved or undeserved. In the meantime, I know that God is good, and only good. I know too that he is all-benevolence, love, justice, and righteousness. And I accept that he must have a sufficient reason for allowing evil and pain to continue during the present time.

SEARCH FOR PROSPERITY

Two things are forbidden in scripture –

A PASSIVE AND HELPLESS FATALISM

While it may be true that we cannot avoid some experiences, that is no reason to fall into supine, pessimistic, despair. Nothing could be more contrary to the affirmative and positive stance of scripture, which we are expected to emulate. Christians are not fatalists. We are never merely helpless victims. No matter what is happening there is always some grace to be had from God, some cause to rejoice, some victory to assert in Christ, some quality of divine life to be found and outworked. While it cannot always be done, sometimes we <u>can</u> rise up in faith and hush a storm, move a mountain, raise up what has been cast down, and cast down what has been raised up. Sometimes we <u>can</u> and <u>should</u> change our world for the glory of God (Je 1:9-10; Mt 17:20; Mk 11:22-24; etc.)

Think about the roll call of the heroes of faith in *Hebrews 11:32-40*. Some by faith overthrew nations; others by faith were cruelly slaughtered. Some were imprisoned by faith, others by faith escaped imprisonment. Some by faith turned aside the sword, and by faith others accepted death by the same sword. *"Time and chance,"* as the Preacher said, *"happened to them all."* But within those happenings they all found a place of faith that ultimately made them, not victims, but gloriously victorious.

A MORBID CRAVING FOR PAIN

Some welcome pain, even go looking for it, in the belief that if they suffer they will be better people. Unhappily, there is more chance that severe pain will break you than make you. Many, like Job's wife, become soured, embittered, and destroyed by suffering. Not all martyrs are brave or strong. There have been many who, faced with shrieking their lives away under a torturer's savagery, chose instead to renounce Christ and go free. So, since none of us truly know how much we can stand, if suffering can be avoided, then avoid it. If it comes anyway, then embrace it in Christ, and seek wisdom from God in how you should handle it (Ja 1:5-8). It may be that the promise of God will enable you to throw it off by faith; or it may be that the promise will give you strength to cope with it. Even if you find that you cannot actually quiet the storms of life, where you are, there should still be an epicentre of peace.

So despite the mystery of life, we are given plenty of encouragement to seek boldly, and to expect, good health, happiness, prosperity, success, and fulfilment. Jesus himself taught us to pray for our daily bread and to ask for escape from times of trial (Mt 6:9-13; Lu 11:2-4). Notice, too, that the word "bread" certainly includes all that we need for a healthy, prosperous, and happy life. As someone has said, we should ask for our daily *bread*, not daily *crumb*. So pray confidently, and expect bravely, and believe strongly, and enjoy the goodness of the Lord.

GET READY FOR THE JUDGMENT

When Jesus was confronted with the problem of human tragedy (Lu 13:1-5), he insisted that the real question was not, *Why did this happen?* but rather, *Am I ready to meet my God?* Whether suffering does you good or harm will depend solely upon how you handle it. Dealt with rightly, those darkened days can enrich you in this present life, and build into you a strength that will carry you irresistibly on toward the eternal glory of God.

Does this provide an adequate theodicy? [41] No. It is useful only to a certain level of torment. Pain can reach such hideously agonising proportions that a person loses all reason and will say or do anything to escape it. Suffering can become so tortured that no possible benefit can be seen in it, nor can any argument break through the barrier of screaming torment. So there always remains an element of deep mystery in the problem of pain. No theodicy ever written has ever been wholly satisfactory. Always there is a degree of suffering that remains inexplicable, too terrible to allow that any value can come out of it.

---

41) "Theodicy" is the branch of theology that tries to explain why and how God is good, all-powerful, and the God of love, despite the presence of vast evil.

But that does not often happen, and even then, enduring the most mind-shattering torments, many saints in the past, men, women, even children, have been able to grip Christ and bear it, and triumph over it. But not all were so strong, and many martyrs were broken by their torturers, and cursed Christ and died, sometimes made insane by their anguish.

But the justice of God cannot be less than that of man, and our law insists that any confession extracted by force is illegal and not admissible in court. So too, the Lord will surely be merciful to those whose pain was more than they could bear. But still a problem remains. Did God, despite his promise (1 Co 10:13), truly allow them to be tried beyond their strength? I cannot believe so. Yet, if they did indeed fail him, his mercy remains large enough to wash away that stain and welcome them into his kingdom.

So we come back to Jesus, and his insistence upon being ready to meet God, no matter what happens. Perhaps, like the people Jesus spoke about (Lu 13:1-5), an assassin's knife might suddenly strike, or a wall collapse, or your car run off the freeway, or a disease might bring unexpected death – the question then will not be, *Why did God let it happen?* but, *Were you ready to meet your God?*

On this matter, let us note that Jesus foretold two judgments–

THE NATIONAL JUDGMENT

National judgment upon the Jewish nation was predicted by Jesus in more detail later in the gospel (Lu 21:20-24, 32-33), and true to his word, it was fulfilled in 70 A.D., when the Romans attacked Jerusalem and overthrew it. The city was reduced to a heap of rubble, and the people enslaved.

However, marvellously, the Christians, remembering the warning of Jesus (vs. 21), and also being warned by their own prophets just before the war began, had already fled the city, and not one of them perished! –

> The whole body, however, of the church at Jerusalem, having been commanded by a divine revelation, given to men of approved piety there before the war, removed from the city, and dwelt at a certain town beyond the Jordan, called Pella. (42)

Thus the church in Judea escaped the cataclysm. But the accurate fulfilment (within a generation, as Jesus had said) of that prophecy of national judgment, makes it a symbol of the sure fulfilment of the greater prediction of

THE UNIVERSAL JUDGMENT

The great folly of our time is the failure of people to have any sense of the future – their horizon extends no further than the present day; they are bounded by the immediate, and have no care for tomorrow. But we should live (and we can be truly alive only when we do) with a vision of two things –

HEAVEN

How wonderful are the promises of God, the rich reward offered to those who overcome the flesh, the world, the devil (Re 2:26-29; 3:5-6, 11-13, 21-22; etc). And today, not tomorrow, is the time to prepare for these things!

In April 1914, a Canadian poet, Robert Service, was sitting alone in a Paris cafe, watching people passing by. He describes his state, and the poem that came out of his meditations –

> I have no illusions about myself. I am not fool enough to think I am a poet, but I have a knack of rhyme and I love to make verses. Mine is a tootling, tin-whistle music ... (Tonight) I am at the end of my tether. I wish I knew where

---

42) Eusebius (A.D. 263-339), Ecclesiastical History, 3.5.3; Baker Book House, Grand Rapids; 1977.

tomorrow's breakfast was coming from. Well, since rhyming's been my ruin, let me rhyme to the bitter end!

Then he composed a poem whose title has since entered into common speech, *It is Later Than You Think!* In this poem he describes the passing parade – a band of merry and rioting students; a willing young blonde; a successful playwright; a beggar destroyed by alcohol; and others. He warns them all; then finally turns to address his readers –

> Lastly, you who read; aye, you
> Who this very line may scan;
> Think of all you planned to do ...
> Have you done the best you can?
> See! the tavern lights are low,
> Black's the night, and how you shrink!
> God! and is it time to go?
> Ah! the clock is always slow;
> It is later than you think;
> Sadly later than you think;
> Far, far later than you think! (43)

But for those who are ready to meet their God, the time is always just right!

HELL

The preaching of hell has become unpopular. Admittedly, we do not want to return to the gory, lurid, and almost gloating proclamations of former years; but with tear-drenched souls

---

43) Robert Service (1874-1958) was an Englishman who moved to Canada when he was 21. He rightly recognised that he was a second level poet, but his several books of poems were immensely popular during the early 20th century and brought him considerable wealth. Despite his assertion above, he was far from penniless during his years in Paris. His poem *It is Later than You Think* (in which he pretends to be a young and penniless versifier in Paris just before and during the First world War) comes from Ballads of a Bohemian, which was first published in 1921, but my copy is quoted from The Best of Robert Service, pub. Dodd, Mead & Co., New York, 1953; pg. 105.

we still must accept the duty to warn all people about the coming wrath – see *2 Thessalonians 1:7-10a; Revelation 19:11-16; 20:11-13; etc.*

This need not, of course, be gloomy news; rather, it can be the greatest word you will hear, because it points to the reality of requitement! Requitement for every wrong the righteous have suffered and recompense for every sacrifice they have made. Divine justice, the righteous government of the universe, ensures that there can be no heaven without a hell; nor can there be any hell without a heaven! Indeed, it has been said that no one is truly ready for heaven until he has first faced hell. The choice is yours. Choose which will be your destiny.

Now then, let us turn again to the words of Jesus, and notice that even while he was speaking to his disciples about the murdered Galileans, he knew that Pilate would spill his blood too, and that he himself would become the sacrifice to expiate human sin. Yet he had no word of criticism for Pilate; he was far more concerned about the eternal destiny of his hearers, and also to help us face pain. He himself, despite fervent, even agonising pleas that he might escape it, knew that he had to face the cross (Mt 26:37-45; Lu 22:42-44). And he was flogged, beaten, abused, crucified, and died. But despite being engulfed by the seeming tragedy of the cross, Christ rose again, and in that glorious victory silenced every question about suffering in this present life.

Which leads us to the idea –

FIX YOUR EYES UPON THE CROSS

The final and only answer to the problem of pain, for us Christians, is to gaze upon the sufferings of Christ. If the Father could look upon the awful pain of his only Son, and do nothing to help him, it is not surprising if he sometimes fails to remove the causes of *our* pain.

The most appalling statement in all literature is the stark and despairing cry of Jesus – *My God! My God! Why have you forsaken me?* (Mt 27:46) If God was willing to abandon his own Son to limitless grief and the ugliest of deaths, then no one can accuse him of injustice toward us; he asks of us no more than he was willing to endure himself in the person of Jesus.

We notice, too, that heaven vouchsafed no reply to the lament of Christ. That terrible *"Why?"* – which we too throw at heaven in our grief – brought no response, only silence, except for the jeering voices of his torturers. The answer given to Christ came in his mighty resurrection three days later, and his ascension into heaven and endless majesty at the Father's right hand.

So too, we should find ultimate consolation in the promise of our own resurrection and glorification when Jesus comes again.

CONCLUSION

The apostle makes two great statements about the pain of Christ –

- Because he suffered, he is able to comfort us who suffer (He 2:18).
- Because he defeated suffering, he can carry us to endless victory (He 2:9) in heaven.

Then there will be no more pain, nor tears, nor death.

Then there will be only laughter, peace, prosperity and gladness for ever and ever.

WHISPERING HOPE

> *I eagerly expect and **hope** that I will never do anything that would shame me, but rather, with my body, whether in life or death, that I will always bravely bring full honour to Christ. . . . I **hope** in the Lord Jesus. (Ph 1:20; 2:19).*

One of the most renowned song-writers of the latter half of the 19th century was Septimus Winner (1827-1902). He composed more than 200 popular songs and wrote or edited more than 200 volumes of music. One of his songs was *Listen to the Mocking Bird*, for which his publisher paid him the grand sum of five dollars. In the next few years, it sold 20 million copies! [44]

Septimus composed only one hymn (in 1868) – *Whispering Hope* – which he published under the name of Alice Hawthorne, one of his several pseudonyms. It too was immensely popular, and is still being recorded today –

> Soft as the voice of an Angel,
> Breathing a lesson unheard,
> Hope with a gentle persuasion,
> Whispers her comforting word. ...
> Whispering hope,
> Oh, how welcome thy voice,
> Making my heart
> In its sorrow rejoice!

Is there a lovelier or more welcome word in our language than *hope*? I doubt it. Is there a life more dreary than one from which all hope has vanished? I cannot conceive it.

---

44) From the eponymous article in Wikipedia.

There is a popular saying, "While there's life, there's hope." But that is wrong. Rather, let us say, "While there's hope, there's life!" Take away hope and nothing remains but despair. Until hope speaks again with the voice of an angel, there can be no joy in the sorrowing heart.

Hope is the sound of heaven, whispering a comforting word, bringing welcome joy to replace the deepest grief. So Paul gave his ringing cry, *"I hope in the Lord Jesus!"* – thus declaring that darkness could never overwhelm him, that every new day brought him something to live for, and that he was certain to press on toward the prize of the upward call of God in Christ.

I want to put before you two major aspects of our Christian hope –

THE PROMISES OF GOD

> *Because of the blood of my covenant with you, I will bring your prisoners out of the waterless pit. Return to your fortress you prisoners of hope, for today I promise you double what your enemy stole from you! (Zc 9:11-12).*

Samuel Johnson, whom I have mentioned a couple of times above, was once told about a man whose marriage had been very unhappy, but who had married again shortly after the death of his first wife. Johnson responded, "It was the triumph of hope over experience!" [45]

Johnson meant his comment to be a quip; yet, at least for a Christian, hope should always triumph over experience. There is surely no life more bleak than one without hope, no word so barren as "hopeless". But for us who believe, that must be impossible! Zechariah uses the beautiful expression *"prisoners of hope"* – that is, we who have entered into the

---

45) Boswell, op. cit. 1770 *Aetat 61*.

blood covenant with our God are firmly held by the silken cords of hope, unable to despair, because upon us some light is always shining, some rescue is always beckoning!

The Lord, speaking through the prophet, gives us two immutable promises –

- *"I will free you from the waterless pit"*
- *"I will restore double what was stolen from you"*

"I WILL FREE YOU FROM THE WATERLESS PIT"

The dungeons of many old castles still contain such pits. They are called *oubliettes*, from a French word that means, terribly, "forgotten". They were deep holes dug into the floor of the lowest dungeon, with no windows or doors, accessed only by a hatch in the ceiling, out of reach above the wretched victim's head. Prisoners were dropped through the trap door and any broken bones from their fall were left unattended. There they were forgotten and starved to death, crazed by thirst, wracked by pain, driven insane by the total blackness. Sometimes, if the gaolers desired to prolong a prisoner's sufferings, scraps of food were dropped to him (or her) from time to time, and a little water. But from an *oubliette* there was no possible escape. To be cast into one of those hideous pits, often onto the bones of former prisoners, was to fall into a pitch-black nightmare of hopeless, tortured despair.

One notable case in history was James Hepburn, the Scottish Earl of Bothwell. He was briefly married (in 1567) to Mary Queen of Scots before the Scottish lords drove him out of the country. He sought refuge in Denmark, but was arrested by order of the king and imprisoned in the notorious Dragsholm Castle. There he was cast into an oubliette and chained to a post in the middle of the floor. He died ten years later. The prison still exists, along with its post and chain, and there is a groove worn around the post that Bothwell is said to have carved into the stones with his feet as he endlessly circled the post. Food was tossed down to him, but often just out of his reach, adding to his torment. He was never offered any facilities to keep himself clean. Filthy, starving, dressed in rotting rags, surrounded by his own excrement, it is hardly surprising that for the last few years of his incarceration he was utterly deranged. [46]

That is the appalling image conveyed by the expression *"a waterless pit"*.

It is a metaphor of life, which sometimes seems as awful as an *oubliette* – that is, circumstances arise, things happen, which rob us of hope, load us with chains, and snatch away our freedom and joy. The physician says your disease is incurable; the accountant says your business is bankrupt; Satan says your sin is unpardonable; the world, or perhaps your own conscience, tries to build around you a high wall of despair, leaving you without hope, casting you into impenetrable blackness.

That is just the time when we who are prisoners of hope rise up in hope, knowing that not even the deepest of life's *oubliettes* can prevent the Saviour from finding a way to lift us up, rescuing us from the waterless pit to serve him again in laughing freedom.

"I WILL RESTORE DOUBLE WHAT WAS STOLEN"

Now we face a paradox. Many times people cannot regain what was lost. A loved one has died. A business has been sold. An opportunity has gone for ever. A sin cannot be undone. The apple has been eaten and it cannot be restored. Yet there still remains hope in the promises of God, who assures us that he will *"restore"* twice what was stolen.

This is one of the great expressions in scripture – *"I will restore!"* In the OT it occurs in one form or another more than a *thousand* times. This is a serious promise! Far from

---

46) Accounts of the imprisonment and death of Bothwell vary in their detail. The description given above was gathered from several sources. It is certainly true in its portrayal of the horrors of an *oubliette*.

being hidden in a corner it marches boldly across almost every page! Our God is a God who *restores!*

Yet still there are times when we feel like the people in prison pits described by the prophet Isaiah –

> *This is a people plundered and looted; they are all of them trapped in holes and hidden in prisons; they have become plunder with none to rescue, spoil with none to say, "Restore!" (42:22)*

Can those captives of the *oubliette* ever hope to be free? Will they never hear a voice crying, *"Restore!"* ? Yes! Of course they will, for the Lord has spoken –

> *I will restore to you the years that the swarming locust has eaten ... You shall eat in plenty and be satisfied, and praise the name of the Lord your God, who has dealt wondrously with you. And my people shall never again be put to shame. (Jl 2:24-26, ESV).*

A key to the fulfilment of this promise must be to live in the fullness of the Holy Spirit, for the oracles of Joel are all grounded in the promise of a great outpouring of the Spirit in the latter days (2:28-32). From those who are baptised in the Spirit, who have received the gift promised by the Father (Ac 2:33), there arises a flowing river of life (Jn 7:37-39) that carries away every prison wall and advances the soul from freedom to glorious freedom (2 Co 3:17-18).

And where the Lord of Restoration cannot restore the actual thing that was lost, then his promise will embrace a better thing – a new life, a new opportunity, a new happiness, a new prosperity.

THE PRISONERS OF HOPE

Now here is another arresting paradox! To escape one prison they must allow themselves to be captives in another! Do you wish to be lifted out of the ghastly *oubliette*? Then become instead the prisoners of gentle but invincible hope!

Thus Paul declares himself to be hope's willing hostage – *"I hope in the Lord Jesus!"* (Ph 2:19), and he urges his readers never to allow anything to *"shift them away from the hope of the gospel"* (Cl 1:23).

Is there anything so strong, so unchangeable, so infrangible, so reliable, so eternal as the hope that we find in Christ through the gospel? Hope is our strongest fortress. And we who are its prisoners rest safe within its walls, for we have nothing to do except abide there. Prisoners are not called upon to defend the walls that enclose them. Battle may rage without, but they remain safe, deep within the castle's ramparts!

Yet the prophet visualises them as having somehow got outside the walls, and he urges them, *"return to your fortress you prisoners of hope!"* (Zc 9:12). What a haunting and beautiful expression! We are pictured as being so firmly bound to hope that no one can break those chains from us. But we ourselves can cast them off, and wilfully leave the protection of our stronghold. So the prophet cries, *"Come back!"* Once again make yourself so much hope's prisoner that you will never again be severed from those happy bonds, nor ever again abandon your stronghold in Christ.

Zechariah's vision has an echo in the legends of Camelot and of Sir Lancelot's castle, which had the delightful name of *Joyous Guard*. It wasn't always so gladly named –

> After setting out for adventure, Lancelot comes across a castle (known as the *Dolorous Guard*) ruled by the Copper Knight. To overcome this challenge, Lancelot must battle ten knights at the first wall, ten knights at the second wall, and finally the Copper Knight himself. However, after defeating many more than twenty knights . . . , he discovers that the Copper Knight has fled. The townspeople lead Lancelot to a cemetery, where he finds a metal slab stating that only one knight can lift the

slab and that this knight's name is written beneath the slab. Lancelot (who has heretofore been known as simply the "White Knight") is able to lift it and discovers that his name is, in fact, Lancelot. The name of the *Dolorous Guard* is changed to the *Joyous Guard* and becomes Lancelot's home. [47]

The previous lord of the castle had kept the townspeople under an imprisoning curse, so they cheered Lancelot's triumph right lustily. He liberated them, and led the town into a new era of prosperity and happiness.

When I first read the story of Lancelot, more years ago than I care to remember, I was delighted by the name *Joyous Guard*. It seemed so improbable for a great military fortress! But how apt it seems for Lancelot, a Christian knight, who in the legends sometimes stands as a metaphor of Christ, the pre-eminent Liberator. His stronghold, too, might well bear the name *Joyous Guard*, for there we prisoners of hope are captives to laughter, knowing that while we remain within that bastion we cannot be overthrown.

WHAT IS THIS HOPE?

"Hope," says the Macquarie dictionary, "is an expectation of something desired." That seems rather flabby and dull when compared with the biblical use of the word. Hope, in the Bible, is active and energetic. It has no tremble of uncertainty, but brims with staunch confidence. This hope is not merely *hoping* (in the sickly modern sense of the word), rather, it *knows* that what is hoped for will be! Of this hope we may say that –

---

47) See www.timelessmyths.com/arthurian/ The massive Bamburgh Castle on the coast of Northumberland, UK, is popularly thought to have been Lancelot's *Joyous Guard*. Sir Thomas Malory so identified it, as also did the 19th century English poet, Algernon Swinburne, in his great epic *Tristram of Lyonesse*/Joyous Guard/*Sec. 93*. Others, of course, insist that the Lancelot tales are all fictitious, including *Joyous Guard*.

IT IS A WAY OF LOOKING AT THE PRESENT

How do you see your world? Does it seem like a sequence of midnights or of noondays? More dark valleys than sunny peaks? As barren as a desert, or flourishing like a lovely garden?

I like the attitude of McLandburgh Wilson, an American poet and author who flourished a hundred years ago –

> 'Twixt the optimist and the pessimist
> The difference is droll.
> The optimist sees the doughnut,
> But the pessimist the hole. [48]

Sometimes, of course, doughnuts have thick rings and small holes, and sometimes the reverse, so that either the hole or the ring may be more prominent. But whether life for you at the moment seems more doughnut or more hole, we Christians are called always to *"hope in the Lord Jesus"* – that is, to be confident, and optimistic, expecting always the best from the Father. Why be pessimistic anyway? No valley is so dank and gloomy that it lacks a corresponding bright peak. Even the most arid desert eventually finds its edge in fertile fields and green pastures. What midnight has ever been so dark that it was not followed by a radiant dawn? Has any tide ever gone out, never to come back in? Nor is any tomb so black that it will not be torn open to the light of Christ on the day of resurrection!

Prisoners of hope live in that light already, and cannot succumb to despair.

IT IS A WAY OF LEAPING TOWARD THE FUTURE

I once heard that our word "hope" comes from the same old Anglo-Saxon root as "hop", with the idea of "leaping" toward

---

[48] The jingle is sometimes wrongly attributed to Oscar Wilde. I have been unable to locate which of Wilson's many works contained it, although it is often quoted.

a goal. As far as I can discover, that derivation is wrong, but I like the idea anyway! It certainly captures the meaning of "hope" in the Bible, which is far from the passive modern meaning of the word, with its undertones of uncertainty and of probable disappointment. No! Biblical hope knows nothing about wishful thinking, nor doubtful outcomes! Biblical hope, built upon the sure promises of God in Christ, is a powerful expectation of an assured result! We know that God is working irresistibly in everything for our good and for the fulfilment of his purpose in our lives (Ro 8:28). We know that God does not make losers, he makes only winners! We live, says the old liturgy, "in sure and certain hope of the resurrection" and of everlasting victory in Christ.

So, if you have wandered away, then return now to your stronghold, and make yourself once more altogether a *"prisoner of hope"*!

ANCHORED BY HOPE

*When God desired to show to the heirs of his promises how absolutely they could depend upon the unchangeable nature of his purpose, he guaranteed it with an oath. Thus by two immutable things, in which it is impossible for God to lie, we who have fled to Christ for safety find all the reason we need to cling onto the **hope** he has set before us. This **hope** has become a strong and steadfast anchor for our souls, for it is lodged in the holy of holies behind the veil, where Jesus has already gone as a forerunner on our behalf. (He 6:17-20)*

Two things are required of an anchor – that it be *strong* – that is, big enough to hold the ship that carries it; and *secure* – that is, well dug into the ocean bed. Thus the apostle says that our anchor – "hope" – is indeed both *"strong"* and *"steady"*, able to keep us safe despite the worst of life's storms –

WE HAVE A SAFE ANCHOR

Priscilla Owens wrote a poem 130 years ago that captures the essence of our hope –

> *Will your anchor hold in the storms of life,*
> *When the clouds unfold their wings of strife?*
> *When the strong tides lift and the cables strain,*
> *Will your anchor drift, or firm remain?*
>
> *We have an anchor that keeps the soul*
> *Steadfast and sure while the billows roll;*
> *Fastened to the Rock that cannot move,*
> *Grounded firm and deep in the Saviour's love.*

How furiously the billows of life sometimes roll over us, seeking to tear us loose from our moorings, and to bring ruin on every hand. Will your anchor drift? Will it remain firm? Will you ride out each storm? Your anchor will certainly hold if it is *"grounded firm and deep in the Saviour's love."* This is the same Jesus in whom we hope. And so long as that hope remains secure, so does our anchor, immovably embedded in Christ.

WE HAVE A STEADY ANCHOR

The biggest and strongest anchor will fail if it cannot find firm sand in which to dig deep its flukes. Here too our hope becomes such an anchor when it finds its ground only in the Cross and depends upon no other security. But then we discover an extraordinary thing about our anchor – it is grounded in the _past_, the _present_, and the _future_ –

IN THE PAST – AT CALVARY (1 CO 1:18)

> *For the preaching of the cross is nonsense to those who are perishing; but to us who are being saved it is the power of God.*

IN THE PRESENT – IN THE HEAVENLIES (HE 6:18-20)

> *By two immutable things, in which it is impossible for God to lie, we who have fled to*

> *Christ for safety find all the reason we need to
> <u>hold fast to the hope</u> set before us (vs. 18).*

What are those two immutable things that make it impossible for God to lie? The question has occasioned much debate among scholars, and no one can provide a final answer. But the most common view, based on the wider context of the text, is that the apostle is referring to God's *promise* and God's *oath*. He has made a <u>*promise*</u>, which, being God, he cannot possibly break. But if any doubt remains, he has confirmed that promise with an <u>*oath*</u>, in which it is even more impossible (if such a redundancy can be allowed) that God should speak falsely.

Are there still waverers, still people who are unsure that hope, the anchor of the soul, will remain firm? Then he adds this arresting statement –

> *Our anchor is lodged in the holy of holies
> behind the veil, where Jesus has already gone
> as a forerunner on our behalf (vs. 19:20).*

Your hope does not stand alone, it is not undefended, it does not lack a secure anchor. Has it not found its ground in Christ himself? Is it not linked with Christ by an unbreakable chain? Is Christ himself not already gone into the holy of holies, as our forerunner, ensuring that both the pathway and the door are wide open for us to follow? Are you not yourself now in the heavenlies in Christ? Then doubt no longer! Believe and let hope burn brightly!

Thus in Mr Winner's lovely song –

> *Hope, as an anchor so steadfast,*
> *Rends the dark veil for the soul,*
> *Whither the Master has entered,*
> *Robbing the grave of its goal!*
> *Whispering hope, Oh, how welcome thy voice!*
> *Making my heart in its sorrow rejoice.*

IN THE FUTURE – AT THE SECOND ADVENT
(PH 3:20-21)

Our citizenship is in heaven, whence we look for our Lord Jesus Christ to come as Saviour, for he will transform our decaying bodies to be like his glorious body, by the power that enables him even to subject all things to himself.

Here is a mark of every true Christian – we are people who are looking forward with unquenchable hope to the coming of the Saviour! Nor is our vision uncertain, nor our hope vain. We *know* that one day – perhaps today – Jesus will come again to take us to himself (1 Th 4:14-18). *"Amen! Even so, come Lord Jesus!"* (Re 22:20)

CONCLUSION

Despite everything, someone may still be asking, "How can I be sure that this hope belongs to me, or that I can apply it to myself?"

Hearken back to the word of Zechariah. He called the people *"prisoners of hope"* because they were the beneficiaries of the blood covenant that God had struck with them – *"Because of the blood of my covenant with you, I will bring your prisoners out of the waterless pit"* (9:11).The idea is that when God looked at Israel, he saw neither their vices nor their virtues, but only the blood-stained altar and the promises he made to all who placed hearty trust in the sacrifices presented there.

So it is with us who hope in Jesus. God looks first at the Cross, where the Saviour died, as a sacrifice for our sins. Then he looks at the empty tomb, the sign of the limitless triumph Jesus gained over sin, sickness, death, and indeed every work of the evil one. Then he looks to his right hand, where Christ, having risen from the dead and ascended on high, now sits for ever, reigning in measureless power, ever interceding for us who believe. Only then does he look at you and me, standing in the shelter of the gospel with unquenchable hope in our hearts. And what he sees pleases him, and he bids us enter Paradise.

So, because of these things, and the blood covenant God has made with us in Christ, we too are become prisoners of hope, knowing that the Father will welcome us on that great day toward which we are all hastening.

Like the great apostle in our text then, let your bold cry be always, *"I hope in Jesus!"*

SEVEN

MADE IN THE IMAGE OF GOD

> *"God is always working in you, helping you continually to please him by who you are and what you do. . . . Strive to be blameless and innocent, behaving like **unblemished children of God** even though you are surrounded by crooked and corrupt people. Then you will shine among them like stars in a dark sky." (Ph 2:13-15)*

Have you ever realised that angels don't laugh? We do, and it shows that in some sense all humans, unlike angels, are replicas of God. Let us explore that fascinating idea!

Scripture says that we are God's people, made in his image and according to his likeness (Ge 1:26). It says also that we Christians should let the Holy Spirit change our thinking, because we have become new people in Christ, created to be even more like God (Ep 3:23-24). Hence our text insists that God's intention is that we should be his children, reflecting his likeness in all that we are and do.

But what does that mean? According to many interpreters, our likeness to God lies in our –

- moral nature
- spiritual essence
- reasoning mind
- power of speech
- creative skill.

All of those are no doubt true, but here is a rather different list –

WE LAUGH AT A JOKE

"He who sits enthroned in the heavens, laughs!" (Ps 2:4).

Perhaps the weirdest idea ever to grip Christians has been the notion that laughter is impious. When God himself laughs, it can hardly be wrong for his children to do so. If we humans have a sense of humour, who placed it within us, if not God? And this capacity for laughter is unique to us. No angel can appreciate a good joke! Nor can any other creature. Try telling a funny story to your cat. "But hold on," you cry, "how do you know that angels don't laugh?" Well, it depends upon what you mean by "laugh". No doubt angels can "laugh" in joy, as they praise God around his throne, or observe his irresistible triumphs. But you will waste your time if you try to tell a joke to an angel. A capacity for humorous laughter cannot be part of an angel's being.

How is that so?

A sense of humour, as we understand it, depends upon culture and training. For example, pick up any journal from a century back, and few of the jokes will seem in the least funny to you. Indeed, humour is one of the most difficult things to carry across the barriers of time or of culture. Even among contemporaries, people often react differently to comic scenes. What one deems hilarious may raise only a smile in another, or even leave him completely unmoved. Some years ago I went to a movie theatre in Los Angeles with a couple of Australian friends. The feature film was a British comedy, a spoof on medieval chivalry. We Aussies annoyed most of the American audience by laughing loudly at the subtle and sly British humour. Only a few of the Americans were able to appreciate it. Most of the viewers, as far as I could tell, thought the movie was serious, and had little or no idea that it was a very droll parody. But then, on other occasions I have remained dull while American friends were hooting with mirth. I couldn't see what they were laughing at! What brings hilarity to one may leave another apathetic.

Humour, in the end, is inexplicable, but it remains a strong part of the divine image in human beings, and it is singularly ours.

Indeed, if you have ever tried to share a joke with a dog, you will know the meaning of futility! Pleasure, dogs can experience; humour, they utterly lack. So too are the angels. I presume they feel pleasure. They rejoice as they dance around the throne of the Lord. They may even experience happiness – but don't tell them a joke. Even the choicest punch line will leave them wondering why we are laughing so heartily!

So, only humans truly laugh; and among humans, *only we Christians* have any reason to laugh! For without Christ, and the hope of heaven, what is there to laugh about? If the gospel is untrue nothing remains except a life that can have no possible value, nor any lasting purpose, nor any goal except death, nor any destiny except the grave, nor any use except to provide a banquet for worms.

THE COSMIC WAGER

Blaise Pascal, the renowned French philosopher, mathematician, and physicist, who is credited with one of the greatest minds that has ever flourished in Europe, pointed out 400 years ago that any person of good sense would choose to believe in God. In his opinion, the risks of being an atheist are enormous. He argued that whether we wish it or not, we are all engaged in a cosmic wager – what will happen after we die? The atheist replies, nothing. The Christian says, resurrection and judgment. Neither of them can prove their propositions beyond doubt. Yet we must all choose between them. We cannot evade making a decision, because we are now alive, yet must die, and the wager is already set – will there or will there not be life beyond the grave? Are we mortal or immortal?

Some try to escape this choice by postponing it until after death, but it will then be too late. We *must* choose now, and we must do it, said Pascal, without access to any certain answer about the existence of God and of life beyond the grave. (49)

But what are the consequences of those choices?

Suppose the Christian choice is wrong? We have lost nothing, because we will never know it! Death would simply then mean the end of all awareness. But in the meantime we have had a wonderful life, indeed the best of all possible lives! So we will die happy, with never any possibility of being awakened to disillusionment!

Suppose the atheist choice is wrong? He has gained nothing in life, and will lose everything after death! But hold on, says someone, what about all the things atheists can do that are forbidden to Christians? And what about all the things Christians have to give up? Well, what about them? Are they worth keeping? As a Christian I have been obliged to abandon nothing that I really want or need for life, health, and abounding happiness – except lying, cheating, cursing, fornicating, drunkenness, violence, fraud, infidelity, and such like. But I have not the least need or desire to do such things anyway! And if anyone thinks that he or she is better or happier for being free to do them, then I can only wonder at such folly.

So atheists have nothing worthwhile to gain by their unbelief, and everything to lose if they are wrong; whereas Christians have nothing to lose by their faith, even if it proves to be wrong, but everything to gain if they are right!

As Pascal said, the only rational choice is to embrace faith. Or, to put it more succinctly, "God's existence is a better bet than his non-existence!" (50)

---

49) The full argument is known as *Pascal's Wager*, and it can be easily found by doing an internet search. I discuss it myself in more length, but not fully, in my book, Attributes of Splendour, ch. 7; and also in Strong Reasons, *ch. 6/Addendum.*

But we are not dependent upon mere speculation and wagering, because, vastly more convincing, we have the assured fact of Jesus' victory over the grave, which has *"abolished death and brought life and immortality to light!"*

So we are a laughing people! And while humour is part of the human condition, and is a mark of the image of God in every person, there is no laughter so pure, so holy, so heavenly, so rich with delight as the joy of the people of God. They have discovered eternal life in Christ! They and they alone have every reason to laugh and to keep on laughing. In every vicissitude; in pain, in grief, in loss or conflict; in green pastures and by pleasant waters; in life, in death, in sickness, in health, in prosperity and poverty, in weakness and in strength – in them all and more we find some reason to rejoice in the Lord and to be merry! Our God is laughing in heaven. and we laugh with him!

WE CREATE BY SPEAKING

Nothing so marks the divine likeness in us as the power of speech. Its origin is inexplicable; its qualities are unique. Every normal child is born with a linguistic potential and an innate sense of grammar, for which no adequate explanation has yet been offered by anybody, except the one given in the Bible – *we are made in God's image.*

The first thing we are told about God (Ge 1:1 ff.) is that he created the heavens and the earth simply by speaking. He said, *"Let there be!"* – and it was done. He calls things into existence out of nothing (Ro 4:17). But then, the very next thing we learn is that he made us <u>*in his image*</u>! But only one thing was known about God at the time he created the first humans to be exemplars of himself – he makes things out of nothing, just by speaking a few words. This speaking God is

---

.... *continued from previous page.*
50)   Mark Porter, in a letter to the *Sydney Morning Herald*, April 17, 2012.

the one in whose image we are made, and whose likeness we share. Thus we are all born with this divine attribute – to bring things about just by the spoken word. Jesus demonstrated this in his own life and ministry, and he urged his disciples to exercise the same bold faith –

> *Jesus instructed them, "If you have the kind of faith God has, then, I solemnly tell you, whoever **says** to this mountain, 'Be taken up and thrown into the sea,' and does not doubt in his heart, but believes that what he **says** will come to pass, it will be done for him." (Mk 11:22-24)*

Notice, the Lord did <u>not</u> instruct his disciples to <u>ask</u> God to remove the bothersome mountain. Rather, he said, they themselves should **<u>tell</u>** it to be gone! There is a time to <u>*pray*</u>, and there is a time to **<u>say</u>**! Failure to act on the latter is one reason why many Christians are deprived of the best God wants to do for them. They want *him* to call something into being, while he is insisting that **<u>they</u>** should do so! [51]

Ausonius cried, "Why should I say that I cannot do what Caesar says I can do?" He was a provincial poet, and envious people complained when he caught the attention of the emperor and was elevated to high office. They pointed to his obvious lack of qualifications, and argued that he should modestly decline the appointment. But Ausonius thought that true modesty forbade him to plead *inability* when his king had reckoned him *able*. He accepted the promotion, and succeeded so well that he eventually became governor of

---

51) Obviously, there are some qualifications that must be added to this business of moving mountains. It cannot be done on a whim, but only in accord with the will of God. For more on what Jesus meant by his astonishing words, see my book Mountain Movers, Vision Publishing, Ramona, Ca.

Gaul and of other provinces, finally achieving the exalted rank of a Roman consul. (52)

There are Christians, less bold than Ausonius, who, despite their King's willingness to grant them spiritual authority and the right to speak with power in his name, choose to declare themselves unworthy. They pretend to humility, when in reality they are proudly rebellious. If God says you can, then you *can* – and you *should*!

WE YEARN TO WORSHIP

The Peak is high, and flush'd
At his highest with sunrise fire;
The Peak is high, and the stars are high,
And the thought of a man is higher.
A deep below the deep,
And a height beyond the height!
Our hearing is not hearing,
And our seeing is not sight. (53)

The poet is affirming that there is more splendour and divinity in the human spirit than in all the mountain's grandeur, or in the wonders of the starry sky, or in the mysteries of the ocean's depth. There is a matrix in our souls designed for occupancy only by God, without whom life remains dully empty. This is why worship (which to some people seems an affront to human dignity, a denial of human liberty) is to a believer highly exalting and richly fulfilling. In worship, deep answers to deep, and the true worshipper finds profound satisfaction. Instead of enslavement, worship brings freedom, and instead of debasement, elevation to the throne of God. In worship, our true nature as people who carry a divine likeness is both revealed and realised.

---

52) Decimus Magnus Ausonius (*circa* 310-395); *Epigrams 1.12.*
53) Alfred, Lord Tennyson, *The Voice and the Peak*; st. 8 & 9.

"Our hearing is not hearing, and our seeing is not sight," said the poet, because unless you have an ear to hear the voice of God, and an eye to see the vision supernal, then you are really deaf and blind. You are not seeing anything worth seeing, nor hearing the only voice that deserves to be heard. Worship is the vehicle by which we are trained to hear the still, small voice of God (1 Kg 19:12), and to see the face of the Almighty.

Yet worship is like a tender orchid. It may easily be crushed by the clamour of the world. Hence it must be carefully nurtured as our highest gift and sweetest joy, and as the ultimate origin of all true happiness, the first taste of Paradise. Indifference will scar it; neglect will wither it; unbelief will render it dumb. If the sound of our worship is to reach the ear of heaven it must be genuine, hearty, rich with love, zealous for God, impassioned by his beauty, offered in his holiness, and presented for his glory.

Those who forget to worship will be forced to weep.

WE LOVE OUR NEIGHBOUR

"See how much these Christians love one another!" cried the pagan enemies of the church during its early decades. But it was a cry of scorn, not admiration. Christian love was reckoned a weakness, not a strength, a mark of servility not authority, a thing for slaves to practise and for the strong and powerful to mock. [54]

But in the end, the affirmation of Jesus proved to be stronger – *"Because you love each other, everybody will know that you are my disciples!"* (Jn 13:35)

And they did love each other, so well, and so truly demonstrating the unquenchable, indestructible power of the love of Christ, that tens of thousands of ordinary people

---

54) The saying originated with the North African lawyer and Christian apologist Tertullian (*circa* 155-230), and is found in his *Apologeticus 39*.

ignored the jeers of their pagan rulers and gladly embraced the gospel. Thousands, too, once they had tasted that love, rather than deny it or lose it, suffered unspeakable tortures and joyfully yielded their lives. They died gladly, proclaiming Christ as Saviour and Lord. But their deaths were not futile, for those who had derided Christian love were themselves finally overthrown, and invincible love conquered the known world.

Perhaps a shortage of that love is the cause of the weakened Christian witness of our time? Perhaps a resurgence of that love would again cause a river of revival to surge across the land!

Yet it does still exist, and true Christians do truly love each other in Christ, and the presence of that love, so contrary as it is to the way of the world, marks Christians especially as people made in the image of God.

WE CAN SEE TOMORROW

"What is man, if his chief good and market of his time be but to sleep and feed? A beast, no more." [55]

Perhaps the sorriest aspect of modern life is that people have lost the capacity to see beyond today. Yet this faculty is a major divide between humans and animals. *We* know that there is a tomorrow; *they* don't. We know that we are alive and must die; they don't. Even when animals seem to plan for tomorrow, such as gathering food before winter sets in, it is a matter of instinct not foresight. Despite the fable of the grasshopper and the ants, no insect or animal is able consciously to choose play over work, leaving other creatures toiling to fill their larders. Yet even those who are working have not actually chosen to do so. They did not say to themselves, "It will soon be cold, and there will no longer be food in the fields, so we must collect as much as we can while

---

55) William Shakespeare, Hamlet, *4.4.33*.

we may!" No, they are driven by urges of which they have no understanding, and which they obey without knowing that they are obeying them.

We humans alone are fully aware that we have needs, why we have them, how to meet them, and what lies before us. The wise, of course, plan for the future, even gaining inspiration from insects to do so (Jb 12:7-8; .Pr 6:6; 20:4) In this we share an attribute of God, who is Lord of the past, the present, and the future. But it is also a fearful burden. How can we live happily today when all those unknown tomorrows lie before us, and beyond them, beyond the grave, the awful expanse of eternity?

Many decline to think about it. They can hardly be persuaded to plan their own *immediate* future, let alone set up an insurance for an *after-life*. So they mar the image of God in them. But we Christians should have a double vision –

IN THIS LIFE – A SET OF <u>GOALS</u>

I cannot imagine living without goals. From my teen years on I have had a purpose in living, a set of goals I hoped to achieve, dreams to fulfil, tasks to complete beyond the ordinary routines of making a living, of performing the duties required by each day. I have had short-, medium-, and long-term goals related to Christian service and ministry, career enhancement, and hobbies. I have had both vocational and avocational goals – some failed, some succeeded, some were changed, some abandoned, but they all added zest, meaning, value, and purpose to life. And of course, none were (are) more meaningful, more zestful, than those connected with serving the church and Christ.

But here is where there is a disastrous failure in our modern church and society – there are so many people who live only for today, who not only lack any plan for the future but seem to have lost even the ability to see past the present moment. I remember reading about a group of young adults who were asked to write a story set, first, in the past, then in the present, then in the future. Generally, writing about the past and the present gave them no problems. Their stories were colourful, detailed, tangible, and successful. But when they came to write about something that might happen in the future, they were lost. A veil settled over their minds, and they were unable to imagine anything happening. The future, to them, was an impenetrable, grey, and misty fog. At best they could see a few shadows. Vivid perception eluded them. Hardly more than one or two of the students wrote successful stories.

Are you in that sad state? Is the future dark to your eye? Do you lack any true goals? Then you are less than fully alive! Get to prayer, ask the Lord, and you will soon discover wonderful things to do, be, and become! I do not mean, of course, that God will disclose your future in any detail, but that he will guide you onto the pathway that will best enable you to realise his plan for your life, and bring you to a sense of ongoing fulfilment, satisfaction, challenge, and joy.

IN THE NEXT LIFE – A CROWN OF <u>GOLD</u>

Here is the most terrible yet most divine aspect of our capacity to see the future – we alone of all creatures know that we must die, and after that comes the Judgment (He 9:27). Here also is the most baffling aspect of human character, that knowing they must one day die, so many people behave as if death were a fiction, and will never touch them!

Yet you *will* die. And what then?

Many of course hope that death is the end of all life and all awareness, bringing with it utter annihilation of body, mind, soul, spirit – everything. Thus, more than twenty centuries ago some Greek poets were already writing cynical epitaphs–

> Do the dead in truth sleep beneath these stones? What is the underworld really? Nothing but a great darkness. And what of the resurrection? A lie! And Hades? A fable! We perish utterly. This my tale to you is true. But if

you insist upon believing the myth, then I am a large ox in Hell!

How was I born, and for what purpose? Why did I come here, only to leave again? Why learn anything, to end up knowing nothing? I was born from nothing, and now I am again as I was. I was not – I was born – I was, and now I am not. That is all. Anything else you may say is a lie. I shall not be again. (56)

Likewise, the world-weary Persian philosopher Omar Khayyam, whom I have quoted before, intoned –

Ah, make the most of what we yet may spend,
Before we too into the Dust descend;
Dust into dust, and under Dust to lie,
Sans wine, sans Song, sans Singer, and – sans End! (57)

Another Voice, when I am sleeping, cries,
"The flower should open with the Morning skies."
And a retreating Whisper, as I wake –
"The flower that once has blown for ever dies." (58)

Oh threats of Hell and Hopes of Paradise!
One thing at least is certain – this Life flies:
One thing is certain and the rest is lies;
The flower that once has blown for ever dies. (59)

---

56) From The Greek Anthology, ed. Peter Jay; Penguin Classics, 1986. The book is a fascinating collection of more than 800 ancient Greek poems and epigrams, spanning more than a thousand years from 700 B.C. Some of them are hauntingly beautiful, some remarkably crude, some humorous, covering a gamut of human experiences and emotions, situations and events.

57) The Rubaiyat of Omar Khayyam, *Quatrain 26*; tr. by Edward FitzGerald (1809-1883). His was the first, and is still the most famous translation into English of *The Rubaiyat*.

58) Ibid. Quatrain 28.

59) Ibid. Quatrain 66.

But for most people across the entire span of history, the idea that death means extinction has been unacceptable. They cannot believe that like a withering flower, human life simply and finally ends. They are sure there must be some kind of continuance. How can love and friendship, truth and joy, perish? How can the sense I have within me of immortality be a delusion? So have countless people asked – and they have searched for an answer. Indeed, all the great religions of the world, with their countless millions of followers across the centuries, have presented some kind of hope of immortality, some vision of Paradise.

But their visions have failed.

All their struggles to penetrate the veil in the end either created the kind of cynicism shown by the Persian sage, or else resulted in deeper despair. For example, many of the poems in the *The Greek Anthology* show the helplessness felt by people in the ancient world when they confronted unexpected death. They discovered how futile were their foolish myths –

- On the death of his wife –

> Atthis, you lived for me and breathed your last in my presence. You were formerly the source of all joyfulness, but now of all tears. Virtuous, much lamented, now sleepest thou the mournful sleep, thou whose head was never laid away from thy husband's breast, leaving thy Theius alone as one who is no more; for with thee the hope of my life went into darkness.

- On the death of a young wife –

> O black winter of savage death that froze the spring of your unnumbered charms. The tomb tore you from your brilliant day in this, your bitter sixteenth year. Your husband and your father – blind with uncomforted grief – lament you, Anastasia, for you were our sun.

- On the death of a child of seven –

> Hermes, dread messenger of Death, why usherest thou this child into the laughterless abyss of Hades? What hard fate snatched Ariston from the fresh air at seven years old? God of Death, delighting in tears, are not all mortal spirits allotted to thee? Why then gatherest thou the unripe grapes of youth? (60)

Those weeping people clung to their myths, because without them they had nothing; yet they could find no comfort, no hope, no joy in their doctrine of Hades.

But centuries later, in his cynicism, the Persian sage unwittingly revealed the very thing that would have solved both his dilemma and theirs –

> *Strange, is it not? that of the myriads who*
> *Before us pass'd the door of Darkness through*
> *Not one returns to tell us of the Road,*
> *Which to discover we must travel too.* (61)

Ah! But One <u>has</u> returned from the dead, even Jesus Christ our Lord, who has abolished death and brought life and immortality to light through the gospel! (2 Ti 1:10) James, too, describes this contrast between the apparent ephemerality of human life and the real eternal life we discover in Christ –

> *What is human life? Little more than a swirl of fog that appears briefly but is soon burned up by the sun . . . But God has promised a crown of life to those who love him . . . Indeed, by his word of truth he has already given us life and*

---

60) Op. cit.
61) Op. cit. Quatrain 67.

made us the most glorious of his creatures. (James 4:14; 1:12, 18)

Never, then, accept either Satan's or the world's evaluation of your life. We are God's <u>*creation*</u>, and also his <u>*new creation*</u> – doubly made in his image and likeness! Therefore, in the words of our text –

> *Strive to be blameless and innocent, behaving like* **<u>unblemished children of God</u>** *even though you are surrounded by crooked and corrupt people. Then you will shine among them like stars in a dark sky." (Ph 2:13-15)*

EIGHT

THE MYSTERY OF THE ATONEMENT

"Jesus humbled himself, by becoming obedient to the point of death — even death on a cross!" (Ph 2:8)

One of the most startling things in Christian theology is that across 20 centuries no one has conceived a definitive theory of the "atonement".

Many different ideas have been advanced by scholars about the meaning of what Christ achieved for us at Calvary, but no doctrine of the atonement has ever been accepted as final by the entire church. How then should we think about the Cross? What *did* Christ do there? Was it

- an act of **substitution**, with Jesus taking our place, suffering the death penalty in our stead, so that we could finally escape death?
- a **limited** atonement for the benefit of the church alone, which excludes the rest of mankind, and brings salvation only to those who believe?
- a **vicarious** atonement, with Jesus bearing our punishment, and satisfying our debt to God, thus releasing us to serve God with joy?
- a **ransom** paid to Satan so that he would be obliged to free us from the grip of Hades, and open the way for us to overcome all the powers of darkness?
- a **quenching** of God's anger against our sin, so that he could look upon us with kindness and enrich our lives with his favour?

- a ***moral example*** for us to follow, constrained by love to offer all that we have to God in return for him offering us his own priceless Gift?

Or we could ask – is the atonement an act of

- propitiation?
- expiation?
- reconciliation?
- redemption?
- demonstration?
- subjugation?
- all of those, none of them, some of them?

Out of all the discussions, at least three major theories have emerged and been embraced at different times by different groups of Christians. They are ...

1. ***The Satisfaction Theory*** – the Cross was a punishment for human sin, endured by Christ on our behalf. This theory was formulated by **St Anselm**, a 12th century Italian monk.

2. ***The Exemplary Theory*** – the Cross was an illustration of God's unfathomable Love. This theory was formulated by **Peter Abelard**, a 12th century French monk.

3. ***The Dramatic Theory*** – the Cross was a place of warfare against Satan and all the forces of darkness. This theory was formulated by **Martin Luther**, a 16th century German monk. [62]

---

62) There were, of course, many ideas about the atonement expressed by many teachers, writers, and preachers across the centuries before Anselm, Abelard, and Luther. I mean only that those three men are usually

....*continued on next page.*

Although each of those theories does present an aspect of what Christ accomplished on our behalf at Calvary, in the end the Cross remains a conundrum. As Paul himself said, *"Who can deny the profound mystery of our religion, of how Christ appeared in human form and was shown by the Holy Spirit to be righteous!"* (1 Ti 3:16) Even the holy angels cannot plumb the depths of this secret! (1 Pe 1:12)

Still, because *everything* cannot be known it does not follow that *nothing* can be known. So it is useful to explore the major theories of the atonement and to learn from them what we can.

But before we do so, perhaps we should ask: *"Why do we need an atonement?"*

Why? Because we are sinners, deserving the severest penalty of God's broken law, and must perish unless God finds a way to rescue us. Indeed, this is one of the unique themes of scripture, for from beginning to end it insists that we are a fallen race, under sentence of death. Yet outside the Bible that is an uncommon idea! For example, think about

- ***other great religious literature***, such as the various scriptures used by Muslims, Buddhists, Hindus, and others. In none of them is there anything comparable to the biblical insistence that we have all sinned and that sin is an offence against God, which must be adequately requited, and for which he alone can provide a sufficient atonement.

- ***philosophical and secular literature***, which universally argues that the human race is advancing steadily toward perfection, and scornfully derides any

---

.... continued from previous page.
  accredited as the first to express their particular ideas on the atonement in some kind of systematic and comprehensive form.

- **<u>the good opinion people have about themselves</u>,** who generally feel, despite their faults, that they are nice people with nice manners, and deserve to go to heaven. Just visit any cemetery and look around for a tombstone that openly admits the sin of the person buried there! As the little girl asked her mother when they were walking through a cemetery, reading the inscriptions, "But Mummy, where are all the wicked people buried?"

But the Bible is unequivocal – *"Not only have we all sinned, but we all keep on falling short of the glory of God."* (Ro 3:23) And the penalty for that moral and spiritual failure is death and hell –

> *"God is the one you must fear,"* said Jesus. *"Not only can he take your life, but he can also throw you into hell. You should certainly be afraid of God!"* (Lu 12:5)

But of course, that is not the whole story! The Bible is equally emphatic that God loves us so much that he is willing to make any honourable sacrifice to rescue us from our terrible doom. Hence the Bible insists that punishment, rather than redemption, is God's *"<u>strange work</u>"* – *"For Yahweh will rise up ... he will be angry ... that he may do his work, his <u>strange</u> work, and fully perform his act, his <u>strange</u> act."* (Is 28:21)

The prophet calls judgment God's "strange" work because the Lord, out of his eternal love, would rather *save* than *destroy*. See *Jeremiah 31:3; John 3:16; 1 John 4:8,16.* So the gospel culminates in the great declaration, *"God was in Christ reconciling the world to himself!"* (2 Co 5:19)

Here are the Father and the Son, equal in love for each other and for us, jointly effecting our salvation. And two things are an inseparable part of this salvation –

- ***The work is as much the Father's as the Son's.***

Banish the pernicious idea that Jesus, by his sufferings, forced a reluctant Deity to abandon his implacable anger. The Cross was the focus of the love of <u>both</u> the Father and the Son. As eager as Jesus was to rescue us, the Father was just as eager. But then also –

- ***The Cross was an indispensable part of that work.***

This too is unique to Christianity. No other great religion offers a divinely wrought pathway to atone for sin. And just what <u>was</u> accomplished at Calvary? <u>Answer</u> – our everlasting salvation! But how? For it is not at all obvious how one man's death can atone for many, nor how sin and guilt can be passed from one person to another. We can understand someone paying another's <u>penalty</u>, but not embracing the offender's <u>guilt</u> ! Yet Jesus at Calvary did both.

Theories of the Atonement are attempts to find a biblical answer to that question. The first of them is –

THE SATISFACTION THEORY

This idea was devised by <u>St Anselm</u> (died 1109), an Italian monk who moved to England and became Archbishop of Canterbury. Refusing to compromise his spiritual principles, Anselm twice quarrelled with the king and was twice exiled. But on each occasion a reconciliation was effected, and he returned to England with his authority enhanced. Reckoned in his own time as the greatest thinker since Augustine, he lived only for Christ and the church, and died full of honour at 76.

Prior to Anselm, the common theory was that Christ's death was a ransom price paid to Satan to compel him to release his captives. The idea was that God tricked the devil by offering Jesus to him on condition that he release all the souls he had in captivity. The devil agreed, and thought that he had won a great victory when Jesus plunged into hades.

But Satan failed to realise that Jesus still possessed his deity, and was stunned when the Saviour rose from the dead and rescued the imprisoned souls. A popular illustration was that the devil is like a fish; it sees the enticing bait, but doesn't know there is a hook inside it.

Anselm shrank from such notions, which seemed blasphemous to him. What possible interest could the Almighty have in buying *anything* back from the devil? And how could God engage in the sly deceit the theory proposed?

Instead, Anselm argued that our sin left us deeply in debt to God. How deep? Almost fathomless!

Jesus himself used various devices to state this, but none more pungent than Luke 17:4 – *"If someone offends you or harms you seven times in one day, and each time he comes back saying, 'I'm sorry; I won't do it again!' you must forgive him every time!"*

Which of us has ever risen to the challenge of such demands? They show how deeply sin has penetrated us, and how far we have to climb even to approach the standard of God. They show how much, despite our best endeavours, we keep on falling short of the glory of God! (Ro 3:23) But great as our debt may be, at Calvary <u>*Christ fully paid it*</u>. Thus the offended law of God is *satisfied* and the Father is now able to treat us who believe as his innocent children.

THE EXEMPLARY THEORY

This idea was devised by Peter Abelard (died 1142), a French monk and philosopher. He saw the Cross primarily as an example of God's measureless love, an example that we are called to follow. Abelard did not find any vicarious aspect in the death of Christ, or at least he refused to see this as the major reason for the Cross. Rather, he viewed Calvary primarily as a call to recognise and respond to the love of God.

Perhaps this was a result of his experience with romance. When still a young man, he fell in love with Heloise, the teen-age niece and ward of a high-ranking cleric, and after she bore him a child, married her. Her uncle took a fearful revenge. He hired a bunch of thugs to beat up the young man and then castrate him. Mutilated and humiliated, Peter fled from Paris to the country. He struggled to re-establish his career, and eventually did attain high renown as a theologian and philosopher.

After many years he ran foul of the church authorities once again, this time for his writings, which were publicly burned. Various troubles followed, his spirit was broken, and he died, aged 63.

In the meantime, Heloise had retired to a convent. She corresponded with Peter, and many of their letters have survived, and are still in print. Here is a selection from her first letter to him –

> To her master, or rather her father; husband, or rather brother; his handmaid, or rather his daughter; wife, or rather sister; to Abelard, from Heloise.
>
> Recently, my beloved, by chance someone brought me the letter of consolation you had sent to a friend. I saw at once from the heading that it was yours, and was all the more eager to read it since the writer is so dear to my heart. Having lost him in reality I hoped at least to create an image of him from the words. ...
>
> You know, beloved, as the whole world knows, how much I have lost in you, how in one wretched stroke that supreme act of flagrant treachery robbed me of my very self in robbing me of you ... For a man's worth does not rest on his wealth or power ... and a woman should realize that if she marries a rich man more readily than a poor one, and desires her husband more for his possessions than for himself, she is offering herself for sale. ...

> Certainly any woman who comes to marry through desires of this kind deserves wages, not love; for clearly her mind is on the man's property, not himself ...
>
> And so, in the name of God to whom you have dedicated yourself, I beg you to restore your presence to me in the best way you can – by writing me some word of comfort, so that in this at least I may find increased strength and readiness to serve God. ... I beg you, think what you owe me, give ear to my pleas, and I will finish a long letter with this brief ending: farewell, my only love." (63)

When Abelard died, Heloise had his ashes conveyed to her convent (of which she was now abbess). When she died 22 years later, her ashes were interred with his. In 1817 their remains were carried to Paris and buried together in a single ornate tomb, which still exists. They were esteemed for the perfection of their spiritual love. In a passion of pure love they had sacrificed their physical union for each other's sake and for the cause of Christ.

That is how Abelard saw the Cross. He said that when we look upon the Cross we must be profoundly affected by its witness of God's love.

Think also about *John 3:16*, which ignores any focus on substitution, redemption, or reconciliation, and focuses on loving, looking, and believing (cp. the Serpent in the Wilderness).

So for Abelard, the idea that the cross was a place where the Father cruelly punished his Son for our sins seemed unjust, immoral, and unethical – it repelled him. Rather, with love

---

63)   From an internet page, The Letters of Abelard and Heloise.

the Father allowed his Son to be put to death, hoping to inspire in us a similar self-sacrificing love.

Many others have echoed Abelard. Here is one famous example, Isaac Watts' great 18th century hymn, *When I Survey the Wondrous Cross* –

> *When I survey the wondrous cross*
> *On which the Prince of glory died,*
> *My richest gain I count but loss,*
> *And pour contempt on all my pride.*
> ....
> *Were the whole realm of nature mine,*
> *That were an offering far too small;*
> *Love so amazing, so divine,*
> *Demands my soul, my life, my all.*

Thus, when we look upon the Cross and the Christ who suffered there for us, we are freed from fear, and moved to repentance, love, faith, and a Christ-like life. The Cross is a call to recognise and respond to the measureless love of God. **If God has so loved us, how can we not love and serve him in return?**

THE DRAMATIC THEORY

This idea was devised by a German priest, Martin Luther (died 1546), who argued that the cross was a place of warfare against Satan and all the forces of darkness. At Calvary Christ totally defeated the devil's might and broke every chain. But he did so not by an exercise of domineering power, but by overcoming the devil's chief weapon, <u>death</u>. There were two vast consequences –

- by his resurrection from the dead Jesus showed himself to be *"the Son of God with Power"* (Ro 1:4); and

- he put all the forces of hell on public display (Col 2:15)...

> *God stripped the rulers and authorities of their power and made a public spectacle of them as he celebrated his victory in Christ.*

That victory we are now challenged to enter into by faith, ourselves in Jesus' name *"treading on serpents and scorpions"*, and taking authority *"over all the power of the enemy"* (Lu 10:19).

And more than anyone before him, Luther argued for the primacy of the Word of God as the sword by which we may defeat Satan in Jesus' name. This was exemplified by his famous casting of an ink bottle at the devil. He was toiling in his study one day, translating the *New Testament* into German, when he thought he saw Satan standing in front of him, mocking him. Declaring that the words he was writing would rout the devil's kingdom, Luther cast an ink bottle at the apparition, which at once vanished. It is said that the ink stain can still be seen on the wall! [64] At any rate, there is no doubt that Luther's writings transformed Europe and helped to send out an army of people emboldened by the Word of God, asserting the triumph of Christ over all the powers of darkness.

CONCLUSION

The infinite mystery of how the death of Christ enables our salvation will always be beyond our full grasp. But the various theories of the atonement (which in the end are only ways of understanding an array of biblical declarations) can give us insight into the gift of God. Jesus did indeed die in our place, bearing our penalty and guilt, thus setting us an example of love to live by daily, and providing us with a means of treading Satan underfoot (Ro 16:20).

---

64) No doubt refreshed from time to time by enterprising tour guides. The story probably evolved from someone saying that with "a bottle of ink", that is, by his writings, Luther had routed Satan, renewed the church, and changed the course of history.

With utter assurance we can affirm with Paul –

Just as scripture foretold, Christ died to take away our sins and then three days later rose from the dead, so that if you declare that Jesus is Lord, and heartily believe that God did indeed bring him back to life, <u>you will be saved</u>." (1 Co 15:3-4; Ro 10:9)

NINE

THE FIVE "SOLAS"

> ***Grace*** *to you and peace from God our Father and the Lord Jesus Christ. ... It is right for me to feel this way about you all, because I hold you in my heart, and because you all share with me the **grace** of God, both in my imprisonment and in the defence and confirmation of the gospel. ... The **grace** of the Lord Jesus Christ be with your spirit. (Ph 1:2, 7; 4:23)*

Paul begins and ends his letter with **_grace_**, that wondrous gift of God, which comes to us through Christ. I want to use the idea of divine grace as a basis for exploring the five great principles of the 16th century Protestant Reformation. It is a theme that follows on well from the focus of the last chapter, the *atonement*.

INTRODUCTION

On October 31, 1517, in Wittenberg, Germany, Martin Luther composed a document that shook the world. It was not, however, written in the most auspicious environment, for he suffered from chronic constipation and composed it mainly while enthroned in an outhouse! The square stone pan still exists, and is now a tourist attraction; but while one may gape at it, no one is permitted to sit on it! [65]

Luther's document was called *The 95 Theses*, and it was an invitation to debate many abuses he had observed in the

---

65) I have read this story about the outhouse several times in different places, but I have not been able to confirm it

Roman Catholic Church. Luther nailed his paper to a church door in Wittenberg, which was then a common way of calling for a public debate. That event began what we now call *"The Reformation",* and out of it arose all the Protestant churches that now exist worldwide.

Luther challenged the claims of preachers who offered indulgences for sale. [66] He also asserted his views about the nature of true repentance and faith, questioned the absolute authority of the papacy, and insisted that the Roman church had corrupted the gospel.

He was soon joined by many other Reformers, whose concepts finally resolved into five foundational principles, namely, that salvation comes to us –

- by **_grace_** alone
- through **_faith_** alone
- in **_Christ_** alone
- from **_scripture_** alone
- to the **_glory_** of God alone. [67]

"SOLA GRATIA"

This means that salvation comes to us by **_Grace Alone_**. It is the doctrine that salvation is unmerited and rests solely upon God's kindness toward us in Christ. If he chooses not to save us then nothing we do can avert ruin. But the Father has

---

66) Those preachers were called "pardoners" and they were authorised by the pope to offer, for a price, remission of the punishment in purgatory that was thought to be still due for sins even after absolution. The pardoners made their living and Rome's coffers were enriched, by selling such "indulgences".

67) For a more formal and detailed explanation of the *Five Solas* see *"The Cambridge Declaration of the Alliance of Confessing Evangelicals"* (April 20, 1996) – (http://www.reformed.org/documents/index.html?mainframe= http://www.reformed.org/documents/cambridge.html)

indeed acted in Christ to make his gracious pardon and deliverance from death available to everyone who believes.

Unhappily, most people, because they are confident either in their personal right to be saved or in their ability to save themselves, scorn the Father's precious gift. Indeed, because of our fallen human nature, even the best of us find it immensely hard to surrender to grace alone.

But against all human self-confidence our cry must ever be –

> *My hope is built on nothing less*
> *Than Jesus' blood and righteousness;*
> *I dare not trust the sweetest frame,*
> *But wholly lean on Jesus' name!*
> *On Christ the solid rock I stand,*
> *All other ground is sinking sand!* [68]

So we must insist that every person has failed both morally and spiritually and is irrefragably cut off from Paradise unless the Lord graciously intervenes to rescue them. See *Romans 6.23; 9:16; Ephesians 2:8-9; Titus 3:5a*; etc. This dominance of grace precludes any salvific claim upon God based upon birth, rank, wealth, achievement, virtue, ethnic identity, or anything at all apart from the free gift of the righteousness of Christ.

Therefore, unlike the Jews of whom Paul speaks, we must reject every attempt to build some kind of personal righteousness, and cheerfully submit ourselves to the righteousness that God alone can give (Ro 10:3). And how foolish it is to do otherwise! What madness makes us prefer the menstrual rags of our own righteousness (Is 64:6) to the lovely and limitless righteousness of God? I have said it

---

68) Edward Mote, in Hymns of Praise, published circa 1834. Mote was pastor at Rehoboth Baptist Church in Horsham, West Sussex for 26 years. He was so loved by his congregation that they offered him the church building as a gift (which meant that he could keep all the pew rents for his own use). Mote replied, "I do not want the chapel, I only want the pulpit; and when I cease to preach Christ, then turn me out of that."

already, but let me repeat it here – even if I had never sinned, and were utterly spotless and pure, I were still ten times a fool if I preferred to depend upon my own righteousness rather than submit to his! Would a man cling to a mud hut when he's offered a mansion in its place? Could he sensibly prefer a fig leaf to a new garment?

But in reality, we *have* no righteousness of our own – nor can we ever have any – not even a fig leaf's worth! Human methods, techniques or strategies by themselves cannot lift us from sin to holiness. On the contrary, one might as well try chasing a cloud on foot.

It is said that the Turkish philosopher and wise man, Nasr'eddin Hodja, was once seen running down the road as fast as he could go, shouting at the top of his voice. Someone saw him, ran up to him, and asked him what on earth was the matter? The hodja [69] kept on running, and puffed, "I want to know how far my voice travels, so I'm chasing after it." Thus he mocked all who pursue the absurd.

Yet his quest was less futile than those who think they can run fast enough, or do anything, to catch salvation by their own efforts.

Surely, though, church history alone is enough to show the futility of trying to obtain the grace of God by paying a price, or making a sacrifice, or exerting an effort. Think about the "saints" and hermits of old. What pains they endured! What sacrifices they made! How much they suffered! Yet in vain, for they were no closer to God at the end than a simple confession of trust in the gospel would have brought them at the beginning.

Let the following passage suffice for them all –

---

69) "Hodja" is a title, much like "mullah", and means a learned or wise man, particularly in a Muslim context.

One hermit, hoping to subdue the flesh and achieve a state of holiness, spent 10 years in a bucket slung between two poles. James and Alexander of Cyr imposed upon themselves the sentence of standing in the open for the rest of their lives. Acepsemus shut himself in a cell for 60 years, refusing to see or speak to anyone, while another hermit lived alone in a cave on the top of a mountain, and never once turned his face toward the west. They all became a pattern for many others who locked themselves alone in caves for life, slept on beds of thorns, laced their food with bitter herbs, twisted thorns and thistles into their garments, and inflicted on themselves countless other pains.

One of the most renowned hermits was St Simeon Stylites (390-459), who sat on a 60-foot pillar for 36 years. But he was outdone by St Simeon the Younger. The early historian Evagrius says that while this Simeon was still a child he befriended and tamed a young panther, which he led to a nearby monastery. The preceptor, who was ensconced on a column himself at the time, saw in this a sign of special sanctity. He invited the boy to join him on his column, which Simeon agreed to do, and then spent the next 68 years on pillars of ever-increasing height, including 45 years on his last. Many miracles of healing, exorcisms, accurate prophecies, and the like were attributed to him.

But both Simeons were exceeded by St Alypius, who combined the idea of standing in the open with that of a pillar, and so he *stood* on his pillar for 53 years, until he lost the use of both his feet, after which he spent his last 14 years lying only on one side of his body. (70)

Likewise, in the 6th century, in convents, it was not uncommon for a nun to have herself bricked into a small space, leaving only a slit through which food was passed, and there remain until death. Possession of such a "living relic" brought enormous prestige to a convent, along with large numbers of pilgrims, and of course much additional revenue. (71)

Measured against such intense passion, such unshakable dedication, the petty denials that modern Christians are prone to use as bargaining points with God turn into a bad smell! A day of fasting, reading a few more chapters of the Bible, spending a little more time in prayer, going to more church meetings, forsaking some lawful pleasure – such are the things some people hope to use to pressure the Almighty. But if St Alypius, rotting away on his lofty and exposed stone pillar for 67 years, got not one hair's breadth closer to God, for all his privations, how can you suppose that any effort of yours will succeed any better?

No, salvation is not in any sense a human work. It is a gift of God that can only be brought to us supernaturally by the Holy Spirit, who unites us with Christ. Thus *by grace alone* we are carried from endless death to eternal life, becoming the very children of the Father.

"SOLA FIDEI"

We are saved by _grace_ alone, through **_Faith Alone_**, because of _Christ_ alone! Any diluting of that proposition brings

---

70) For more information on his life, see the eponymous article in Wikipedia. His presumed head is preserved in the Monastery of Koutloumousiou.

71) From my book The World's Greatest Story, *Ch. 6*, where you will find more details, and supporting references.

ultimate spiritual death. It is the rock upon which the church must be built. Abandon or weaken it, and the church, like a house built on sand, will soon begin to crumble away.

The gospel declares, not what *we* must do to reach God, but what *God* has done for us in Christ to bring us to his throne. It is not about what *we can do* to gain heaven, but about what *God has done* by his own grace to carry us there. The pattern was established way back in the Garden when the Lord God, in the cool of the evening, went looking for his erring children, and calling, "Where are you Adam?" It is a scene, not of Adam searching for God, but of God looking for his wayward child. It is the difference between *religion* and the *gospel*. *Religion* is the story of man's futile quest for God; but the *gospel* is the story of God's effective quest for us (Ge 3:8-9). *Religion* leads to gods made in the image of man; but the *gospel* leads to people restored to the image of God.

Is there then *nothing* at all that we can do to help us toward salvation? Yes, there is! We are called to *repent* and to *believe* and to *confess* the good news that Christ came, died, and rose again to rescue us from sin and death, and to give us eternal life. (Mk 1:15; Ro 10:9-11). And that is sufficient. Nothing more is required from the worst among us; nothing less is needed by the best.

Yet we cannot claim any credit even for those actions. For it is the Holy Spirit who draws us to repentance and trust. Indeed, we must in the end see *faith*, not as some personal virtue, but simply as the instrumental means of our salvation. That is, faith is nothing more than a tool God uses to link us with Christ, and that tool is itself a gift of God (Ep 2:8). So we are left with no opportunity to commend ourselves, not even for our faith; rather, we must simply thank God, not only for our salvation, but also for giving us a heart to believe.

If faith is the sole pathway to salvation, then all human works are excluded. So much is this true that Paul himself, that great servant of God, was compelled to say –

> *We know that no one can be justified by keeping some law, but only by trusting in Jesus Christ. That is why <u>even we apostles</u> have put our faith solely in Christ Jesus, so that we may be justified by faith in Christ and not by observing the law. This much is certain: no one will ever be justified by keeping the law!" (Ga 2:15-16).*

Did you notice the words, *"<u>Even we apostles</u>"*? Surely if anyone had a human claim upon the grace of God, it must have been the apostles? What relentless sacrifice and toil they suffered in fulfilling their ministry! But no, even they dared to offer God nothing but the merits of Christ.

This exclusion of all human works (whether good or bad, noble or ignoble, loving or hateful) as a pathway to God offends human pride. But, offended or not, we have to accept that we have no basis upon which to approach God except unwavering trust in the saving work of Christ. We cannot allow any exceptions. We must insist that every person abandon all pretence to merit, cast off all pride, embrace humility before God, and acknowledge faith in Christ alone as their only hope of eternal life.

> *Nothing in my hand I bring,*
> *Simply to thy Cross I cling;*
> *Naked, come to thee for dress;*
> *Helpless, look to thee for grace;*
> *Foul, I to the Fountain fly;*
> *Wash me, Saviour, or I die.* [72]

Paul's splendid refrain rightly became the great battle cry of the Reformation: *"We are justified by faith in Christ alone, apart from any work of ours!"* (Ro 3:20-22, 26, 28; 4:5; 5:1; Ac 13:39; 1 Co 6:11; Ga 2:16; 3:8, 11-14, 24; Ph 3:9; Tit 3:7).

---

72) *Rock of Ages Cleft for Me*, by AM Toplady; 3rd. stanza. From The Church Hymn Book; 1872.

Calvary alone can placate the fury of God's offended holiness and requite his violated justice. But the Cross must remain ineffective for us until we have heartily embraced its message by faith.

Where such faith exists, all other pathways to God are scorned. No trust will be placed in shrines and relics. Icons and artefacts will never again be relevant to salvation. Faith becomes its own authenticator, an all-sufficient anchor for the soul, an assured key to eternal life, an open door to the throne of God.

However, never imagine that faith is nothing more than some kind of mental assent to a piece of dogma. Rather, it must have about it a lively quality, a vigour that boldly and joyfully seizes the promise of God —

> *Faith, mighty faith, the promise sees,*
> *And looks to that alone;*
> *Laughs at impossibilities,*
> *And cries, "It shall be done!"* [73]

See *Ephesians 2:8-9; Philippians 3:9; 1 Peter 1:9*; etc.

Saving faith sparkles; it takes hold of Christ firmly; it is wrought by the Holy Spirit in response to the preaching of the gospel – how then can it ever be dull, lifeless, void of life? Perhaps it waxes more mightily in some than others, but it must always have some throb of life that enables the believing heart to entwine itself with Christ and find peace.

"SOLUS CHRISTUS"

This means that salvation comes from **_Christ Alone_**. There is no salvation outside Jesus Christ, nor is there any other Saviour. His sinless life, his sacrificial death, his triumphant resurrection and ascension are altogether sufficient to reconcile us to God. We need no other hope. We accept no other Redeemer. There is nothing to add to what Christ has

---

73)   Charles Wesley, Hymns and Sacred Poems; 1742.

achieved, nor can any human work reduce the value of the Cross.

So Calvary, the Saviour who died there, and the empty tomb become the only claim we can make upon God. In Christ alone we trust, and to him alone must be given pre-eminence in all things (Cl 1:18).

When that message is blurred there will soon be a substitution of —

- wholeness for holiness
- recovery for repentance
- intuition for truth
- feelings for faith
- chance for providence
- programmes for trust
- ritual for worship
- and immediate gratification for enduring hope.

See *Acts 4:12; Colossians 1:18; 1 Timothy 2:5*; etc.

Solus Christus means that Christ has no rivals, nor any equals. We cannot partner Christ with any other prophet nor allow any other leader to usurp his right. He is Lord of lords and King of kings. No higher sovereign exists, nor any other final authority. The gospel he proclaimed is not one among many peer religions. He is *The Truth*, they are false. Thus Christ precludes the relativism that is popular in our time, as if he were no longer solely *The Way* (Jn 14:6) but only one of several ways to God.

There is in fact an exclusivity to the gospel, even an intolerance, that many find offensive. But we will not apologise for it. There is truly no other name under heaven but the name of Jesus by which fallen humanity can be saved (Ac 4:12). We cannot condone wild fanaticism, nor allow the harsh dogmatism that leads people to violence against each other, for we Christians must be ruled by love. But neither will we compromise our faith merely to relieve the discomfort caused by the gospel. Jesus is still today, as he has been from the beginning, a Rock over which many will stumble, and a Stone of Offence (Ro 9:33; 1 Pe 2:8; Mt 21:44; Lu 20:18). The fable of *The Man, the Boy, and the Donkey* is relevant –

> A Man and his Son were once going with their Donkey to market. As they were walking along by its side a countryman passed them and said: "You fools, what is a Donkey for, but to ride upon?"
>
> So the Man put the Boy on the Donkey and they went on their way. But soon they passed a group of men, one of whom said: "See that lazy youngster? He lets his father walk while he rides."
>
> So the Man ordered his Boy to get off, and got on himself. But they hadn't gone far when they passed two women, one of whom cried: "Shame on that lazy lout, riding while his poor little son trudges along."
>
> Well, the Man didn't know what to do, but at last he took his Boy up before him on the Donkey. By this time they had come to the town, and the passers-by began to jeer and point at them, declaring, "Aren't you ashamed of yourself for overloading that poor donkey with you and your hulking son?"
>
> So the Man and Boy got off and tried to think what to do. They thought and they thought, till at last they cut down a pole, tied the donkey's feet to it, and raised the pole and the donkey to their shoulders. They went along amid the laughter of all who met them till they came to

Market Bridge, where the Donkey, getting one of his feet loose, kicked out and caused the Boy to drop his end of the pole. In the struggle the Donkey fell over the bridge and was drowned.

"That will teach you," said an old man who had followed them. "Try to please everyone and you will please no one." [74]

Two essential corollaries of *Solus Christus* are –

- **_The sufficiency of the royal priesthood of Christ_** before the Father's throne, thus dethroning the Virgin, for in Christ we have full and free access to God.

We need no other Intermediary, no other Intercessor, no other Priest, nor any other Name upon which to call. Christ alone is our Priest, indeed, our High Priest, forever making intercession for us at the throne of God (He 7:25). Why should it ever be supposed that we need any other Mediator? Who could ever give us better freedom to approach God? And how can it be imagined that we need anyone, even Mary, to bring us to Christ? Are we not enjoined to *"come boldly to the throne of God"* in the name of Jesus? (He 4:16), having no other claim than *the blood of the everlasting covenant* (He 10:19-22). Or as Paul puts it –

> *Through Jesus alone, and depending upon nothing more than our faith in him, we may approach God boldly, and with all confidence! (Ep 3:12, paraphrased)*

If we cannot enter the holiest by a simple confession of faith in Christ, then we will never stand in the presence of God. If Jesus alone is inadequate, then no one else can carry us there.

---

74) Taken from *Aesop's Fables* at http://www.aesopfables.com .

- ***The splendour of the royal priesthood of each believer***, thus dethroning the saints, and removing any need of their intercession along with any need of their goodness.

Whatever rights the departed saints had to approach the throne of God, in Christ we have the same. Whatever virtues the saints accumulated in Christ we gain better from Christ. Their works may earn them a certain status in the coming kingdom of God, but our works may earn the same for us. There is nothing they can do for us, nor can they add anything to us, in our present pilgrimage. They are as dependent upon the merits of Christ as are we. And if they were members of God's royal priesthood, then so are we in Christ!

As God's royal priests we have the two-fold right that belongs to all true priests –

- ***A right of unfettered access to the throne of God***, which we should never allow anyone or anything to deny us.

Just as the ancient priests had a right of entry to the holy place solely by virtue of their birth, not because of any personal merit, so do we. We need no other dependency save that we are the children of God by faith in Jesus Christ. On that basis alone we come boldly to the throne of grace. There is no sacrifice to make, no special prayer to offer, no song to sing, no task to fulfil, no holiness to achieve, no goodness to display, no pains to undergo, nor any training, effort, or price to pay to arrive at the footstool of the Almighty. Let any believing heart do no more than whisper the name of Jesus and at once that person will be nearer to God than any archangel or angel has ever been! Never allow anyone to tell you otherwise.

- ***A right of speaking in the authority of the King***, which we should exercise in bold faith against all the works of darkness, speaking as the ambassadors of Christ (2 Co 5:20).

Therefore we must keep Christ and the Cross at the very centre of our faith and vision.

But that introduces another major idea. It is impossible to separate Christ from his church, which is his Body on earth, and of which he is the Head. Whoever wishes to be in union with Christ the Head must also be in union with the church, his Body. Can a man wed only a girl's head? Hardly! It's a package deal! No matter if he finds her head lovely but her body repulsive. If he wants the one, he must take the other. So with Christ. There is no fellowship possible with Christ apart from fellowship with his Body, the church, by which I mean a local church.

Remember how Paul wrote all his major doctrinal letters to local churches – at Rome, Colosse, Corinth, Ephesus, and so on. The presumption must be that the truth he revealed is generally applicable only within that context and therefore belongs only to those who are actively involved in a local church. [75]

However, I say "generally" because there are plainly situations when godly people are denied access to a local church, or find themselves irrevocably cut off from attending worship with other Christians. In such cases, the Christian is obliged to serve the Lord in isolation from other believers, and may indeed serve him very well.

Thus there is a need for balance. Indeed, the _Protestant_ heresy says that salvation is entirely a private and

---

75) The so-called "universal" church – ethereal, invisible, spiritual – has no real existence. The church the apostles knew consisted of local companies of Christians, bonded together in love, fellowship, worship and discipline, under the lordship of Christ. To them the worst punishment that could be inflicted upon an erring saint was to cast him out of a local church, thus *"consigning him to Satan"* (1 Co 5:1-5). How foolish then is the notion that one can serve God as well outside the church as within it. Some people may be obliged by circumstances to serve Christ outside of any bond with a local church, and they may serve him well; but they would serve him even better if participation in the life of a church were open to them.

individualistic matter; but the _Roman Catholic_ heresy says that salvation is entirely a public and corporate matter. The one makes salvation solely dependent upon personal faith and private communion with God; the other makes salvation entirely dependent upon the church and public attendance at its services.

Both claims are wrong. Salvation is neither wholly private nor wholly public, neither fully personal nor fully corporate; it is an amalgam of both. Where a local church is available and the believer is able to become an active participant in its life, then it is spiritually perilous to abandon the church. But where circumstances make any connection with a church impossible, then private faith is sufficient to sustain spiritual life and carry the believer from earth to glory.

So while salvation _can_ be gained apart from the church, and without any contact with the church, it must be said that if there were no church there would be no salvation for anyone. Christ is present in the world primarily through his church, his Body on earth, with himself as its Head, and the church is the channel through which the gospel is carried worldwide. All who wish to be sure of their place in the kingdom will cling to the church, and will discover Christ and serve him though the worship, work, and witness of a local company of believers.

This does not change the proposition that salvation comes to us through faith alone, for that proposition does not stand alone – it is allied to the assertion that salvation is from Christ alone, and Christ is found in his church. Nor can salvation be gained simply by joining a church, nor even by working very hard in it, for without _faith_ it is impossible to please God (He 11:6). Salvation comes to us as a gift of God's grace, through hearing and believing the word of God, which unites us with Christ, especially in his church, and all to the glory of God.

"SOLA SCRIPTURA"

This means that ultimately we look for spiritual direction and authority in **_Scripture Alone_** (Re 22:18-19).

We hold that the Bible is the sole arbiter of two things –

CHRISTIAN FAITH

No authority outside of scripture can be allowed to bind a believer's conscience. We give nothing precedence over it – neither church, nor creed, nor council, nor state. No personal experience, no matter how wonderful it may seem, can be allowed to contradict or weaken the force of scripture. Everything must be measured against biblical truth. Other revelations, visions, dreams, omens, and the like, if they deny what the Bible teaches, must be scornfully rejected, even if they come in the shape of an angel or seemingly of Christ himself. [76] The Holy Spirit will never speak contrary to what is written in the Bible, nor will any vision from God. Whatever purports to come from God will harmonise with scripture and will in some way glorify Christ.

We insist that the Bible is inerrant in all that it actually teaches and that *it is the only written divine revelation,* and that *it alone can bind the conscience.* This is because the Bible alone teaches all that is necessary for our rescue from sin and death; in its pages alone is there an uncorrupted picture of Christ; it alone can inspire the kind of faith that brings people separated from God into dynamic union with

---

[76] Over the years several people have approached me saying that Jesus had appeared to them, telling them to do this or that, or promising them some boon, or revealing some future event. But even while listening I knew that they were wrong. I cannot say what they saw, but I was sure it was not a genuine vision of Christ. Why? Because in one way or another, their words were a mockery of scripture. Had they heeded my warning, they would have been spared the trouble that all who failed to listen eventually fell into. I am not saying there are no genuine visions of Christ, of course there are, but these are always in harmony with Scripture and therefore do not lead to error.

the Father (Ph. 2:16; Cl 3:16; 1 Ti 6:3-5; 2 Ti 2:15; 3:16-17; He 4:12; 1 Pe 1:23-25; 4:11;.2 Pe 1:19-21; Re 22:18-19; etc., etc.).

CHRISTIAN PRACTICE

It is folly for the church to succumb to the pressures of the surrounding mass culture. We cannot be ruled by market demands, popular acclaim, songs that fail doctrinally, nor by any demand to accommodate the gospel to current mores. The gospel is not a commodity that can be sold by clever promotion and smart marketing. Unless the Holy Spirit draws a person to repentance no quantity of clever talking will provoke genuine faith. Salvation cannot be purchased with gold, nor can we choose to follow Christ apart from the Father's call, which commonly comes through preaching the gospel (1 Pe 1:18; Jn 6:37; 14:6; Ro 10:13-15).

If the preaching of Christ and him crucified is not enough then the church has already failed.

An understanding of cultural and sociological trends, of human psychology, of good ways and bad ways to present a message, are all useful, but we dare not depend upon them. To an extent we may, and indeed probably must, adapt to modern secular trends, current forms of music, architecture, communication, and the like, but nothing can be allowed to transcend the pulpit. If the church is not built upon and sustained by the preaching of the word of God, then it will fail. The word of God must reign supreme. Scripture, wisely and rightly interpreted, must be seen as the only inerrant rule for the life, work, worship, and witness of the church. Anything that claims a higher authority or presents a contrary path must be rejected.

And mark that our call is not to be successful, but *faithful*; not to pursue happiness, but *holiness*. We are not trying to emulate some prosperous commercial enterprise, but to build the family of God. While sound business principles should not be ignored, neither are they paramount. Our guiding rule is not *profit* but *love*, for by love alone will the world know that we are truly disciples of Christ (Jn 13:35). If we are deficient in love then our beautiful churches, our sophisticated music, our grand productions, our clever marketing, are all dust in the wind. The entire enterprise will deserve only to be blown away.

But we cannot know what divine love truly is, nor how to walk in that love, apart from the faithful preaching of the word of God. Therefore we must demand preachers who deliver the whole counsel of God, without fear of human opinion, and without compromise. We cannot endorse any attempt to appease current secular demands or prejudices that requires us to weaken the proclamation of Christ as the only Way, Truth, and Life. Popular opinion is no basis upon which to determine the righteous message of the gospel. The Bible must remain our sole criterion of truth.

I do not mean that there is no truth outside of scripture, for that would be ridiculous, but that all claims to truth must be measured against the Word of God. Anything that denies what scripture positively affirms must be rejected as error.

THE ESSENTIAL PULPIT

In his Great Commission Jesus told his disciples to go into all the world and **_preach_**. Not hold prayer meetings, nor sing songs, nor write books, nor even build churches – good and useful though they all are – but **_preach_**! (Mt 28:19; Mk 16:15; Ac 1:8).

This emphasis upon the authority of the Bible, and especially upon preaching, sharply distinguishes the church from the mosque. In Islam the pulpit is an option; but for the church it is a necessity. This idea was enforced a thousand years ago by a story about the Hodja, Nasr'eddin –

> It was Friday evening, and a large crowd had gathered to hear the renowned Hodja preach. But he was weary of the acclaim and of the demands of preaching, so when he entered the pulpit he asked the people if they knew what he was going to preach about. They all said, "No."

Whereupon he cried, "If you don't know, then how can I teach you?" And he left the pulpit and went home.

The next Friday, the Hodja asked the same question. Not willing to be tricked again, the people all said, "Yes!" Whereupon he cried, "If you know already, then what can I teach you?" And he left the pulpit and went home.

Next week the mosque was once again packed, and again Nasr'eddin asked if they knew the topic of his sermon. Determined not to be cheated of their sermon a third time, some replied, "Yes!" while others shouted, "No!" Whereupon he said, "Let those who know tell those who don't." And again he left the pulpit and went home. [77]

Thus he showed that the pulpit was not an essential part of Islamic worship, and that it could be occupied or not, as the leader chose. As far as I know, that is still the case in Islam, although commonly someone does preach at the regular Friday service in each mosque. But there is no ordained clergy in Islam, and therefore no one upon whom the task of preaching falls automatically.

But that is not the case with the church. For us the pulpit is not an option; rather it is *preach* or *perish*! Where there is no pulpit there is no true church; [78] and where the gospel is not fully preached from that pulpit, there is no true church; and where the word of God is not strongly expounded from that pulpit, there is no true church; and where the people are

---

77) I have read this story in several places over the years, some reverent, some cheeky. Here is one of the latter–http://www.cs.biu.ac.il/~schiff/Once/ rst4.html

78) I do not mean, of course, merely a piece of furniture, but a place from where a preacher can proclaim the full counsel of the Almighty, and the preaching itself.

not regularly called to obedience to God from that pulpit, there is no true church.

Paul rating preaching so high in spreading the gospel and building the church, that even when the preachers were wrongly motivated he rejoiced. So long as Christ was *preached*, for whatever reason, the great apostle eagerly thanked God! –

> *Most of the brothers, having become confident in the Lord by my imprisonment, are much more bold to speak the word without fear. Some indeed preach Christ from envy and rivalry, but others from good will. The latter do it out of love ... The former proclaim Christ out of rivalry ... What then? Only that in every way, whether in pretense or in truth, Christ is proclaimed, and in that I rejoice. Yes, and I will rejoice! (Ph 1:14-18, ESV)*

So whatever else the local church may lack, this it must have – *a pulpit with an open Bible from which the word of God is proclaimed, and Christ is preached, constantly and faithfully.*

"SOLI DEO GLORIA"

This means **<u>Glory to God Alone</u>**, and it expresses the doctrine that no one nor anything outside God should receive credit for our salvation and that he alone is worthy of our praise and adoration. *We must live our entire lives before the face of God, under the authority of God, and for his glory alone.* Two great composers, Bach and Handel, often appended this motto to their music, using the initials *SDG*. Other composers and writers have done the same, and at least in spirit, so should we.

This rule has been called the "over-arching principle of the Reformation", and in one way or another all the battles engaged in by the Reformers against the corruptions that were endemic in the church in their time, were ultimately a fight for the glory of God. The Reformers were determined to unseat pope and bishop from what they reckoned a wrongful usurpation of the rule of God. They fought against the exalting of images and the worship of Mary. They rejected the right of the church to add to or take away from the Bible. They resisted any arrogation of power by church or state that brought honour to humans rather than God. As the *Westminster Shorter Catechism* (1647) asks, "What is the chief end of man? *Answer:* Man's chief end is to glorify God and to enjoy him forever."

The Reformers also argued against the common division of the world into secular and sacred, for to them all things were sacred, and God could be, and must be, as well served in so-called secular vocations as in priestly ones (Ep 6:5-8).

However, living solely for the glory of God does not mean that life will always go as we feel it should, nor that we will be treated fairly. Injustice will continue, and the most devout Christian may sometimes have to endure deprivation of one sort or another. Jesus himself warned –

> *Do not lay up for yourselves treasures on earth, where moth and rust destroy and where thieves break in and steal, but lay up for yourselves treasures in heaven, where neither moth nor rust destroys and where thieves do not break in and steal" (Mt 6:19-20).*

This principle of the divine economy is well illustrated by another tale from the Nasr'eddin Hodja collection – [79]

> One day four boys came to the Hodja, carrying a bag of walnuts. They asked him to divide the nuts between them. He said, "Do you want me

---

79) There are several collections of stories about Nasr'Eddin, both in print and online. They are a kind of Muslim version of the *Fables of Aesop*. Unlike Aesop, few of them have an attached moral, but they are nearly all amusing and instructive in some way. A search of the internet will quickly take you to several locations that contain collections of the Hodja stories.

> to do it God's way or man's way?" They replied, "Oh! Surely God's way!" thinking this would lead to a fairer division.
>
> But the Hodja gave a large handful to one boy, lesser ones to the next two, and hardly any nuts to the fourth.
>
> The boys protested angrily.
>
> But he said, "If you had asked me to divide the nuts according to man's way, I would have given each of you the same number; but you asked for God's way, who gives to some people much and to others very little."

Thus the Hodja taught the boys that the ways of Providence are inscrutable, and that we can do no more than trust God, whatever happens.

So we are called to live entirely for the glory of God and to be governed solely by his will. His purpose alone must be ours. Of course, within that framework, there are many lesser goals, dreams, ambitions, and callings that we are free to pursue. But those choices must always be finally subservient to the command of the Lord.

Soli Deo Gloria also holds the idea that the chief aim of Christian life is to glorify God by giving Christ pre-eminence in all things (Cl 1:18), especially in preaching the gospel.

This should prevent us from turning worship into entertainment, or evangelism into a marketing strategy. It should cause pastors to give more consideration to the content of the songs they allow to be sung in church, to ensure that they are true to the gospel, and that they exalt Christ rather than the singers. It should cause us to focus more on holiness than on self-improvement, on righteousness rather than riches, and on giving more than getting. It should also prevent us from offering adulation to any human being, whether pope, priest, pastor, teacher, evangelist, or any other.

CONCLUSION

Though we understand and apply those five slogans in a manner that may differ from the Reformers, they should still be the foundation and the pillars of all our ministry and outreach, to the glory of the Lord our God through our Saviour Jesus Christ.

CONCLUSION

TEN

ADVANCING IN CHRIST

> *Let those who are <u>perfect</u> be thus minded. (Ph 3:14-15)*

The French artist Paul Cézanne was famous not only for his postimpressionist style, in which he produced many fine paintings, but also for the slowness at which he worked, and for his perfectionism. One of his clients, after sitting 115 times for a portrait, was astonished to hear him murmur, "I am not altogether displeased with the shirt front." [80]

Some people think that God demands that sort of perfection from each of us, and they are terrified of falling short of it. Are they right or wrong?

In the text just above, Paul uses an important word, *teleios*, which is quite properly, translated as "perfect". But it does create a problem. The Greek word lacks both the absoluteness and the abstract character of the English terms. In English, "perfect" and "perfection" can stand on their own, conveying a concept or an ideal of perfection; but the Greek word always had a practical sense. That is, something (or someone) could be called *teleios* only by becoming "perfect" for fulfilling some purpose, or for doing some task – such as we might say of a tool, "it's just perfect for the job". The tool itself might be blemished, or even poorly made, but if it does well what it was made for, then it is *teleios*.

Thus *teleios* is better rendered as "finished", or "sufficiently developed", or has "all the necessary qualities". It could be

---

80) The Book of Anecdotes; ed. Clifton Fadiman; Little, Brown and Co; Boston, 1985; art. *Cézanne*.

paraphrased as, "this object is as good as it can be expected to be, or needs to be, at this time, or for this purpose." When applied to God, of course, *teleios* does mean absolute perfection in every conceivable way. But when applied to anything else, it carries a lesser, limited meaning, thus –

> *You must be as perfect (teleios) as your Father in heaven is perfect (teleios)." (Mt 5:48)*

Now that is one of those verses Bible readers are prone to hurry past, hoping it will not catch up with them! If it does, they react with dismay, and lift up their complaint, "Only a relentless tyrant would make such an impossible demand!" They protest angrily (like Joram, when Ben-hadad summoned him to cure Naaman's leprosy), *"See how he is seeking a quarrel with me!"* (2 Kg 5:7).

But God does not command what we cannot perform. The solution lies, of course, in understanding the actual meaning of what Christ said, which is much softer than what is implied by the English word "perfect", as in this paraphrase–

> *Just as the Father is everything you expect him to be, so you should be everything the Father expects you to be.*

So the "perfection" demanded is relative – absolute for God, but only what is fair and reasonable for us. For God, total moral perfection is expected; but for us, only a kind of down-to-earth, pragmatic perfection. For God, we assume perfection fully realised, unblemished, ideal; but for ourselves, perfection that is qualified, incomplete, and that never will be absolute. [81]

---

81) I presume that after the resurrection of the dead, when we return with Christ to heaven's glory, we will be rid of all corruption and made "perfect"; but no creature can ever possess the absolute perfection that is an attribute only of the Almighty.

Teleios, then, carries the idea of attaining a proper rate of growth, reaching an expected goal, arriving at a required standard, achieving a desired purpose. It defines practical behaviour rather than an abstract ideal. So when Jesus insisted that, like the Father, we too must be "perfect" (*teleios*), he was not demanding any higher perfection than is commensurate with our human nature, along with the opportunities we have had, the influences that have worked on us, and so on. He was saying that for each of us, each ongoing day, there is a level of maturity, of growth, that we should have reached. Just as we expect the Father to be fully perfect, so he expects us to be as perfect as we should be at this stage of our life. He wants no more of us; but neither is he satisfied with less.

The New Testament uses *teleios* in several different ways, which all convey this idea of growth or development. I want to express them in one word, *ADVANCE*. That is, you can call yourself "perfect" if you know that you are –

ADVANCING TOWARD THE PURPOSE OF GOD

In our main text from *Philippians* (3:12-15) Paul uses *teleios* to describe a person who is aware of his true self; that is, he is not deluded about himself, but is mature and honest in appraising himself. He insists that such a person can make only one sensible decision, and that is to *"press toward the goals God has established"*. This he twice says is the mark of a "perfect" Christian.

This self-knowledge has often been lauded as the mark of a truly mature person (a Greek would say *teleios*), well balanced, scorning self-delusion, possessing a quality of serenity, a sure purpose, poised and confident. For example, the 2nd century Greek travel writer, Pausanias, tells of an inscription that was carved at the entrance to the Temple of Apollos, at the Delphic Oracle, on the heights of Mt Parnassus in central Greece –

> In the fore-temple at Delphi are written maxims useful for the life of men, inscribed by

> those whom the Greeks say were sages ... (who) came to Delphi and dedicated to Apollo the celebrated maxims, *"Know thyself,"* and *"Nothing in excess."* (82)

The idea presumably was that there was little use in seeking to know the gods until one had a fair knowledge of oneself. Delusion about oneself would almost certainly produce delusion about heaven. If I am unwilling truly to know myself, then it will be impossible for me truly to know even another human being let alone God. Paul had much the same idea when he wrote –

> *Do not think about yourself more highly than you ought to think. Think rather with sober judgment, each according to the measure of faith that God has assigned you. (Ro 12:3)*

And I would say it is just as much a sin to think yourself less than you are than to think you are more. We should strive to know just what we are, and what we are not, and to live happily and comfortably within that framework.

Then a companion aphorism was, *"Nothing to excess."* This too was echoed by Paul –

> *Let everyone see how moderate you are, for the Lord is near! (Ph 4:5)* (83)

The idea of moderation as an ideal is very ancient. It goes as far back as the worship of the Sumerian god Enki, some five thousand years ago. By the time it had become a motto engraved upon Apollo's temple at Delphi (4th century B.C.) it had been part of the received wisdom of mankind for two

---

82) Description of Greece, *Book X.24*.1; tr. by WHS Jones; William Heinemann Ltd., London, 1918.

83) You will find an extensive discussion of what Paul means by the word he uses here (*epieikes*), in my book Christian Life, Vision Publishing, Ramona, Ca.

millennia. Three hundred years later, Paul too endorsed it, and made it one of his prescriptions for Christian life, pleasing to God and to the church. The two Delphic sayings belong together. Those who know themselves well will likely behave moderately toward others. And those who are moderate in all things, will be more likely to know themselves well. So, "nothing to excess," but let a pleasant balance be a rule of the good life in Christ. Screaming fanaticism, frothing hysteria, wild emotions, irresponsible chaos, unrestrained action of any sort – these all violate the rule of moderation and ought to be shunned by right-thinking people.

So then, following the rules of sober thinking and moderate behaviour, you can pronounce yourself <u>*perfect*</u> if you set yourself to fulfil the three goals God has made you for –

SELF-FULFILMENT

See vs. 12-13 –

> *Not that I have already (reached my goal) nor am I already perfect, but I press on to make it my own, because Christ Jesus has made me his own. Dear friends, I do not reckon that I have yet made it my own. But one thing I do – forgetting what lies behind I keep straining forward to what lies ahead!*

Can you say the same? Indeed, what other final purpose can any true believer have, other than to discover the will of God, then do it? And the will of God (contrary to foolish claims I sometimes hear people make) is most likely to match who you actually are, your personal talents and character, personality and abilities. So, *"Know yourself!"* And make it the quest of your life to fulfil as completely as possible all that you are, and have, and can be.

I once heard a story about an old rabbi – let us call him Johanan – who was on his death bed, with a group of disciples gathered around him. One of the young men summoned the courage to ask the dying man for one last word of wisdom, a piece of sage advice that he deemed the most important thing he could say to them.

Rabbi Johanan lay still, with his eyes closed, while the young men wondered anxiously if he had heard the request, and if he would be able to speak. Suddenly, he seemed to find a new surge of energy. He sat up, looked sternly at his followers, and spoke these last words – "My sons, I have learned this lesson above all. When I meet my Maker in a few moments, he will not ask me why I was not more like his servants Abraham, or Moses, or Elijah, or Ezra, or anyone else. He will ask me only one question – 'Rabbi Johanan, why were you not more like Rabbi Johanan?'"

So too with us. God is not wondering why you are not more like some famous saint, or some renowned preacher, or some successful Christian leader, or like anyone else at all, not even Jesus of Nazareth, but only why you are not more like *yourself!* [84] If he had wanted you to be someone else, he would have made you like that person. Instead, he made you as you are, and he likes what he has made (Ge 1:31).

The anonymous author of the *Wisdom of Solomon* [85] expresses the idea beautifully –

> *Everything you have created is precious to you, O Lord, and you hate nothing that you have made, otherwise you would not have made it. Can anything remain in existence*

---

84) We must of course be like Christ in the sense of following his example of obedience to the Father, of emulating his character, and of reflecting his beauty. Nonetheless, if I may say it reverently, I will never be Jesus and he will never be me; nor should either of us wish to be other than what the Father ordained from the beginning.

85) Probably written about 150 years before Christ. During the first three hundred years or so of church history the book was treated by the church as scripture. It was finally banished from the canon early in the 5th century, but remains part of the Old Testament *Apocrypha*. It remains in the canon of the Roman Catholic and some other denominations, although it is recognised as having only secondary authority.

> *except by your choice? Can anything even come into being unless it is by your will?"* (11:24-26)

So let us be content to be who we are and determined, as much as lies within us, to bring into reality everything that God has made us both to be and to become.

REWARD

See vs 14 –

> *I press on toward the goal for the prize of the upward call of God in Christ Jesus. (ESV)*

Some people hold the peculiar notion that Paul's words in these few verses show that he was unsure of having a part in the resurrection of the righteous dead, which is to happen when Christ returns. To me, that seems absurd. One only has to remember what he says in chapter one (vs. 21-23) to realise he was utterly confident of his place in the Kingdom of God. And he certainly included himself in the last words of this chapter – *"But our citizenship is in heaven, and from it we await a Saviour, the Lord Jesus Christ, who will transform our lowly body to be like his glorious body, by the power that enables him even to subject all things to himself"* (vs. 20-21, ESV).

Yes, he does use terms of aspiration in the passage, but he is talking about the *extent* to which he will enter into the *power* of the resurrection of Christ, and of how well he will merit the *prize of the upward call of God in Christ*. But of his participation in the resurrection itself when Christ comes, he could have had no possible doubt.

"I am stretching toward the mark," he cried, like an ancient runner, leaning forward, his arms outstretched, straining to be the first to touch the ribbon at the end of the race. In a normal contest, of course, only one person can be first, but in this Christian race of ours, every runner can win. But only if the believer is running with a *determination* to win! No prize comes to the lazy, the careless, the backslidden, those with

no interest in the laurel crown. Hence Paul's strong language – *by any means* – *pressing on* – *straining forward* – *stretching out*. He sees himself as an athlete, training hard, running the race with fierce zeal, and straining every nerve, determined to win the highest prize that can be gained.

Nor can we ever relax from this race. Adam Clarke says,

> When it was said to Diogenes, the cynic, "Thou art now an old man, rest from thy labours;" to this he answered – "If I have run long in the race, will it become me to slacken my pace when come near the end; should I not rather stretch forward?" (Diog. Laert., lib. vi. cap. 2. sec. 6.) [86]

So must our attitude be. We are not engaging in a recreational stroll, where we may go here or there, as the fancy takes us, but we are runners in a race. There is a course that must be strictly followed, or else face disqualification. There is a goal – the finish line – to be attained, or else lose the prize. We cannot depart from the course, nor cease running, until the race is ended, and the mark reached. Only then will the runners merit the prize.

And what is that prize?

It is not specified, except that reward will come to those who heed the *upward call of God*. That is, the call God gives his people to fix their minds, not on earthly things, but upward, on those that are heavenly (Cl 3:1-4; Mt 6:19-21). For such people, the prize will indeed be rich, splendid beyond description. Why doesn't Paul say what it will be? I presume, because for each overcoming Christian it will be different. Think about the metaphorical words of Jesus, when he said that some would rule five cities, and some ten (Lu 19:17-19; and cp. Mt 5:21-23). Think too about the diverse promises

---

86)   Commentary on the Bible (1832).

that the ascended Christ makes to those who *overcome* (Re 2:7,11,17,26; 3:5,12,21). To each person will come the prize appropriate to his or her calling and achievement. Despite popular opinion, not everybody will be the same in heaven, nor occupy the same place in the hierarchy of the Kingdom of God.

Elsewhere, Paul does give some idea about what he was expecting to receive from the Master's hand, and he declares that we may have the same expectation if we too run well and fight well –

> *Henceforth there is laid up for me a crown of righteousness, which the Lord, the righteous judge, shall give me at that day: and not to me only, but unto all them also that love his appearing. (2 Ti 4:8)*

To some degree, for each of us, the *prize of the upward call of God* on that day will be partly determined by divine sovereignty and partly determined by how well we have run the race set before us now. Anyone who thinks that he or she is a mature Christian, says Paul, will recognise this truth, and resolve to merit the highest possible reward –

> *Let us therefore, as many as be perfect (teleios – mature), be thus minded. (Ph 3:15).*

And if you are struggling to grasp these matters, or wonder about how true they are, then, says Paul, *"God is willing to make everything clear for you"* (vs. 15b). If you sincerely ask God to show these things to you, he will, and you will then *know* how important it is to run the race as a true competitor, and to hunger for the prize.

WORSHIP

See vs 17-19 –

> *Dear friends, join together in imitating me. Take us as the pattern you should copy, and follow the example of those who walk in the same way. I have often told you before, and I*

> *am telling you again now, even with tears, that there are many who behave like enemies of the cross of Christ. Their only end is ruin. Their god is their stomach. They are proud of behaviour that should make them ashamed; and their minds are fixed on earthly things.*

This is a troubling passage. Were those disgraceful people ever Christians? Presumably they were at least in the church, but had they ever been born again? If Paul is indeed speaking about people who had once been saved, but are now backslidden, then this passage offers proof that salvation can be lost. Paul clearly states that they are destined for destruction. No doubt scholars will continue to quarrel about how far the terms can be pressed to mean one thing or another, but at the least it provides a solemn warning against presuming on the grace of God.

Their god was their stomach. This at first seems merely to be an injunction against greedy eating; but it probably means much more than that, including excess greed for anything earthly. The ancients located the soul and human emotions in the belly, so Paul's warning must include those who go to church simply because pomp and circumstance appeal to their senses, or because they gain some kind of ascetic or emotional satisfaction from religious ceremonies. We might say today that our *hearts* were moved by a lovely service; but the ancients would say that their *bellies* were stirred. Yet in this case, it was all carnal. Those people were never moved to repentance, they never came into real union with Christ by faith. They approved an easy and undemanding religion, having no stomach for truly striving to win the race.

They are proud of behavior that should make them ashamed. – about which Albert Barnes (1798-1870) makes the following comment –

> They glory in things of which they ought to be ashamed. They indulge in modes of living

which ought to cover them with confusion. *Who mind earthly things* – That is, whose hearts are set on earthly things, or who live to obtain them. Their attention is directed to honour, gain, or pleasure, and their chief anxiety is that they may secure these objects. This is mentioned as one of the characteristics of enmity to the cross of Christ; and if this be so, how many are there in the church now who are the real enemies of the cross! How many professing Christians are there who regard little else than worldly things! How many who live only to acquire wealth, to gain honour, or to enjoy the pleasures of the world! How many are there who have no interest in a prayer meeting, in a Sunday school, in religious conversation, and in the advancement of true religion on the earth! These are the real enemies of the cross. It is not so much those who deny the doctrines of the cross, as it is those who oppose its influence on their hearts; not so much those who live to scoff and deride religion, as it is those who "mind earthly things," that injure this holy cause in the world. [87]

<u>Their minds are fixed on earthly things</u>. In the 5th century before Christ, the Greek playwright Euripides composed his satyrical *Cyclops*, in which the one-eyed god captures Odysseus and his companions, and proposes to eat them. As he forces them into his cave, he says –

> *The earth, by force, whether it will or no,*
> *Bringing forth grass, fattens my flocks and herds,*
> *Which, to what other god but to myself*

---

87) Notes on the New Testament; Kregel Publications, Grand Rapids, Michigan; 1966; *Philippians, in. loc.*

> *And this great belly, first of deities,*
> *Should I be bound to sacrifice? I well know*
> *The wise man's only Jupiter is this,*
> *To eat and drink during his little day,*
> *And give himself no care.* (88)

Thus the Cyclops scorns all gods, and pretends to worship only one divinity, his belly, "the first of deities". He mocks law, he despises care; he lives for himself alone and his own pleasure. Even the supreme god Jupiter is to him found only in worshipping and satisfying his careless and carnal appetites. And he has had a multitude of followers over the centuries, some of whom can be found even in the church.

The Cyclops suffered a horrible fate. Ulysses cunningly managed to put out his one eye with a red hot poker. Which is perhaps an apt metaphor of the kind of people Paul is castigating – since they refuse to see the truth, they become blinded to the truth, and will never see the way of life until it is too late. Their minds are fixed on earthly things. Heaven remains invisible, and they cannot capture a vision of the beautiful City of God, toward which the real pilgrims of Christ are resolutely marching.

This capacity to see the invisible is something that must be cultivated. Indeed, consign any creature to perpetual darkness and it will lose the ability to see. So are many Christians. They have for so long looked only at earthly things that heaven has become impenetrable. Indeed, we all need to exercise our spiritual sight (cp. Ep 1:17-18; Cl 1:9), so that we look beyond the visible world, which is only temporary, and learn to see ever more clearly the world that is truly permanent (2 Co 4:18). Our spiritual faculties need exercise and training as surely as do our physical. This

---

88) From the poetical rendering by Percy Bysshe Shelley (1792-1822) of the play, *lines 316-321.*

requires prayer, discipline, concentrated effort — but the resulting vision splendid provides a vastly adequate reward!

THE CONSEQUENCE

Through the entire passage Paul steadfastly pushed toward his real purpose, introduced by the forceful conjunction, "but" –

> *But we are citizens of heaven, from whence we are waiting with eager longing for our Saviour to come, the Lord Jesus Christ. He will transform our corrupt bodies to be like his glorious body, by the power that enables him to bring everything that exists into subjection to himself.* (Ph 3:20-21)

We cannot behave like those whose god is their belly; indeed, we turn from them in shame, because we now belong to a different country, heaven, with a different King, the Lord Jesus. We are citizens of the New Jerusalem. We live by a higher standard and under a godly law.

CITIZENSHIP

Paul's citizenship analogy had particular relevance for the Philippians. Although Philippi had existed as a Greek city for many centuries, by the time Paul visited it in 49 A.D. it had become a Roman colony. [89] This meant, despite its location in east Macedonia, that it had adopted Roman culture, lived under Roman law, followed a Roman style, kept to a Roman polity, and its citizens had the same rights, privileges, and responsibilities as if they lived in Rome itself. In appearance

---

89) This was done by the decree and actions of Octavian (later, Augustus Caesar), across the span of a dozen years from *circa* 42-30 B.C. He did so, to celebrate his military victories and to reward his troops who were settled there. To strengthen the Roman population of the city, Roman soldiers from the defeated armies were also forced to move there. And so Philippi, once thoroughly Greek, almost overnight became thoroughly Roman.

and manner Philippi had become a Roman city in a Greek land.

So the Philippians well understood what Paul meant when he spoke to them about a new citizenship, with a different set of loyalties, operating under a heavenly ruler, and requiring a changed lifestyle. All around them, in the secular world, they were surrounded by Greek people and Greek culture and law; but within the walls of their city, Rome was replicated. They were immensely proud of their connection with Rome, and strove to be as much like the mother city as possible. [90] But now the Christians among them had to lift the scene to a higher dimension. Now they were to call themselves citizens of a vastly greater and more glorious city than Rome, with a higher demand upon their love, their loyalty, their pride. Just as a good citizen of Philippi would scorn to emulate Greek rather than Roman manners and customs, so should Christians reach for a heavenly style, following the rules and polity of the Kingdom of God and of the New Jerusalem.

ASPIRATION

The chief mark of our new citizenship, says Paul, is an unquenchable awareness of the Second Coming of Christ. We live with a constant expectation of his return, an eager scanning of the clouds above (*"they shall see the Son of Man coming in clouds with much power and glory"* Mk 13:26), and a frequent question, "Will it be today?" This is an irresistible quality in a genuine Christian –

> *We are waiting with eager longing for our Saviour to come, the Lord Jesus Christ (Ph 3:20)*

---

90) They did, however, continue to speak Greek, which was the *lingua franca* of the ancient world, as English is today. Even when he wrote to the Christians in Rome, Paul did not use (as one might expect) Latin, but Greek. *lingua franca*

So we who believe, who are filled with the Spirit of Christ, cannot help but yearn for that wonderful day when we shall see him coming, and all the holy angels with him, when the church will be raptured (91) to join with him in heaven's bliss for ever.

Christians quarrel about many aspects of the Second Coming – its manner, its time, its place, its immediate result, and the like – but there can be no lack of certainty about its *reality*. *"This Jesus will come from heaven just as you have seen him go to heaven!"* (Ac 1:11) So we who love him look for him. We hope he will come today, but if not, we shall still live as those who are truly cut off from this world, and who belong to a higher and better land. For us, reality lies, not in this world, but the next. This world is but a passing shadow; the world to come will endure for ever. Who but a fool would try to catch and keep the shadow while allowing the substance to pass by without heeding it? Shall we prize the fragrance more than the rose, the photo more than the person, a candle's flicker above the radiant sun? Rather, we stand with the wise who scorn the folly of esteeming a transient world above the eternal and imperishable City of God. Our home is heaven, and we press toward it with eager joy. As the gospel song proclaims –

> *This world is not my home I'm just a-passin' through,*
> *My treasures are laid up somewhere beyond the blue!* (92)

Indisputably, from the time of Abraham until now, the real people of God have deemed themselves strangers and pilgrims who can find no lasting residence in this world. As the apostle says, they know that God has prepared for them an eternal city that has an indestructible foundation, and

---

91) "Rapture" is the term used to describe the resurrection of the righteous dead and the ascension of the church to meet Christ in the air on the Day of his Return.

92) Albert E. Brumley (1905-1977), who composed over 800 songs (Wikipedia).

they remain restless travellers, looking for that better and heavenly country (He 11:10,16).

Gill beautifully describes the pilgrim's true nature –

> Their thoughts are often employed about (the city of God); their **affections** are set upon it (Cl 3:2); their **hearts** are where their treasure is (Mt 6:21); the desires of their **souls** are towards it, and they are **seeking** things above, and long to be in their own city, and **Father's house**, where Christ is; and to be at home with him, and for ever with him. This is the work and business of their lives now, and what their hearts are engaged in. (93)

TRANSFORMED

The bodies of the faithful, says Paul, will be transformed into the likeness of the glorious body of Christ – *"He will transform our corrupt bodies to be like his glorious body."* (Ph 3:21)

I have used the word "corrupt" to translate the Greek term, which probably has more the sense of "humiliation" than of vileness. (94) At the time he wrote, Paul was thinking, not about a body decaying in the earth, but about his living body. Indeed, Paul's words contain no suggestion that the Second Coming might be centuries in the future. He writes as if he were expecting that wonderful consummation to occur at any time – *"**we** are waiting with eager longing ... he will transform **our** corrupt bodies."* Yet he was constrained by

---

93) John Gill, Exposition of the Whole Bible, 1763; *in.loc* (emphasis mine).

94) In an excess of enthusiasm, the 17th century translators of the KJV rendered the phrase *"our vile body"* (singular, not plural), which may be colourful but is not very accurate. Indeed, it has probably done a lot of harm among the more pious by causing them wrongly to denigrate their bodies. Of course, that may even have been the intention of the zealous, puritan-influenced scholars employed by King James.

the Holy Spirit to express himself in such a way that twenty centuries later his words are still relevant. Hence, when we read them, we think about our bodies rising from the corruption of the grave. (95)

But if he was thinking about his living body, what did he mean? Certainly not that the body is in itself "vile" (to use the KJV term), or in some way despicable. Hardly! Our bodies are designed and fashioned by God, and the Saviour himself was pleased to take on human shape. They are also the present temples of the Holy Spirit (1 Co 3:16-17; 6:19). Yet for all their worth and divine likeness, our bodies are also the vehicles of sin; by them or through them we are tempted; they have often been the scene of our humiliation; and we cannot hope to enter heaven until they have been transformed by the resurrection and re-fashioned into the likeness of Christ (1 Jn 3:2). So they are to be changed and made to be *"like his glorious body"*.

But what does that mean?

GLORIFIED

Many scholars have offered diverse opinions on how much change will be seen in the resurrection – all the way from improved versions of our present shape and appearance to radical alteration in every way. We should probably be content to stick with John – *"What we will be like when Jesus comes isn't very clear yet. But we do know this — when Christ appears we will be like him because we will see him as he is."* (1 Jn 3:2)

Paul adds a few more ideas when he discusses the resurrection elsewhere, but still leaves the matter uncertain (see 1 Co 15:43-53; 2 Co 5:1-4); and Jesus adds a snippet in his comment that in heaven the saints will neither marry nor

---

95) Paul later seemed to assume that he would die prior to the return of Christ – see 2 Ti 4:6-8, which, if written by Paul, dates about five or six years after his letter to the Philippians.

be given in marriage, but will be like the angels (Mt 22:30). Then, since we will be like the risen Christ, perhaps the awesome vision John saw may give us a clue – *Revelation 1:13-18*.

We shall certainly be **immortal**, never again to experience any sort of sickness or death (Re 21:4; 22:2-3); **spiritual**, no longer bound by physical law (cp. Jn 20:19,26); **recognisable** for we shall know each other and Christ (cp. Mt 17:3); **powerful**, having authority to rule (Lu 19:17,19), and the strength to smash nations (Re 2:26-27). Other qualities could be added from other passages, which altogether convey an image of extraordinary splendour and privilege.

ADVANCING TOWARD MATURITY IN GOD

See Hebrews 5:11-14, *"But solid food is for the mature (teleios)."*

The people whom the apostle is addressing could no longer be called *teleios* because they still needed *"milk"* when they should have advanced to *"meat"*. Notice the contrast between infants and adults (vs. 13-14). To its parents, a baby is "perfect" at each stage of its growth. But if its development does not keep pace with its increasing age, parental joy will soon be replaced by anxious tears. Behaviour that is delightful in a baby is repulsive in a grown man.

Thus the Father will think you and me *"perfect"* so long as we maintain the spiritual growth he rightly expects from us. But if you allow yourself to be spiritually retarded, he may be as exasperated with you as the apostle was when he called those Hebrew Christians "dull" – an insulting term that actually means *"lazy sluggards"*, or *"thick-headed numbskulls"*! (vs. 11).

Call yourself *teleios*, he says, when you have advanced so far in spiritual maturity and in discernment, through constant endeavour, that you can readily *"distinguish good from evil"* (vs. 14). Do you truly wish to remain a suckling babe? I cannot believe it. Indeed, I would suppose that your very reading of this book marks you as a person who is continually growing up in Christ, and will continue to do so, ever learning, until you are marked as a person possessing *teleios* – coming ever closer to *"the measure of the stature of the fulness of Christ"* (Ep 4:13, ESV).

ADVANCING TOWARD THE MYSTERY OF GOD

See 1 Corinthians 2:6-7, *"Yet among the initiated* (teleios) *we shall impart wisdom."*

In the Greek world, *teleios* was also a technical term used to describe a person who had been initiated into the mystical rites of a religion. We who believe are *"perfect"*, says Paul, because we have been initiated into Christ and the Church.

In particular, Paul links this initiation with the charismatic ministry of the Holy Spirit (vs. 10-12). Even more particularly, he joins *teleios* (vs. 6) with glossolalia (vs. 13-14, which should probably read, *"interpreting spiritual truths in the language of the Spirit"* – that is, in other tongues, which are folly to the unspiritual man, but are *"discerned"* by those who possess the Holy Spirit.) This is our "secret" rite; this is our "mystery" (compare 1 Co 14:2).

This means more than simply speaking in tongues indifferently, without thought, focus, or prayer. It implies such principles as the following –

- the spiritual man discerns the presence and power of God in glossolalia, and is enriched by that;
- revelation comes to the church through tongues/ interpretation, and prophecy (1 Co 14:5, 26-31);
- the person who speaks in tongues is *"edified"* (vs. 4);
- those who speak to God in tongues (vs. 2,28), are *"blessing God"* and *"giving thanks well"* (vs. 14-17), which is a source of life both to the glossolalists and to the whole church; and so on.

So God will consider you *"perfect"* if you remain filled with the Holy Spirit, constantly building up yourself and blessing God as you sing and pray *"with your understanding and with your spirit"* (1 Co 14:14,15; Ju 20).

ADVANCING TOWARD SURRENDER TO GOD

See Matthew 19:21, *"If you would be perfect* (teleios), *go, sell what you have."*

The Greeks described a man as *teleios* when he reached a certain standard, or fulfilled certain requirements – as a student who had passed his exams; an athlete who had qualified for the games; an apprentice who had become a tradesman; a young musician who had become adept on an instrument; and so on.

For a Christian, the standard required is simply this: *surrender to the will of God*. It is not so much a work as a condition; not what you do, but what you are; not what you have accomplished, but what you are becoming; not the labour of your hands, but the attitude of your will; not sacrifice, but obedience.

So for that rich young man whom Jesus was instructing, *"perfection"* involved giving away his wealth. But had he obeyed, that would have rendered him perfect only until Christ demanded another task from him. If he were then to disobey, his *"perfection"* would at once be lost, or at least marred. He could be *"perfect"* only so long as he obeyed each heavenly command (as it came to him) and continued to grow in the willingness and depth of his obedience.

Jesus meant that the young man would become *"perfect"*, not when he was *poor*, but when he was *obedient*. Neither riches nor poverty are anything in the kingdom of God, but obedience is everything. The man whom God desires to be rich cannot be *"perfect"* if instead he chooses poverty;

neither can the man be *"perfect"* who clings to wealth when God has commanded him to embrace poverty. (96)

Perfection, therefore, does not necessarily require you either to gather riches or to give them up; nor does it depend upon any single or final act of obedience. Rather, we are required to maintain a daily attitude of surrender to the will of God, whatever that might be for each one of us. Those who do so are rightly called *"perfect"*.

Obedience is a habit that grows. The pleasures that result from each new surrender to the will of God create an increasing eagerness to receive new and more challenging opportunities to serve God. That service also becomes more mature, deeper in wisdom, stronger in faith, wiser in performance, more joyful in fulfilment, more truly dependent upon the enabling grace of God.

ADVANCING TOWARD THE LOVE OF GOD

See Matthew 5:43-48, *"You must be perfect* (teleios) *just as your heavenly Father is perfect* (teleios).*"*

---

96) There have been two occasions across the 60 years (so far) of my public ministry when the Lord has told Alison and me to give away almost all of our possessions and to follow him into a new venture. We did as we were told, ridding ourselves of everything but our clothing and some personal possessions, such as her engagement ring, our wedding rings, some special gifts from loved ones, and the like. Because we *knew* that we had heard from God, it was not hard to do (otherwise it would have been impossible!), and we went out, believing that the Lord would replace it all and more – which he did. But no one should foolishly copy our action supposing it will please God. On the contrary, it will deeply displease him if you are not obeying his explicit instruction. There was also a third, involuntary, occasion when we were moving from Minneapolis to San Diego and our large furniture truck was stolen, containing almost everything we possessed in the world, including my library, lecture notes, and sermons for the previous 25 years. It took me a whole month of prayer before I was finally able to surrender the truck into God's hands, truly forgive the thieves, and set about with Alison to rebuild our lives and ministry. The *very next day* the police called and said they had found the truck 100 km away! Our goods and chattels were all gone, but my library, lecture notes, sermon outlines, were all still there!

That is, just as each new day God is everything you expect him to be, so you should be everything he expects you to be – remembering always that God's expectations are limited to the level of growth you should have attained at this point in your Christian life. He does not expect you today to be what you cannot reasonably be expected to be until tomorrow.

Can you then ever proclaim yourself *"perfect"*? Yes! Whenever you have a sense that you have as nearly as possible equalled the Father's expectations of you, then joyfully cry *teleios*! That should be, not an uncommon, but the ordinary state of Christian life. Every Christian should feel that he or she has reached the point they should be at in the process of *"following after holiness"* (He 12:14) and of *"pressing on toward the prize of the upward call of God in Christ Jesus"* (Ph 3:12-16).

Christ linked this demand for perfection especially to an attitude of love toward other people. Our love for our neighbour must reflect the Father's love. That means -

- We should see people as God sees them; not as "things" to be exploited, but as immortal beings made in his image.

When devout Jews celebrate the Passover, the ceremony requires them to take a cup of wine, recite the list of plagues that ravaged ancient Egypt, and then, for each plague to spill a little wine out of the cup. This is intended to teach them to be sad when human life is destroyed, even that of their enemies. For the same reason, the rabbis long ago attached a midrash to the biblical account of the Exodus. It tells how the angels in heaven, when they saw the Red Sea rushing in to engulf the Egyptian army, began to dance and rejoice before the throne of God. Sorrowfully, the Lord reproved them – "The work of my hands is perishing and you sing praises to me?" ⁽⁹⁷⁾ That is truly the way we should think about people if we would be *teleios* in the eyes of God.

- We should adopt God's attitude of universal benevolence (vs. 46-47).

This does not require you to have affection for every person, nor even to consider everyone a friend. Wisely, scripture does not say, "You must *like* your enemy," but "you must *love* him!" You can show that divine benevolence by praying for your enemies and by seeking to do them good.

Thus, divine benevolence is a matter of good will, of liberality, and is not necessarily linked with fond feelings. Notice how God shows his benevolence, and how Jesus says that we must do the same (Mt 5:43-47; and compare also Ro 12:14-21).

I once attended a meeting, along with about ten thousand other people, at which Francis McNutt suggested this exercise to us. He said that we should read *1 Corinthians 13:4-8*, replacing the word "love" with "Jesus". Nothing will more clearly show you the character of Christ that we are called to emulate. Then read the passage again, but this time replace "love" with "I". You will at once realize how far short we all come of actually emulating the Saviour!

Nonetheless, if we are reaching for that quality of love, striving to exhibit it in word and deed day by day, then the Father will reckon us as possessing *teleios*.

CONCLUSION

The demand of Jesus is not, *"from this time on, try to be perfect"*; rather, it is imperative – *"be perfect NOW!"*

---

97) The Passover Haggadah, by Rabbi Shlomo Riskin; Ktav Pub. House, New York; 1983; pg. 90. Also, What the Rabbis Said, by Ronald L. Eisenberg; pub. ABC-Clio, Santa Barbara Ca.; 2010; pg. 12.

But if you understand what *teleios* means, then you should be able to say, *"I am indeed perfect — I am all that the Father expects me to be at this moment."* And that will be true if you if you are committed to growth both in spiritual maturity and in Christian character. Then, despite many blemishes, you will be each day as perfect as God can expect you to be; that is to say, you will be as perfect in the admiration of the Father as the Father is perfect in your admiration.

For that reason, Paul was able, not only to call his fellow pilgrims "perfect", but to allow that he (like they) was <u>not yet</u> "perfect"! – *"Not that I have already obtained this, nor am I already perfect* (teleiso), *but I do press on, striving to make it my own, just as Christ Jesus has made me his own." (Ph 3:12)*

So, he is perfect; he is not yet perfect – which is how we all should be; "perfect" today, because we are what we should be; but not "perfect" tomorrow, unless we are continuing to grow in knowledge and maturity in Christ.

So let us all fix ourselves into a pattern of always advancing

in the love of God
in the purpose of God
in surrender to God
and toward God himself.

If you are thus minded, then you will indeed show yourself to be a *"mature"* (teleios) Christian! (Ph 3:15)

ELEVEN

YOU DON'T KNOW ME

One of Elvis Presley's popular songs in 1967 was *You Don't Know Me*. It was written in 1955 by Cindy Walker and Eddy Arnold, and contains the lament of a forlorn lover whose sweetheart has gone off with someone else –

> *You give your hand to me,*
> *And then you say hello;*
> *I can hardly speak,*
> *My heart is beating so,*
> *And anyone can tell*
> *You think you know me well –*
> *But you don't know me! ....*

On the surface it is just another romantic pop song about love. But it is actually rather profound. Whether wittingly or not, I don't know, but the lyrics reflect a universal sorrow, that sharp pain, that twisting of the heart, that we have all felt on occasion.

<u>Sometimes</u>, it takes the form of an unrequited yearning for love that can never be – a piercing stab into the soul, a poignant sense of infinite regret and of deep loss.

<u>Sometimes</u>, it is not pain we feel so much as frustration, or even anger, because people stubbornly refuse to recognise our true motives, or to see our true selves.

<u>Sometimes</u>, we feel very alone and quite unable to communicate our real feelings, or even our thoughts.

It is our doom to be cut off from each other, even sometimes from those who are nearest and dearest. The sad, remorseful cry rises, *"You don't know me; you just don't know me!"*

How can we break down these barriers? How can we learn to understand both ourselves and each other? How can this aching loneliness, this bitter isolation, this deep regret, be cured?

The only real solution is found in the gospel, and it lies in one remarkable Greek word – *koinonia = fellowship,* which occurs some 20 times in the NT letters. In *Philippians* it is found four times, once in each chapter –

> *Whenever I think of you I thank God for you. Indeed, I think of you often, and I am always praying for you with joy, because of the **koinonia** we have shared in the gospel from the beginning until now. ... So if there is any comfort in Christ, any consolation in love, any **koinonia** in the Spirit, any affection and sympathy, fulfil my joy by thinking in the same way, and having the same love ... Everything is trash to me, so long as I may know Christ and the power of his resurrection, and the **koinonia** of his sufferings .. When I left Macedonia, you were the only church that shared **koinoneo** with me in giving and receiving. (Ph 1:3-5; 2:1-2; 3:8-10; 4:15)*

At its simplest level, "koinonia" means "fellowship" – yet it is much more than merely friendship or finding a companion, for the Greek word always entailed some kind of action, some giving or receiving, some measure of lively partnership. Its frequent use by the apostles suggests the importance it had in the life of the early church. Indeed, it was so important that only the death of Christ was sufficient to secure it for us –

> *Once you were separated from Christ. You were strangers and did not belong with God's chosen people. You had no hope and you were without God in this world. But now Christ has created peace between us and made us into one people. With his own body he broke down the wall that separated us and kept us apart.*

> *Yes, by means of the cross he has united all of us into one body and brought us back to God. So we are strangers no longer, but rather, we have become citizens together with all God's people and members of the family of God. (Ep 2:12-19)*

On the cross Jesus broke down the "wall that divided us", caused by sin, and brought us into one great family. And the consequence? Because of Calvary we are now gifted with *koinonia*. John provides a fine summary of what *koinonia* means in his letter –

> *What we have seen and heard we announce to you also, so that you will join with us in **fellowship**, yes, the same **fellowship** that we have with the Father and with his Son Jesus Christ. ... If we claim to have **fellowship** with God while we keep on walking in darkness, then we are liars. But if we live in the light, just as he is in the light, then we will have true **fellowship** with one another, and the blood of Jesus, his Son, will wash away our every sin. (1 Jn 1:3, 6, 7)*

Four times John uses *koinonia* in his opening chapter, showing that it is a foundation of all that follows. Most importantly, he insists that our fellowship with each other rests upon our fellowship with the Father in Christ. *If one is deficient so will be the other.*

THE MEANING OF "KOINONIA"

The scriptures I have cited so far show that *koinonia* is much more than friendship. [98] Rather, it means variously, having

---

[98] The definitions given in the next few pages were drawn some years ago from several different lexicons and commentaries, and I have lost all record of the sources. But assuming the sources were correct, then you can trust my definitions above!

things in common; a partnership; caring; and therefore sharing. It marks an attitude of generous giving in contrast with selfish getting. If you want an example, simply look at Jesus!

A comparison of the way the Greeks and the Apostles used the word, shows the following meanings –

A BUSINESS PARTNERSHIP

This was its most common meaning in secular Greek. It has the sense of two or more people forming a joint commercial venture, and working closely together for their mutual profit.

Thus we in the church should be bonded to each other in loyalty, labouring together with zeal, partners in the work of Christ, committed to the prosperity of the church. In this we find one of life's greatest joys – *living for a cause bigger than oneself*. Indeed, unless you do have such a cause, you are hardly alive at all!

How often we see the contrary – people jostling for position or advantage, seeking personal gain rather than the benefit of the Kingdom of God. Yet do they find any true joy? Real laughter, happiness that endures for ever, is rooted in the service of God. But do remember always that God is ever concerned about character and motivation more than he is about achievement. Let what you *do* arise out of who you *are*.

Nonetheless, the rule remains – where true *koinonia* exists Christians will labour together to exalt Christ, to grow the church, and to expand the Kingdom of God.

A COVENANTED RELATIONSHIP

Koinonia was used to describe the friendship and partnering that is part of a good marriage, and extended also to any similar situation of deep bonding and mutual concern.

Note that both the scandal and the glory of the early church lay in the taunt reported by Tertullian: "How these Christians love each other!" (99) In the reckoning of the wider world, Christian love was a thing to be mocked not admired. They deemed it a sign of effeminacy, of insipid weakness, so contrary to their own ruthless greed. The world knew "fellowship", but always between people of similar tastes and background. The Christian ideal of selfless, even self-sacrificing fellowship stirred their scorn rather than their esteem. And still today secular fellowship is often superficial or merely sentimental.

But in Christ, says scripture, we *"have"* fellowship – that is, we do not merely "enjoy fellowship", but we <u>possess</u> it as a gift from God, one that in Christ binds us together into a profoundly committed and loving relationship.

Indeed, in the church such a communion grew between people of quite disparate backgrounds that it was not unknown for a slave to be bishop in a congregation of which his master was a member!

When all is being done for the glory of God (Ep 6:5-10; Cl 3:22-24), then there is no difference in status or importance between master and slave, worker and employer, bishop and parishioner, men and women, young or old – only a difference in function.

If the church is not such a *bonded family,* then it is merely a *religious assembly,* of scant value to God or man.

AN EXPRESSED FRIENDSHIP

Koinonia was neither a friendship of casual acquaintance nor of mutual interests. Rather, it embodied the deep friendship that arises from frequent association, and from an inner abiding work of the Paraclete. Hence there is a divine quality in Christian *koinonia* that raises questions about the

---

99) I refer to this quote also in *Chapter Seven,* and *Chapter Sixteen.*

genuineness of the faith of people who have no desire to fellowship with the saints. If we already "have" this fellowship as a gift of God, then what must we say about people who think that active participation in a local church is not essential, or who do not care if there is some quarrel between them and another Christian? At best their faith is deficient; at worst, it is a pretence.

Ask yourself again – can one be a true Christian yet not be striving for *koinonia* with and among the people of God?

Nowhere is this commitment of pure love better expressed than in the six-fold injunction, *"you must all greet each other with a holy kiss of love!"* *(Ro 16:16; 1 Co 16:20; 2 Co 13:12; Ph 4:21; 1 Th 5:26; 1 Pe 5:14)* – which is the theme of a later chapter in this book.

A TRUE COMPASSION

This was fellowship demonstrated by helping those in need. It was a fellowship of action not just of feelings or words; it cared; it communicated; it served; it gave; it sacrificed. It was not fellowship experienced only when the church gathered for worship, but involved an ongoing concern for the wellbeing and happiness of every member of the family of God. True *koinonia* cannot ever be merely an abstract idea, a thing only of emotion, a sweet doctrine to be believed but not acted upon. Always, *koinonia* is expressed by *action*. There is something to *do*, not just *feel*.

A HEAVENLY COMMUNION

When Paul began setting out the manner in which a local church should present the eucharist, he used this word, *koinonia* –

> *The cup of blessing that we bless, is it not a **koinonia** in the blood of Christ? The bread that we break, is it not a **koinonia** in the body of Christ? (1 Co 10:16)*

He was saying that through the cup and the bread we "*participate* in the blood and body of Christ."

How many furious debates there have been about what that means! Yet surely Paul himself provides the answer –

> *Do I mean then that a sacrifice offered to an idol is anything, or that an idol is anything? No, but the sacrifices of pagans are offered to demons. (vs. 19-20)*

In the background of Paul's comment lies the pagan belief that when they ate part of an animal that had been sacrificed in a temple, the god entered into that meat and became part of the body and soul of each worshipper. Of course, that was nonsense, because the idols were nothing. Yet, says Paul, behind every idol was a demon, so that, those worshippers *really did* come into union with a spiritual power!

Hence he warns Christians never to share in those meals –

> *I do not want you to be participants with demons. You cannot drink the cup of the Lord and the cup of demons too; you cannot have a part in both the Lord's table and the table of demons." (vs. 20-21)*

So then, as surely as a pagan worshipper was bound to a demon when a sacrifice was eaten, even more so should we come into a mystic union with Christ through the bread and the cup.

Thus our text once again –

> *I speak as to sensible people; judge for yourselves what I say. The cup of blessing that we bless, is it not a participation in the blood of Christ? The bread that we break, is it not a participation in the body of Christ?*

Paul doesn't explain in what sense or how we "participate" (*koinonia*) in the body and blood of Christ, and we are probably wise if we do not engage in futile speculation. But surely "participate" requires more than merely a ritual demonstration of our faith in the efficacy of the cross? Surely there has to be at least some element of fusion with Christ, of sharing in his very nature, of receiving some part of him into our own being? This table cannot be just an "ordinance", but is rather a "sacrament" – that is, the bread and the wine do not just *remind* us of Christ, but do bring us into some sort of dynamic union with him, an actual "communion" (*koinonia*), that imparts some real quality of divine life to us.

But that is true, of course, only when one eats and drinks <u>in faith</u> – just as the water of baptism is ineffective apart from faith, or the printed page of the Bible, or the bricks and mortar of the church.

So participation in Christ through the eucharist does not depend upon some magical mutation wrought by a priest, but by the worshipper heartily believing the promise of God, and taking the elements with a fervent expectation of encountering, as he or she eats and drinks, the life of Christ.

It is worth adding that Christ is not intrinsically present in the elements, that is, the bread and the wine. Rather, in response to each believer's faith, our union with Christ is wrought by the immanent [100] presence of the Holy Spirit, and by the empowering presence of the Word of God. [101]

A LIVELY WORSHIP

The ancient Greeks used *koinonia* in connection with worship. It held the idea that the worshipper entered into partnership with the gods, and that they in turn would graciously commune with the worshipper, and bestow many desired blessings.

---

100) "Immanence" means pervading, or thoroughly indwelling; "imm*i*nence" means drawing near, or about to happen.

101) I appreciate that some denominations insist that Christ is indeed present in some form in the actual bread and wine. I respect that view, though I do not personally hold to it.

There was also a sense that worshippers in a particular temple were inescapably joined in a bond of faith and fellowship, both with each other and with the god who was honoured there. Hence one worshipper might feel, say, an affinity with Mars, and with those who revered the same god, while another might be drawn to Minerva, or to Apollo, or Fortuna, and so on.

Likewise in the church, but with vastly greater richness and true substance, the source of all human fellowship lies in the believer's communion with God through Christ.

Where this divine fellowship becomes cold and formal, there *koinonia* among the people soon withers also. That idea was strongly expressed by John when he drew attention to three false claims that were being made by some people in the church (1 Jn 1:7-10) –

> *<u>If we say</u>, "We have fellowship with God," and yet continue to live in darkness, we're lying. … <u>If we say</u>, "We aren't sinful," we are lying to ourselves, and the truth is not in us. … <u>If we say</u>, "We have never sinned," we turn God into a liar and his Word is not in us.'*

But let us here note especially the first of those statements –

> *If we say, "We have fellowship (koinonia) with God," and yet go on living in darkness, we are lying and no longer living in the truth. But if we live in the light just as God dwells in the light, <u>then we have fellowship (koinonia) with each other</u>. And the blood of his Son Jesus washes away our every sin.*

How startling to hear John placing a condition upon divine pardon – if we do not have fellowship with each other, then our sins will not be washed away! We believe that redemption comes to us without strings, freely, by the unmerited grace of God. And so it does. But anyone who truthfully claims to be saved will show it by the way he or she behaves, and especially by reflecting the love of Christ. Jesus himself said as much, namely, that if we do not forgive each other, truly forgive, from the depths of our hearts, then God will not forgive us! (Mt 6:14-15; 18:35; Mk 11:26) They are words to make any humble Christian echo the sentiment of the old spiritual song –

Oh! Sometimes it causes me to tremble, tremble, tremble.
Were you there when they crucified my Lord?

But if you *were* there, by faith, and if you have truly discovered the pardoning grace of God in the crucified and risen Christ, then you will have no other heart than to forgive anyone who ever offends you or sins against you.

Knowing that I do heartily and freely forgive anyone who has ever done me harm, and that my sins are washed away, and that I am in true fellowship with the people of God, then two great prizes become mine –

- I can now enjoy the fellowship that will be ours in heaven.
- I am assured of a place in the resurrection when Christ returns!

So let *koinonia* flourish among us! In the love of God and in the fellowship of the saints in Christ we find a true and eternal family, a bonding that can never be severed!

TWELVE

ESCAPING THE PAST

> *This I am resolved to do – forgetting what lies behind me, I strain forward to what lies ahead, pressing on toward the goal, and reaching for the prize of the upward call of God in Christ Jesus. (Ph 3:13-14)*

Just over 400 years ago, Thomas Heywood wrote a play which has been described as "the apex of dramatic achievement during the early 17th century".

It is titled, "A Woman Killed with Kindness," and at its heart is a wife who has betrayed her husband. In one place, the cheated husband laments –

> *Take from th'account of time so many minutes,*
> *Till he had all these seasons call'd again,*
> *Those minutes, and those actions done in them . . . .*
> *But, oh! I talk of things impossible,*
> *And cast beyond the moon.*

Ah! All those minutes and "the actions done in them"! How much we regret them! How we wish to recall them and remake them! How impossible it seems! But Paul insists that we can indeed thrust the past behind us, and press forward with a clear vision, unfettered by any chains from yesterday.

INTRODUCTION

Human beings, alone among life on earth, are able to remember and record the past, and alone are obliged to live under the weight of it – for good or ill.

Likewise, we alone can and must anticipate the future, an anticipation that is heavily influenced by our past. But for us the problem is that our past can't be changed, because there is nothing to go back to, since it exists only in memory. [102] The clock cannot be turned back so that we can get a second chance to get it right. Yet that does not destroy the reality of the past, for it is an essential element in our being. Much of what we are today is a compound of all that has filled our former days.

What then can be done? How can we cast off the shackles of the moribund past?

THE GUILT OF THE PAST IS REMOVED

> *I have swept away your offences like a black cloud, and your sins like the morning mist. Return to me, for I have redeemed you. (Is 44:22)*

Can this really be true? Can God change what has become part of an unchangeable history? No, the story itself remains unalterable; not even God can re-write history, nor revise anything we have ever thought, said, or done. The record, for good or ill, is fixed for ever. But God, as a Judge, <u>can</u> remove our iniquities from the legal record, and declare null and void all charges that have been laid against us.

---

102) Time is a great mystery. The present we comprehend well enough – although we do find it hard to grasp each moment as it comes and goes; as soon as we try to look for it, it is gone – but the past seems to have no existence save in our memory of it; nor does the future, save in our anticipation of it. We have only the "now". Time travel seems impossible, since there is really nowhere to go to. If it were possible, someone in the future would have invented it and already be travelling back to our time. As far as I know, no visitor from the future has arrived here yet! Nor are they ever likely to do so, since the future doesn't exist. They have nowhere to come from; and when the future does come, they will have nowhere to go back to. How do you wind back time? How do you travel to something that has no existence outside the pages of a history book?

He cannot take that action arbitrarily, for that would make him an accessory to sin. But he *can* do it through the substitutionary work of Christ on the cross, and *will* do so for all who fix their confidence in Christ. Calvary cancels all legal access to the evidence against us. So far as the law is concerned, like a black cloud driven away by a strong wind, or like a mist burned off by the rising sun, so have our offences, all of them, been expunged from the record, and we are declared innocent.

Never again allow the Enemy to burden you down with a memory of the faults of yesterday. God has judicially forgotten them. So should you!

THE MEMORY OF THE PAST IS TRANSFORMED

God says he will forget – *"I will never again remember their sins and their iniquities"* (He 10:17).

But what does that mean?

God cannot actually forget anything that he knows, so he does recall every moment of our past days. But he *can* choose the manner in which he remembers. Hence, he remembers our sin now only as a battle that was won, a triumph gained, a victory secured for ever by Christ, and in each of us through Christ. Furthermore, he insists that every denizen of darkness, and all the holy angels, must also remember us only as we are in Christ, so that no voice can be lawfully raised against us in accusation.

God's memory of the past has also been transformed into the stairway that brings us to Paradise, for our redemption in Christ has gained us a better status than Adam unfallen could ever have gained. That is something to knock out one's breath! Had Adam not sinned, his descendants all would have been born in pure innocence, but would have remained simply unfallen human beings. But now, by an astounding act of divine grace, although we all were both born in sin and have done sin, in Christ, the Last Adam (1 Co 15:45), we have been elevated to the very throne of God! In the entire universe no creature, angelic or otherwise, has precedence over us. In Christ we stand highest below God in the hierarchy of heaven. We have the loftiest privileges. We bear the very likeness of Christ. We will be crowned with glory and splendour beyond imagination! All memory of former things, of death and decay, of poverty and war, of rebellion and crime, will be banished for ever! (Re 21:4)

THE POWER OF THE PAST IS BROKEN

> *"I have swept away your offences like a black cloud, and your sins like the morning mist. Return to me, for <u>I have redeemed you</u>."*

God does take a frightening risk when he offers such free and seemingly easy pardon. Surely such privilege will be abused? Surely people will take advantage of grace and use it as a licence to sin? And indeed, some have done so (Ro 6:1).

But the Lord warns us against using grace as a licence for sin by reminding us of the cost of that grace – he had first to achieve our "redemption", and now he requires us to "return".

You see, the safeguard always is that no one can deliberately continue to live wickedly and still retain a grip on Christ. But we have life only in Christ, and apart from him we are dead and doomed to perish for ever. But how can anyone who is truly redeemed, and loves the Redeemer, do other than strive to please him?

THE THREAT OF THE PAST IS RE-WRITTEN

Behold, the day that threatened a wintry cold and bleak prospect, now shines brightly with a sparkling blue sky! The future that once looked so gloomy, because of the past, now gleams with glad promise of eternal delights! The weight of yesterday's follies might have crushed us each new day, but the Cross has cut the chains that tied it to us, and now we stand tall, and look forward with joy. We are like Christian, in John Bunyan's striking analogy. The pilgrim had complained about the weight of his sin, saying –

> This burden upon my back is more terrible to me than all these things which you have mentioned *(the privations and persecutions he would face as a Christian)*; nay, methinks I care not what I meet with in the way, if so be I can also meet with deliverance from my burden.

So he continued on his way, still carrying that crushing weight –

> Now I saw in my dream, that the highway up which Christian was to go was fenced on either side with a wall, and that wall was called Salvation. Up this way, therefore, did burdened Christian run, but not without great difficulty, because of the load on his back.
>
> He ran thus till he came at a place somewhat ascending, and upon that place stood a cross, and a little below, in the bottom, a sepulchre. So I saw in my dream, that just as Christian came up with the cross, his burden loosed from off his shoulders, and fell from off his back, and began to tumble, and so continued to do, till it came to the mouth of the sepulchre, where it fell in, and I saw it no more. Then was Christian glad and lightsome, and said, with a merry heart, "He hath given me rest by his sorrow, and life by his death." Then he stood still awhile to look and wonder; for it was very surprising to him, that the sight of the cross should thus ease him of his burden. He looked therefore, and looked again, even till the springs that were in his head sent the waters down his cheeks. Now, as he stood looking and weeping, behold three Shining Ones came to him and saluted him with, "Peace be unto thee." So the first said to him, "Thy sins be forgiven thee;" the second stripped him of his

rags, and clothed him with a change of raiment; the third also set a mark on his forehead, and gave him a roll with a seal upon it, which he bade him look on as he ran, and that he should give it in at the Celestial Gate. So they went their way. . . .

Then Christian gave three leaps for joy, and went on singing –

> *Thus far I did come laden with my sin;*
> *Nor could aught ease the grief that I was in*
> *Till I came hither: What a place is this!*
> *Must here be the beginning of my bliss?*
> *Must here the burden fall from off my back?*
> *Must here the strings that bound it to me crack?*
> *Blest cross! blest sepulchre! blest rather be*
> *The Man that there was put to shame for me!* [103]

As Christian joyfully continued his pilgrimage he met a companion, Hope, and together they walked along the path until they met three Shepherds who showed them many things. Then the Shepherds said –

> "Let us here show to the Pilgrims the gates of the Celestial City, if they have skill to look through our perspective glass." The Pilgrims then lovingly accepted the motion; so they had them to the top of a high hill, called Clear, and gave them their glass to look.
>
> Then they essayed to look, but the remembrance of that last thing that the Shepherds had shown them *(a frightening vision of hell)*, made their hands shake; by means of which impediment, they could not look steadily through the glass; yet they

---

103) The Pilgrim's Progress; Part 2; Sec. 2.2,9.

thought they saw something like the gate, and also some of the glory of the place. Then they went away, and sang this song –

Thus, by the Shepherds, secrets are reveal'd,
Which from all other men are kept conceal'd.
Come to the Shepherds, then, if you would see
Things deep, things hid, and that mysterious be. (104)

The "Shepherds" of course represent Christian pastors, good teachers of the word of God, and faithful shepherds of souls from earth to heaven. They wanted to show the pilgrims a view of heaven, but the two men were not ready to see more than a glimpse. Perhaps we can catch a better view of what the future holds for us?

RAISED TO GLORY

There is one glory of the sun, and another glory of the moon, and another glory of the stars; for star differs from star in glory. So is it with the resurrection of the dead. (1 Co 15:41-43)

All who share in the rapture of the church will be ablaze with glory and ecstatic with happiness. Yet not all will be the same. They will differ as the stars in their radiance. Hence Peter urges us so to serve the Lord that we will be assured of an acclaimed entrance into Paradise, shining brightly, worthy of highest honour (2 Pe 1:10-11; cp. also Lu 19:17-19).

MADE LIKE JESUS

It is not yet clear what we shall become. But we know that when Christ appears, we shall be like him, because we shall see him as he really is. (1 Jn 3:2)

---

104) Ibid. 2.36.

Perhaps we do not know just how Jesus *"really is"* today in heaven, or how we will be like him when we are raptured with the church on the day of his coming; but we can surely gain a good impression from this? –

> *I saw one like a Son of Man, clothed with a long robe and with a golden sash around his chest. The hairs of his head were white, like white wool, like snow. His eyes were like a flame of fire, his feet were like burnished bronze, refined in a furnace, and his voice was like the roar of many waters. In his right hand he held seven stars, from his mouth came a sharp two-edged sword, and his face was like the sun shining in full strength. When I saw him, I fell at his feet as though dead. But he laid his right hand on me, saying, "Fear not, I am the first and the last, and the living one. I died, and behold I am alive forevermore, and I have the keys of Death and Hades." (Re 1:13-18, ESV)*

I do not suppose that scene provides a literal description of the actual appearance of Christ, but it does convey an image of glory so supernal, so ineffable, so devastatingly magnificent, that it would throw any rational man onto his face! And on that day, *we shall be like him!*

ENTHRONED WITH CHRIST

> *Everyone who wins the victory will sit with me on my throne, just as I won the victory and sat with my Father on his throne. (Re 3:21-22)*

There have been many quarrels about the meaning of "winning the victory", or to use the KJV term, "overcomers". Some apply it to a particular denomination; some insist on adherence to a body of doctrine; others use it to describe a particular level of achievement in Christian life; and so on. But I prefer the definition given by John –

> *Who is it that overcomes the world except the one who believes that Jesus is the Son of God?* (1 Jn 5:5, ESV)

A person overcomes the world simply by remaining true to his or her commitment to Christ. This is someone who steadfastly refuses all worldly blandishments, holds firmly to faith, stands bravely against persecution, resists temptation, is penitent in the face of failure, and always loving and serving Christ. In other words, a sincere Christian living Christianly. No special achievement is involved, no amazing quality of sainthood, no extraordinary victory, no peculiar body of doctrine, just steadfast faithfulness to Christ, and lifelong service in the church, his Body on earth.

Such people do indeed overcome the world and will one day find themselves enthroned with Christ in heaven! And there they will have the honour of

REIGNING WITH CHRIST

> *I will give power over the nations to everyone who wins the victory and keeps on obeying me until the end. I will give each of them the same power that my Father has given me. They will rule the nations with an iron rod and smash those nations to pieces like clay pots.* (Re 2:26-27)

Again, I presume that the picture is metaphorical rather than literal, simply conveying an impression of limitless authority and irresistible might. But love will still be the ruling principle of heaven, not tyranny; justice, not despotism; and dominion tempered with mercy.

How far will the rule of the saints extend? What will be their inheritance? I suppose, the universe, all 150 billion galaxies, and all their wealth. But no one really knows; so we wait with trembling excitement for that great Day to come, and the Judgment, and the final disposition of all the saints in the new heavens and new earth of the eternal Kingdom of God.

Then indeed, will the past be forgotten and remembered never again –

> *God shall wipe away all tears from their eyes; and there shall be no more death, neither sorrow, nor crying, neither shall there be any more pain: for the former things are passed away" (Rev 21:4).*

One is no longer surprised by the apostle's strenuous, eager language; on the contrary, I make it my own affirmation, as I hope also that it is yours – *"This I am resolved to do – forgetting what lies behind me, I strain forward to what lies ahead, pressing on toward the goal, and reaching for the prize of the upward call of God in Christ Jesus." (Ph 3:13-14)*

THIRTEEN

KENOSIS

*Christ, because he was in the form of God, did not deem it robbery to claim equality with God; yet he **emptied** himself, and having taken on the form of a slave, and being made in the likeness of a human, and fashioned as a man, he humbled himself, becoming obedient unto death, even to death on a cross. (Ph 2:6-8)*

That passage is one about which entire libraries have been written, churches sundered, friends made foes, and divines divided! And still no consensus exists in the church about its true meaning. So perhaps we should stop here, and go no further?

But that would mark me craven, and I am none such. So let us bravely attempt to find, if not all the truth, then at least some of it.

In Greek, the word I have emphasised means "to make empty, or void", and in connection with Christ it is used only here, and only by Paul. From that Greek word, the process is called the *kenosis* of Christ. [105] Paul uses it as a way of explaining –

---

[105] Perhaps half of this chapter on the *kenosis* has been drawn from my book Emmanuel – *Part Two, Chapters 13, 14, 15;* Vision Publishing, Ramona, Ca. You will find there a more extensive coverage of the *kenosis*. However, I felt that it was impossible to leave all discussion of this theme out of a commentary on *Philippians*. The kenotic passage lies at the heart of Paul's letter, and is perhaps the most important part of it, so it seemed appropriate to include this material here.

- the ***infinite mystery*** of how, in Christ, the eternal God of the universe was able to discard the barriers of time and space and confine himself within a human form; and

- the ***infinite love*** of God, who with measureless condescension and self-sacrificing love, humbled himself in Christ to live and die for the redemption of lost humanity.

Only a handful of words, yet they describe

CHRIST AS HE WAS AND NOW IS

- In the ***form*** of God – that is, not just having a similar outward shape, like a plastic banana resembles a real one, but possessing the inner dynamic, the characteristics, the very nature of the real thing, that is, of God.

- Possessing ***equality*** with God. It was no robbery for Christ to assert this claim, but simply true. He was the Son of God, therefore he was, is, and always will be God. No one can be in the form of God, and be equal with God, and not be God. The two words together are an unequivocal declaration of the full deity of Christ.

When the church found those expressions, and others like them, being applied to Christ in scripture, it was compelled to devise the doctrine of the Trinity – that is, there is truly only one God, but he exists in three Persons, all equal in splendour, and differing only in office. If the Bible witness is accepted, then no other explanation is possible. We are driven to cry with the poet –

Holy, holy, holy! Lord God Almighty!
Early in the morning our song shall rise to Thee;
Holy, holy, holy, merciful and mighty!

God in three Persons, blessèd Trinity! (106)

However, certain errors must be avoided. The Trinity does not contain three separate gods. There is room in the universe for only one true God. So the Divine Being is One, but embracing three persons, Father, Son, and Holy Spirit. Nor are the three Persons simply different aspects of God, as if he were in fact just one Person showing himself in three different roles – such as a man might be a father, brother, and uncle, all at the same time, but still only one man. No, the Father and the Son, and the Holy Spirit are individuals, but they co-exist in one Being, whom we call God. (107)

CHRIST AS HE BECAME

Through his *kenosis* Christ took on

- the ***form*** of a slave.

"Form" is the same word that described his former state; thus it means that Christ made no pretence of being a servant, but truly did make himself the slave of all that he might became the Saviour of all.

- the ***likeness*** of a man.

That is, he had a true human nature in a real human body, and was wholly and truly a man, with all the abilities, capacities, and behavioural needs of any other human being.

- the ***fashion*** of a man.

That is, he chose to limit himself to human strength, to behave as a man must behave, not to call upon any outside resources or powers that were not available to other Spirit-filled men and women of faith. He never stepped outside of the human "fashion" of doing things. He did not do things

---

106) John B. Dykes, Hymns Ancient and Modern, 1861.
107) My book Emmanuel *One & Two*, explores these ideas more fully and in greater depth. Vision Publishing, Ramona Ca.

the way an angel would, or even a god, but as a man. Thus he came among us as Brother and Friend, although

> *we were then his enemies; but now we are reconciled to God by the death of his Son ... through whom we have received the atonement. (Ro 5:10-11)*

All of this rested upon his *kenosis*, translated above as he "**emptied** *himself*" But what does that mean?

TWO CONFLICTING OPINIONS

Across the centuries, the church has generally held to one or the other of two main opinions about the *kenosis*, or what has been called *"kenotic theory"* –

- Christ surrendered all his divine attributes before he came down from heaven to earth, and he was therefore born, lived, and died as an absolutely ordinary man, except without sin.

In this case, Jesus was devoid of all divine qualities during his earthly life. They remained his possession only through his bond with the eternal Logos in heaven, but he was not able to exercise them on earth.

- Christ surrendered the independent use of his divine attributes, but nonetheless, during the years of his incarnation, he retained full possession of them.

In this case, in conjunction with the eternal Logos in heaven, Jesus kept all his divine qualities, except those that were incompatible with human existence, such as omnipresence, infinity, immutability, and the like – although even those he retained in spirit if not in the flesh (think about the account of his Transfiguration – Mt 17:1-9; Mk 9:2-8; Lu 9:28-36; 2 Pe 1:16-18).

Under this opinion, some go even further –

> Some say, for instance, that when the Lord Jesus was on earth, He no longer had all-

knowledge or all-power. He was no longer in all places at one and the same time. They say He voluntarily laid aside these attributes of Deity when He came into the world as a Man. Some even say He was subject to the limitations of all men, that He became liable to error, and accepted the common opinions and myths of His day!

This we utterly deny. The Lord Jesus did not lay aside any of the attributes of God when He came into the world.

He was still omniscient (all-knowing). He was still omnipresent (present in all places at one and the same time). He was still omnipotent (all powerful). (108)

However, while it is certainly true that Jesus as the *Logos* in heaven retained every divine attribute, it seems absurd to suppose that Jesus as the *Man* of Galilee did so. In his human form, he could not possibly be everywhere at once, nor hold all power, nor all knowledge. No ordinary human mind could contain the omniscience of God – that is, full knowledge of *everything* that has ever been, or that can be known, such as *every* word ever spoken in *every* language, since the beginning of human speech, along with every fact of science, art, culture, and so on. Indeed, as a man, he could only have known what was accessible to other human beings at that time. He had no knowledge, for example, of trigonometry, calculus, the existence of galaxies, nor of many other modern scientific specialities. Also, he must have lacked many skills. No doubt he was an excellent carpenter, but it is improbable that he was also a genius in art, music, sculpture, architecture, engineering, and so on. If he did possess such powers and such learning, then he was no

---

108) Bible Believer's Commentary, ed. Arthur Farstad; Thomas Nelson Publishers, Nashville; 1995; *in loc.*

ordinary human being, not truly human, and our salvation would be invalidated.

But to get back to our theme, given such diverse viewpoints, it is not surprising that Christians have never been able to reach agreement on just what the *kenosis* means. But this much at least seems clear –

STANDARD DOCTRINE

Standard Christian theology has always held that the presence of a divine nature in Christ did not in any way falsify nor compromise his humanity. That is, although Jesus (in adult life) was fully aware of his divine identity, he voluntarily chose to act within the confines of a human nature. Whether or not he retained, as a man, possession or use of those attributes is not important. The point is, he *lived* as though he had to work only with those things that are proper to a true human nature. He never once actually *used* any inherent divine power, but employed only what is available to every Spirit-filled man or woman of faith. Had he not done so, had he even once either resumed or drawn upon some divine power not available to other servants of God, his work as Redeemer would have unravelled. To achieve our salvation he had to be born as a man, live as a man, overcome temptation as a man, set an example as a man, die as a man, and then, and only then, in the strength of his deity raise himself from the dead. At that moment, he did indeed prove himself to be the Son of God in power! (Ro 1:4) [109]

---

109) This was the point of the *Temptation in the Wilderness*, when Satan taunted him, "If you really are the Son of God, turn these stones into bread!" The devil was enticing him to resume the powers of deity. But Jesus replied with the cutting rebuke, *"Man shall not live by bread alone, but by every word that comes out of the mouth of God!"* It was a declaration that he, Jesus, was not there as God, but as representative Man, to fulfil, as a man, the demands of scripture, and thus make atonement for the people. So he declined the temptation, and was able to go on and fulfil the Father's purpose.

How then, prior to his resurrection, was he revealed as the Son of God? <u>Answer</u>: his divine origin was demonstrated through the following –

- the many prophecies that were fulfilled in him, revealing his unique call, special anointing from heaven, and his heavenly identity.
- his sinless birth, which was the only possible explanation of his sinless life.
- the repeated testimony of the Father, at his birth, at his baptism, and on several other occasions.
- the authority he claimed for his teaching, and the claims he made about himself as part of that teaching.
- his measureless possession of the Holy Spirit, and the expression through him of all the ministry gifts (apostle, prophet, evangelist, teacher, shepherd).
- his Transfiguration, which gave the disciples a glimpse of the infinite glory that always belonged to Christ through his bond with the heavenly Logos.
- the testimony of the demons who on several occasions cried out his real identity.
- above all, his claim that no one could kill him against his will; he alone had power to lay down his life and to take it up again (Jn 10:18), which he demonstrated in his resurrection. (Ro 1:4)

None of those things impinged upon the reality of his humanity. Nor did they give Jesus resources beyond what God has made available to all his servants, namely –

- the Word
- faith
- the power of the Holy Spirit
- prayer, and the

- authority that came from his knowledge of his mission and of his heavenly identity. (110)

Thus, although Christ never lost his heavenly identity as the eternal Logos (Jn 1:1-3), during his years on earth, he was a true man, not a "pseudo-man", not a "deity incognito" wearing a human disguise, like some mythical pagan god. This true *humanity* of Jesus, like his true deity, can be demonstrated in several ways –

- his *birth* of a human mother in squalid circumstances. Although he was conceived (in Luke's lovely phrase, 1:35) by the Holy Spirit overshadowing Mary's womb, his gestation and birth thereafter were quite natural.

- his ordinary *growth*, following the same processes as every human child, being obliged to learn how to walk, talk, think, and behave (Lu 2:40, 51-52; He 5:7-8).

- his *appearance* – as the gospels show, it was quite ordinary; he looked just like any other Jewish man of about 30 years of age; he had no special form or beauty that would compel people to admire him (Is 53:2).

- his *name* – a common one, Joshua, which would have belonged to hundreds of other boys at that time ("Jesus" comes from the Greek spelling of "Joshua").

- his *family* – he had four natural brothers and several sisters who saw nothing exceptional in him, and

---

110) Do you ask, why then can't I do all the things Jesus did – walk on water, raise the dead, hush raging storms, multiply a loaf of bread? The answer is simple. He was able to do those things because they were part of the mission the Father had given him to fulfil, and for which he was empowered by the Holy Spirit (Lu 4:16-21). If you and I were given the same tasks, then, by the power of the same Spirit, we could do them! But of course, God has different plans for you and me to fulfil, and by faith, as Spirit-filled servants of God, we can expect to achieve them.

indeed, thought he was mad when he began to make seemingly outlandish, if not blasphemous claims about himself (Mk 3:21,32; 6:3; Jn 6:42).

- his *life* – in which he was just as dependent as other people are upon proper food, rest, exercise, sleep, and the like; and just as susceptible to bruising and physical injury.
- his *betrayer* – Judas, who had to identify him with a kiss, to prevent the soldiers from mistakenly arresting the wrong man.
- and many other similar proofs could be added.

Out of all this, the proposition is confirmed – during the years of his incarnation, Jesus confined himself to human properties. *Jesus was a man,* and he lived as a man must live, fully human, not semi-divine.

HUMILIATION AND EXALTATION

Succinctly in our text, Paul describes the infinite condescension and grace of Christ. He reveals Jesus' seven-fold *descent* into the deepest humiliation, and then his seven-fold *ascent* into the highest honour –

THE DESCENT

Christ was in the form of God, but did not count equality with God a thing to be grasped; on the contrary, he descended into humiliation by –

1. emptying himself
2. taking the form of a slave
3. being born in the likeness of men
4. being found in human form
5. humbling himself
6. being obedient unto death
7. dying on the cross.

Thus he moved from a position of absolute power to absolute weakness – from the highest position in the universe to the lowest level of human society. But for that very reason, he has been exalted again to the highest pinnacle of honour, for–

THE ASCENT

1. God has highly exalted him
2. and bestowed on him the loftiest name
3. that at his name every knee should bow
4. in heaven
5. on earth
6. and under the earth
7. and every tongue will confess that Jesus Christ is Lord, to the glory of God the Father (Ph 2:9-11).

And that entire process began with the *kenosis* – "though Christ was in the *form* of God he **emptied** himself" – which brings us up to the hard questions: what does it mean, *he was in the form of God*? What was his *equality* with God? How did he *empty* himself, and of what?

Those are difficult questions to answer while avoiding heresy on this side or that. For example, a hundred years ago two famous scholars expressed their opinions – [111]

Canon Gore – "There is room, no doubt, for much variety of opinion ... and in any case the wise interpreter will be very shy of erecting a 'kenosis doctrine' on a phrase the exact limits of which no man can fix with precise accuracy."

Professor A.B. Bruce – "... the diversity of opinion prevailing among interpreters in regard to the meaning of

---

111) Quoted by Dr E.H. Gifford, in The Incarnation; Longmans, Green & Co., London, 1911; pg. 3,4.

(this) passage ... is enough to fill the student with despair and to afflict him with intellectual paralysis."

I am bound to say that a century later the scene is no better! In an effort to arrive at some kind of certainty on the *kenosis* I spent countless hours labouring through various commentaries, lexicons, grammars, biblical dictionaries, and theologies – but I came to the end of my toils feeling rather like Omar Khayyam – [112]

> *Myself when young did eagerly frequent*
> *Doctor and Saint, and heard great argument*
> *About it and about – but evermore*
> *Came out by the same door as in I went!*

But that is too cynical. Despite the many uncertainties, there is still much wisdom to be found. Perhaps we can discover some of it? –

VARIOUS ALTERNATIVES

Scripture says that Christ *emptied* himself – but of what? and how? Did he empty himself of the *form* of God, or of his *equality* with God, or of both, or of neither?

Some commentators choose to remain agnostic in the face of such questions. They argue that Paul did not write, "he emptied himself of this or that;" but merely, *"he emptied himself,"* without any mention of what was poured out. He tells us only the *manner* in which Christ accomplished his *kenosis* (by the 7-fold descent), and then the inevitable outcome (the 7-fold ascent). He does not tell us the inner mystery of the *kenosis*. And his purpose was not to formulate a piece of perplexing theology, but to encourage Christians to follow the example of Christ, by showing his humility and grace, sacrificially serving each other and God (Ph 2:5, 12-13).

---

112) Edward Fitzgerald, op. cit. *Quatrain 27*.

Paul's emphasis is not so much on what Christ *abandoned* as it is on what Christ *assumed* – that is, Jesus took on human likeness, and the form of a servant, and became obedient to death. Perhaps John Gerstner has the right idea –

> The *kenosis* has generally been taken to refer not to the *subtraction* of divinity, but to the *addition* of humanity. [113]

So (it is argued), we cannot hope to guess what scripture does not plainly tell us about the *kenosis*. We cannot presume to say how many of his divine attributes Christ may have abandoned, or in what way he did so. Nor can we tell how, or by how much, he surrendered his position of equality with God. We can do no more than describe what it meant for Christ to be *"in the form of a servant,"* to live on earth as a man, and to die on a pain-wracked cross. The inner counsels and processes of the Godhead must forever remain mysterious to us. We have to be content with the description given in the four gospels of the outer processes of the incarnation – a description that deals with observable fact, not hypothetical mysteries.

ATRACTIVE BUT NOT PERSUASIVE

Those arguments are attractive. There is undoubtedly a strong element of truth in them. They benefit by clearing away a lot of weary speculation, leaving the soul free to concentrate on the main thing – Paul's breathtaking vision of the transcendent Lord joyfully grasping servitude among men, and providing for us a peerless example of humble love. Yet most thinkers are reluctant to stop at that point.

There is within the church an insistent urge to penetrate the mystery of the incarnation as far as thought and scripture will allow. And the fact is, scripture and thought both

---

113) I have lost the source of this quote.

provide more insight into the *kenosis* than the above arguments are willing to admit.

I have already pointed out the two main divisions in the church on how to interpret the *kenosis*. But here is another way of looking at it, which chooses to break up the mystery into –

FIVE OTHER SOLUTIONS

- <u>*the Logos*</u> gave up all of his divine attributes, and thus, during the years of his incarnation, ceased all cosmic functions, and lost all divine consciousness.

That is, the powers of Christ became strictly human, his activities were absolutely earthbound, and he had no personal awareness beyond that of being an adult man – however, he did eventually learn from scripture, and by revelation of the Holy Spirit, that he was the One whose coming had been foretold by the prophets.

- <u>*the Logos*</u> gave up the incommunicable attributes of God (such as omnipotence, omnipresence, omniscience), but not the relational attributes (such as love, holiness, truth, justice, mercy, and so on).

Christ fully retained all those relational attributes and frequently demonstrated them in his life and ministry.

- <u>*The Logos*</u>, since he cannot be separated from God without sundering the deity (which would be absurd) must have remained fully in the heavenlies and in constant possession and use of all his divine powers while embodied in Christ on earth.

That is, Christ remained fully present in heaven as the divine Logos, the second Person in the Godhead, with all the attributes of God, while at the same time he was incarnate in Jesus of Nazareth, who as a man had possession and use only of human attributes.

- *the Logos* surrendered to the Father all control over the exercise of his divine powers, and had no access to them except as the Father himself allowed.

This seems to be confirmed by such passages as *Matthew 26:53;* for if Jesus still commanded the attributes of God why could he not call upon the angels himself, instead of asking the Father to send them?

- *the Logos* retained all his attributes and powers, both in heaven and on earth, but voluntarily refrained from using any of them in such a way as would have disturbed his claim to be a true man living within the confines of human nature.

This seems to be confirmed by such scriptures as *Matthew 4:3*, where Satan takes it for granted that Jesus, as the Son of God, could himself turn stones into bread.

The *first* of those solutions is rejected on the ground that Christ, as the eternal Logos, could not altogether put aside his divine attributes without ceasing to be divine, which would have negated his ability to make reconciliation between God and man.

The *second* and the *third* are rejected on virtually the same ground – the Logos cannot discard any of his attributes without in the process destroying his divinity.

The *fourth* is rejected because it seems to contradict certain statements in the gospels.

The *fifth* is rejected on the ground that it is impossible to conceive how Jesus of Nazareth could embrace in human form such divine qualities as the possession of all knowledge, or being everywhere at the same time.

So we are left with a mystery (1 Ti 3:16) that defies any final solution. We find ourselves obliged to echo scriptures, making statements in one place that seem to contradict what it says in another – because in one place it is talking about the *Man of Galilee*, while in another it is talking about the

Son of God. How those two natures (the human and the divine) can blend into one person must baffle penetration by any finite mind.

Nonetheless, some things can be affirmed. Among them is the proposition already established, that whether or not he actually retained the independent use of any or all the divine attributes of the Logos, the *man* Jesus of Nazareth never once stepped outside the boundaries of his human nature. All that he said and did during the 33 years of his incarnation was done as a man, calling only upon those resources that are available to all believing Spirit-filled people.

Thus he was able genuinely to set us an example that we can follow – that is, as he did, so we too can we live in union with the Father by faith, full of the Holy Spirit, and obedient to the Word and will of God (1 Pe 2:21).

THE KENOSIS OF THE CHURCH

We need to remember that Paul's focus in his great passage about the *kenosis* was not on some dogma about the Incarnation, nor even on some theory about the nature of Christ, but on how Christ set us an example to follow. His purpose was not theological, but practical. So he began with the admonition –

> *You should have the same mind that Christ Jesus had. (Ph 2:5).*

Then, in the next few verses, he explains how Christ was humbly willing to step away from the Father's throne, to be born on earth, live as a man, serve others, and die on a cross to make atonement for our sin (vs. 6-11). Then he comes to his real point –

> **<u>Therefore</u>**, *my beloved ... work out your own salvation with fear and trembling, for it is God who works in you, both to will and to work for his good pleasure. (vs. 12, 13, KJV)*

He means that the *kenosis* of Jesus calls for us to undergo our own *kenosis*. We too should "empty" ourselves of all that we prize, surrendering wholly to the Father's will, setting ourselves to serve him for ever. We too should have such a heart of love and sacrificial service toward each other. We too should embrace the Father's purpose, for God in Christ came from heaven to earth to become one with us, so that we in turn, in Christ, may be carried from earth to heaven and become one with God.

Then he adds this startling revelation to the people at Philippi, and to us. We do not have to rely upon ourselves to live out our own *kenosis*. It is God himself who will work in us, and through us, and for us, both giving us a **will** to serve him continually, and **enabling** us to do his will. And how pleased the Father will be with them when he observes this *kenosis* in his children! For that is the end of the entire passage – that we, following the example of Christ in emptying ourselves of self-will and human ambition, and taking on the mind of Christ, may one day share the glory of Christ in being raised to heaven's splendour!

WORK OUT YOUR SALVATION

Now that is a goal so enticing, so rapturous, that Paul urges us to begin without delay to *"work out your own salvation with fear and trembling"*. No doubt that is paradoxical, perhaps even seems contradictory. But it is not really so. Yes, God works ***in*** us both to will and to do his good pleasure, but then, with God's help, we have to work ***out*** that same salvation day by day.

Mark you, he does not say work ***for*** your salvation, which no one can do, for we depend wholly upon Christ for our rescue, but to work it ***out.*** This has two applications –

YOUR OWN SALVATION

The adjective is significant – *"your **own** salvation."* General salvation is offered to the entire world by God in Christ, as a free gift of his marvellous grace (Jn 3:16). We can't buy it or work for it in any way. But once we have received it, and it becomes our "own", then we must work it out hour by hour.

Christian life, like a good marriage, must be worked at. It doesn't happen of its own accord. Those who "neglect" their own salvation will one day lament their folly –

> *Therefore we must pay much closer attention to what we have heard, lest we drift away from it. For since the message declared by angels proved to be reliable, and every transgression or disobedience received a just retribution, how shall we escape if we neglect such a great salvation?. (He 2:1-3, ESV)*

So then let us apply ourselves diligently to prayer, to reading the Bible, regular worship, resisting the devil, turning aside the blandishments of the world, growing in the fruit of the Spirit (Ga 5:16-25), bearing a steadfast witness, and displaying in every possible way the beauty of Christ.

YOUR CHURCH SALVATION

It is possible that Paul was not thinking so much of individual salvation as of the church at Philippi, which needed rescuing from ruinous strife. Apparently they were lacking unity of purpose, and were troubled by selfish, proud, wrongfully ambitious people, who were endlessly complaining and arguing! (Ph 2:3-4, 14). He wanted them, stirred by the example of Christ, to have a change of heart, to be more concerned about others than themselves (vs. 4), and to become blameless and sincere, so that they might shine like stars in a crooked and depraved world (vs. 15).

That is a worthy goal for any local church! But again, it won't happen by itself. The church has to adopt such a goal purposefully, and work out the grace of God in its people, until, against the darkness of a wicked world, it truly does shine like a star blazing in heaven above!

THE KENOSIS CONSUMMATED

Christ so well fulfilled the purpose of the Father in his *kenosis*, that

> *God exalted him to the highest place, and gave him the name that is above every name! (Ph 2:9)*

Now the decree is immutable. At the name of Jesus, every knee will bow, whether in heaven, on earth, or under the earth (vs. 19) –

- **<u>in heaven</u>** – the myriads of holy angels, and all heavenly principalities, rulers, authorities, and dominions, along with the archangel, the cherubim and seraphim, the four and twenty kings on their golden thrones, and all the redeemed of all time who in spirit are already in his presence.

- **<u>on earth</u>** – all the peoples of the earth, all nations, tribes, lands, cities, cultures, and identities, the criminal and the upright, those who love God and those who hate him, all ethnic groups, and the devotees of all religions –.there will be no exceptions – every creature on the face of the planet, willingly or unwillingly, will bow before the name of Jesus.

- **<u>under the earth</u>** – the dead awaiting the resurrection and judgment, and all the fallen angels and creatures of the kingdom of darkness, including the devil himself.

All, all must one day yield to the sovereignty of Christ, whether or not they choose to do so, and they will all confess with laughter or with tears or with rage or self-pity, or any other emotion, but confess they will, *that Jesus Christ is Lord, to the glory of God the Father!"* (vs. 11)

And if we too follow the path of *kenosis*, then we too will share in that supernal magnificence on the day of his coming.

FOURTEEN

ASCLEPIUS AND HIS ILK

The god Apollo (says an ancient myth) fell in love with Princess Coronis, and she conceived a male child by him. The god had to leave the maiden for a time, and being doubtful of her virtue he sent a raven to spy on her. At that time, ravens were white. The princess was actually in love with a handsome young prince, and the two began to meet in secret. The raven, observing their tryst, at once flew off to report the betrayal to Apollo, and with great fury he slew the maiden. Preparations were made for her funeral, a splendid pyre was built, and the grieving citizens began to lament her untimely death. Meanwhile the goddess Diana, who was jealous of Apollo, placed a curse on the raven for its evil report, changing its snowy plumage into pitch black. That is why to this day ravens are as dusky as a lump of coal. (114)

When the flames began to reach toward the body of the princess, who was still carrying the baby in her womb, Apollo, regretting his hasty anger, rescued the child and gave him to a goat to nurture. The boy's name was Asclepius, who when he reached manhood was found to possess remarkable healing skills. His fame spread far and wide, until it was said that under his hands no sickness was incurable.

ASCLEPIUS APOTHEOSISED

A day came when Asclepius brought a dead man back to life (says the myth). Alarm shivered across Mt Olympus, the abode of the gods. Mighty Zeus, fearful that humans might learn how to escape death altogether, cast a thunderbolt onto

---

114) For more on the Asclepian myth and its relationship to Christology, see my book Emmanuel – *Part Two,* Chapter Eleven, *Perseus and Asclepius;* Vision Publishing, Ramona, Ca; 2006. Also, see the next footnote below.

the earth and killed Asclepius. But his father Apollo pleaded for mercy with such fervour that Zeus relented, and Asclepius was carried up to heaven and took his place among the stars.

Now that he was divine, Asclepius soon became the Greek god of healing, and his fame began to spread even more widely than it had while he was still human. Temples in his honour sprang up all over the land, and his worship rapidly spread to other lands. Even the proud Romans, in the year 293 B.C., when their city was suffering from a terrible plague, sent an embassy to Greece to beg the aid of their healing god. It is said that Asclepius himself came to the rescue of the city, accompanied by a great serpent. When the ship anchored in the Tiber, the serpent slithered from it and took possession of a nearby island, which later became an Asclepian shrine. A temple was built there to commemorate the great physician's art, for he had stemmed the plague and restored health to the Romans.

Asclepius travelled with the serpent, and took its image as his attribute, because of the manner in which snakes renew their skin each year, thus providing a sign of his renovative powers. He also carried a sacred staff, around which the serpent is often shown coiled, and to this day a staff entwined by a serpent remains a symbol for the practice of medicine. [115]

---

115) There are many variations in the several myths about Asclepius, including changes in his name to Asklepios, Aesculapius, and others. But the general story is much as told above. What is certain, is that he was a popular god throughout the Greek and Roman world of apostolic times, with temples, some of them magnificent, everywhere. See The Gods of the Greeks, by C. Kerenyi, tr. by Norman Cameron; Thames and Hudson; 1988; pg. 142-145. The Greek Myths, *Volume One*, by Robert Graves;Penguin Books Ltd; 1975; *Section 50*. A Smaller Classical Dictionary, by William Smith; John Murray, 1882; eponymous article. Bullfinch's Mythology, by Thomas Bullfinch; The Modern Library; pg. 105, 238. The Oxford Classical Dictionary, ed. N.G.L. Hammond & H.H. Scullard; Clarendon Press, 1969; articles *Aesculapius* and *Asclepius*.

. . . .continued on next page.

ASCLEPIUS AND THE APOSTLES

In the time of the apostles the cult of Asclepius, the god of healing, was immensely popular throughout the Greek and Roman world. The ruins of many splendid Asclepian temples can still be found scattered across the former Roman territories. He was called in the Greek tongue *Soter*, meaning *Saviour, which is the very title the apostles gave to Jesus!* And the benefit people hoped to gain from Asclepius was called *soteria* – salvation/healing; which again is *the same word as the apostles used to describe the major benefit of the gospel.*

Consider then the breathtaking boldness of the apostles: they plucked the beautiful title Saviour right out of the hand of Asclepius and gave it instead to Jesus! They were announcing to the world that what people had in vain hoped, across many centuries, to find from a god who had never existed and could not possibly answer their prayers, was now available in reality from Christ!

What did the people turn to Asclepius to find? His title *Saviour* (soter) held a promise (vain in his case) of two things: freedom from all bondage; healing of all disease. Those same two things, the gospel declares, are now truly available in Christ, summed up in the marvellous word *salvation* (soteria). Could we expect less from Jesus than the pagans expected from their mythical deity? Would the people have heeded the apostles if they had suggested that the *Saviour Jesus* could not offer as rich a blessing as they expected from the *Saviour Asclepius*? Hardly! The very fact

---

.... continued from previous page.
> Athenian Popular Religion, by Jon D. Mikalson; University of North Carolina Press, London; 1983; various references. The Illustrated Dictionary of Greek and Roman Mythology; by Michael Stapleton Peter Bedrick Books, New York; 1986; articles *Aesculapius* and *Asclepius*. For a full account, see http://www.theoi.com/Ouranios/Asklepios.html, which embod-ies all the myths.

that the apostles appropriated from the Asclepian cult the terms Saviour/Healer, Salvation/Healing, Save/Heal, show their belief that a humble seeker could find a *better* pardon, a *better* rescue, a *better* healing from Christ than any god of stone could ever give them!

Which brings us now to our text –

> *Our citizenship is in heaven, and from it we await a* **Saviour**, *the Lord Jesus Christ. . . . This will result in my* **salvation** *. . . A clear sign that your* **salvation** *is from God . . . Work out your own* **salvation** *with fear and trembling.* (Ph 3:20; 1:19, 28; 2:12)

There Paul uses the same words we have been talking about, **soter/saviour**, and the related **soteria/salvation**. This salvation, because of the association the words had with the Asclepian cult, meant nothing less than pardon of all sin, release from all bondage, and healing of all sickness. It is inconceivable that in the ancient world, or in the minds of the apostles, they could have had a lesser meaning.

Against that background let us never shrink back from making two great affirmations about the gospel of Christ –

LET US DECLARE
THE SAVING POWER OF THE CROSS
A MULTICULTURAL PRESSURE

Australia is in the midst of an extraordinary multi-cultural experiment, which if it succeeds, will mark us as one of the most civilised nations in human history! Seldom has it been possible for so many races, or so many people of diverse ethnicity from a variety of cultures, to live together amicably. It is a sight that must be pleasing to the Father of us all, although only time will tell if the present inter-racial concord, which is currently quite strong, will prove to be enduring.

In the meantime, this multiculturalism does have an unfortunate consequence for the church. Multiculturalism requires that all ethnic groupings, cultural expressions, creeds, and religions be given an equal place in the sun, with none being superior to another. But the gospel presents an exclusive message, which allows no alternatives, proclaims all other religions false, and insists that Christ is the one and only Way to Paradise. Therefore, in a way that we have never before known, the church now finds itself under great pressure, and in fierce competition with

THE TEMPLE

The dominant idea here is that the soul finds ultimate bliss by total absorption into the divine, in which all individuality, personal identity, and self-expression is lost. It is rather like watching a lump of lead dissolving into a molten pot, leaving only dross on the top. So we die, discard our mortal frame and singular identity, and become dissolved back into the cosmic essence of the universe. We are like a drop of spray, tossed out of the great ocean for a few moments, existing independently only until we fall back into it and are lost for ever.

THE MOSQUE

The dominant idea here is that of fatalism, where the will of Allah is supreme. Pardon depends upon a divine caprice, for no sacrifice for sin is available. People have no final choice except to submit to the decrees of Allah, who will thrust into hell those whom he has chosen to damn, and carry to Paradise those whom he has chosen to honour.

THE SYNAGOGUE

The dominant idea here is trust in ethnic identity and the proper observance of ritual. To be born a Jew and to serve Yahweh and the synagogue faithfully is the pathway to Paradise. Here too pardon must rest upon a whim of Yahweh, for no pathway is shown to rectify sin, nor is there any way to restore lost righteousness, nor to apprehend the power of God to overcome sin and to serve God in holiness.

How different is

THE WAY OF THE GOSPEL!

- <u>Against the **Temple**</u>, with its utter dissolution of the soul, the gospel affirms the value of each person as an individual fashioned in the likeness of God (1 Jn 3:2-3), and destined in Christ, if they embrace him as Saviour, to remain each one a child of God, enjoying and serving him for ever.

- <u>Against the **Mosque**</u>, with its despairing fatalism, the gospel affirms that every Christian is a partner with God in shaping the future, both for oneself and for the kingdom (Mt 6:9-10), and always with an admonition to "choose" ourselves which path we will follow.

- <u>Against the **Synagogue**</u>, with its exclusive nationalism, the gospel widely embraces every nationality and tongue, inviting *"whoever will to come and drink freely of the Water of Life!"* (Re 7:9-10; 22:17).

A CURE FOR TWO ILLS!

Only the gospel offers both **ransom** and **release**; which was expressed beautifully 150 years ago by A. M.Toplady in his poem *Rock of Ages* –

> *Be of sin the <u>double cure</u>,*
> *Cleanse me from its **guilt** and **power**!*

Why then do so few Christians experience both elements of this saving power? The answer today is the same as it was 2200 years ago, when Rabbi Sirach called his young disciples to choose godliness and live with discipline –

> Consider the generations that have gone before us, and see – has anyone ever trusted in the Lord and then been put to shame? Or has anyone ever held firmly to the fear of the Lord and then been forsaken? Or has anyone ever called upon him and then been ignored? Surely

> the Lord is compassionate and merciful, always ready to forgive sin and to rescue people who are suffering affliction. So woe to timid hearts and to limp hands! Woe to the sinner who tries to walk two ways at once! Woe to faint hearts that are lacking in trust! How can you hope to be sheltered? Woe to you who have lost your nerve! What will you do on the Day of Judgment? *(Sirach 2: 10-14)*

> You must never say, "It is the Lord's fault that I wandered from the right way"; for God does not do what he hates. Nor should you ever say, "It was God himself who deceived me"; for God has no use for a sinful man. If it is abominable, then the Lord hates it; and those who fear him will hate it too. Was it not he who created us in the beginning, and has he not given us the power to choose what path we will follow? So if you choose to do so, you can keep his commands; to act faithfully rests entirely upon your own decision. God has placed before you fire and water: stretch out your hand for whichever you wish. In front of you stand life and death; whichever you choose will be given to you. *(Sirach 15:11-17)*

> Turn to the Lord and forsake your sins; come into in his presence with prayer, and your offenses will shrink away. Return to the Most High and renounce iniquity, and set yourself to hate whatever the Lord abhors. *(Sirach 17:25-26)*

In the liberty of Christ, in the knowledge of sin forgiven, we do have freedom and strength to choose right from wrong, and to walk pleasingly before him. How futile it is to accept pardon from God if we do not also seize the promise of victory, and make every effort to resist the devil, and to put off the *"old man"* and all his works while clothing ourselves with the *"new man"* in Christ (Ja 4:7; Ga 5:24-25; Ep 4:22-27; Cl 3:5-12; etc.)

The gospel is the way, the only and all-sufficient way to gain pardon for sin and freedom to live for God. Let us resist the multicultural pressures of our time, and never in the least degree resile from that truth.

LET US DECLARE
THE HEALING POWER OF THE CROSS

While the basic meaning of the title *Soter* held by Asclepius was *Saviour*, the god himself was linked primarily with *healing the sick*. Petitioners would go to one of his temples, and there spend the night. If he or she were fortunate enough to dream about the god, then it was reckoned certain that full healing would follow. In the larger temples, the cure of sickness was also facilitated by the attendance of nurses and physicians, dieticians, physical therapists, and the like. The ancients did not entirely depend upon their superstitions!

There are still in existence a large number of inscribed tablets, from grateful devotees, praising Asclepius, and thanking him for his healing power. Many of those cures may be attributable to mind over matter, or to the skills of the attending staff, but some of them, taken at face value, appear to have been truly a miracle. They are a testimony to the mercy and kindness of God, who sometimes *"winks at our ignorance"* and meets us where he finds us (cp. Ac 17:30, KJV).

In any case, it would have been impossible for the apostles to ignore this bodily healing component of *soter* when they snatched it from the Asclepian cult and made it part of the gospel. To call Jesus "Saviour", then, is also to call him "Healer"; and not just "healer" in some limited spiritual sense, but rather of the whole person, body, soul, and spirit. Thus Paul once prayed –

> *May your spirit, soul, and body be kept healthy and faultless until our Lord Jesus Christ returns. (1 Th 5:23, CEV)*

Indeed, when scripture uses one of the Greek words related to *soter/saviour*, it can often be accurately and responsibly translated as "heal" (*sozo*), "healer (*soter*), or "healing" (*soteria/soterios*). Thus in the following places, along with many others that could be cited –

"SOZO – SAVED"

- "She said to herself, 'If I only touch his garment, I will be <u>made well</u>.' Jesus turned, and seeing her he said, 'Take heart, daughter; your faith has <u>made you well</u>.' And instantly the woman was <u>made well</u>." (Mt 9:21-22, ESV)
- "Everyone who touched Jesus was <u>made whole</u>." (Mk 6:56)
- "Jesus said to the leper, 'Stand up and go your way. Your faith has <u>made you well</u>.'" (Lu 17:19)
- "He was crippled from birth and had never walked. ... But he listened to what he was saying, and Paul, looking at him closely, saw that he had faith to be <u>made well</u>. So he commanded loudly, 'Stand upright on your feet.' And the crippled man sprang up and began walking." (Ac 14:9-10)

"Sozo" occurs some 90 times in the NT, many of which could be understood as well of physical healing as of spiritual salvation. Sometimes the context clearly shows which emphasis is meant; in other places, either choice is valid, and both are probably intended.

"SOTER" – SAVIOUR

- "We know that this man is indeed the Christ, the Saviour of the world." (Jn 4:42)

"Soter" occurs some 25 times in the NT, always as a title of Christ. It is never specifically linked with healing the sick, but its common meaning in apostolic times cannot be stripped of that link. In other words, where Christ is called *Saviour*, it could always be translated equally well as Healer, or Deliverer, or Rescuer. Thus in *Acts 5:31* we are told that "God has exalted Christ at his right hand as Prince and <u>*Saviour*</u>". But that is set against the background of the apostles, in the name of Jesus, healing the sick – *"They brought the sick and those who were demon possessed, and they were **all** healed!"* (vs. 16). Even Peter's shadow touching people was enough to heal "multitudes" of them! (vs.15). Indeed, by the hands of all the apostles, acting in the name of the Great Physician, *"many signs and wonders were regularly done among the people"* (vs. 1).

They understood what it meant to call Jesus *Soter* – he was the One who could at last fulfil the Father's promise, and *"take away from them all sickness and every disease"* (De 7:15).

"SOTERIA/SOTERIOS" – SALVATION

"*Soteria*" and its associated words occur at least 50 times in the NT, nearly always in connection with Christ as Saviour or with the salvation that he offers. In one place it means specifically, "good health" or "well being" (Ac 27:34). But in most of the other references, too, bodily health may be included as part of the "deliverance" that Christ brings to all who believe. In any case, given the culture in which the apostles used the word, their readers would have inevitably embraced physical and mental healing along with spiritual wholeness.

It baffles me how commentators can miss this obvious truth, or how they can relegate the healing ministry of Christ to the past and claim that today only his power to save the soul is relevant. But at least it is impossible to deny sensibly that the apostles assumed that the Great Commission (Mk 16:16-

20) [116] did indeed include healing the sick as well as preaching pardon of sin.

Perhaps one reason why people are blind to the healing commission is the fierce war that Satan wages against the church grasping the power of Christ over sickness and disease. Why would he do that? I suppose because Satan

- hates anything that expresses the will and purpose of the Father.
- wishes to keep the church as impotent as possible and to limit its harvest of souls; and because
- miracles of healing are the first sign of the inevitability of the resurrection of the dead, and of the devil's ultimate defeat and punishment; and because
- any church that keeps miracles in its ministry will never lose its hope in Christ of a glorious triumph over death and the grave; but when miracles vanish, resurrection-faith soon metamorphoses into a misty symbolism.

Hence there are now many churches who no longer believe in a literal resurrection of the dead, not even of Jesus. They treat the "resurrection" language of scripture as simply a pretty way of talking about the mystical existence of the departed in heaven. But when a blind person sees again, or the deaf hear, and cripples walk – when the power of the living Christ is displayed by healing the sick through laying of hands and prayer – it is impossible to deny the conquest of Jesus over the grave. And as he said, if he lives, then we know that we too shall live in him and with him! (Jn 14:19)

---

116) Some deny that those verses were an original part of the gospel. But even if that were so, they are very ancient, and clearly express the opinion of a very early redactor of the text. In any case, the book of *Acts* and church history show that in fact they did do exactly what the passage claims – *"they went out and preached everywhere, while the Lord worked with them and confirmed their message by many miracles"* (vs.20).

ENJOYING DIVINE HEALTH

Our goal should be the enjoyment of divine health by everyone in the local church, and prayer and the ministry of healing should be a vital and continual part of that process. Nonetheless, in working for that admirable goal, our dependency should not be on miracles alone, but on an amalgam of the three ways in which the Father brings good health to his people. Failure to use all three of these ways may result in unexpected and unwarranted disease –

NATURAL LAW

Notice how God's healing covenant with Israel depended not solely upon faith, but upon obedience to his laws, which included rules about diet, exercise, rest, etc (Ex 15:26; Le 26:3,4 ff,14-16 ff.; De 7:12,13,15; 12:28; 28:1-15; etc.). Therefore, people who ignore hygiene, who do not allow themselves adequate recreation, who refuse to eat properly, or who abuse their bodies in some other way, cannot expect a full outworking of the healing covenant, and may indeed find that it has lost all efficacy for them.

MEDICAL SCIENCE

There is nothing in the healing covenant that demands an immediate miracle, or says that God may channel healing only through the prayer of faith, unaided by any natural means. Think about how another promise, that of divine prosperity, is outworked –

- see *Psalm 104:27-28*, and notice that the creatures must gather what God has provided (see also 1 Kg 2:3; Ps 1:3; 90:17; and cp. Pr 21:25.

- thus also Sirach, in a delightful passage, declares that God wants to spread good health in a golden glow across the face of the earth, but he uses physicians to do it –

    Honour the physician with the honour due him, because you will surely have need of him.

> Remember that the Lord created him, for all healing comes from the Most High. Even kings offer rewards to physicians. The skill of the physician gives him a high reputation, and great men admire him.
>
> The Lord created medicines from the earth, and a sensible man will not despise them. Was not water made sweet with a tree in order that God's power might be known? And the Lord gave skill to men that he might be glorified in his marvellous works.
>
> The pharmacist compounds medicines out of the earth, and by them physicians heal the sick and take away pain. God's works will never be finished; and through physicians he spreads good health across the face of the earth.
>
> My son, when you are sick do not be negligent, but pray to the Lord, and he will heal you. Give up your faults, do what the Lord approves, and cleanse your heart from all sin. Offer a sweet-smelling sacrifice, a grateful portion of fine flour, and pour oil on your offering, as much as you can afford. Then give the physician his place, for the Lord created him; let him not leave you until you no longer need him.
>
> There is a time when success lies in the hands of physicians, especially if they too pray to the Lord that he will grant them success in diagnosis and in healing, so that your life may be preserved. But if you are defiant against the physician you will sin against your Maker! *(38:1-15)*

It seems probable that James was thinking of that passage (vs. 9-10) when he wrote his letter to the church (5:14-16). It provides a fine balance, which is as valid today as it was twenty-two centuries ago. The rabbi mingles prayer, confession, medicine, and good sense as his prescription for good health. He even goes so far as to say that people who ignore God's provision of physicians, pharmacists, and nurses may be committing sin. He was probably correct.

COVENANT PRAYER

Trustful prayer, of course, should never be our last resort, but always the first. Let us not make Asa's mistake of turning to the physician but forgetting God (2 Ch 16:12). He should have done both – that is, sought healing from God first, and then had recourse to the physicians for what help they could give him.

Another principle to remember is that prayer based upon the healing covenant should remain constant until full recovery is gained. Let the physicians do what they can, but let all your real confidence be fixed in the power of God. That, in the end, is our greatest healing resource!

CONCLUSION

We cannot evade the challenge to be fully true to both aspects of the gospel – **_salvation_** and **_healing_**. We cannot claim to have "fully preached" the gospel, or to have preached "the full gospel", unless it is done with both *"word and deed"* (Ro 15: 17-19) So let us bravely resist all pressures to compromise this glorious message.

Our final aim is to create a company of people, victorious over sin, abounding in good health, who will be a shining witness to all the riches that lie in the gospel of Christ, the *Soter*, who saves and heals his people!

FIFTEEN

REJOICE IN THE LORD

> *Finally, my brothers and sisters,* **rejoice** *in the Lord ...* **Rejoice** *in the Lord always; and again I say,* **Rejoice***!" (Ph 3:1a; 4:4).*

Two things distinguish Christianity from all other faiths –

- *answered prayer*; and
- *unquenchable joy*.

Indeed, if a company of people have no experience of answered prayer, and if their sorrows are not alleviated by the joy of the Lord, can they be truly Christian?

Someone may say that joy was a vital part of the experience of ancient Israel, and so is not unique to the church. Yes, Israel did know great joy; but as marvellous as it may have been, their experience of the joy of the Lord was usually spasmodic, confined to various seasons, conditioned by circumstances. That is why the prophet promised a greater day of rejoicing, of which we are now the beneficiaries in Christ–

> *The people whom the Lord has redeemed will return and come singing to Zion; everlasting happiness will be given to them, along with gladness and joy. They will never again know sorrow or feel grief. (Is 51:11)*

But is it really possible to be always rejoicing, or truly to "*give thanks always and in everything*" (Ep 5:20). Can anyone hope to fulfil such extraordinary injunctions? Yet Paul makes it worse –

> *Do not worry about anything, but in everything by prayer and supplication, with*

> *thanksgiving, let your requests be made known to God (Ph 4:6).*

Surely there are times when worry is inescapable, or when joy would at best be inhuman, and at worst blasphemous? Well, not really, for the key is –

OUR JOY IS IN THE LORD

Note that scripture does not demand that we must ***feel*** joy at all times, but rather – no matter how bitter our feelings may be – we should **"rejoice in the Lord"**. But what does *that* mean, to rejoice in God himself?

GIVING THANKS ALWAYS

IN SORROW

Here is a paradox! We are sorrowful, yet we rejoice! We weep and we laugh at the same time. How? Simply, because our joy is grounded in our relationship with the eternal, unchanging God. People may fail us. Death may carry off a loved one. Life may harrow us. But the Lord is still there. And not only is he there, but he offers comfort. Can any true believer deny that there is comfort in Christ, and that in him we may find consolation for the deepest griefs? Is he not *"the God of all comfort"*? (2 Co 1:3); and does he not

> **comfort** us in all our troubles, so that we may be able to **comfort** those who are suffering affliction with the **comfort** with which we ourselves are **comforted** by God. (2 Co 1:4).

The Greek word has the sense of calling upon someone to come to one's aid, not merely with sympathetic words, but with whatever actual help the hurting person may need. It is a word redolent not only of *feeling* but of useful *assistance*. And thus is the comfort of the Lord. He *helps* the sufferer.

> *In the crimson of the morning,*
> *In the whiteness of the noon,*
> *In the amber glory of the day's retreat;*
> *In the midnight robed in darkness,*

> *Or the gleaming of the moon,*
> *I listen for the coming of His feet.*
>
> *He is coming, O my spirit,*
> *With His everlasting peace,*
> *With His blessedness immortal and complete;*
> *He is coming, O my spirit,*
> *And His coming brings release,*
> *I listen for the coming of His feet.* (117)

The Lord is always coming to those who love him, and in all circumstances he is at work, shaping everything together for our good (Ro 8:28). But that verse troubles some people. Did Paul say –

> *All things work together for good, for those who are called according to God's purpose. (ASV; ESV; GW; KJV; etc);*

or did he say –

> *In everything God works for good, for those who are called according to his purpose? (CEV; GNB; NIV; NLT; etc.)*

Is the difference worth quarrelling about? In my opinion there is little to choose between them, albeit the first is perhaps a shade more passive than the second. If I had to choose, I would pick the second, because it seems to me to show God more actively involved in compelling every event to turn a benefit for his people. But the end result of either reading is surely the same – no matter what happens, even the worst of human disasters, the man or woman of faith can trust God to work in it and through it, and so find some cause to rejoice in the Lord! Thus the martyrs sang, even as the flames coiled around them and their shrieking children. They made merry even while their homes were being destroyed and their goods plundered (He 10:34). In salt

---

117) Lyman W. Allen, *The Coming of His Feet*, 1914.

mines and prisons, in slave yards and galleys, in unremitting toil and the crack of the lash, torn by the fang and claw of ravenous beasts, still they could find some cause always to give thanks to God.

IN POVERTY

Our sufficiency is in Christ – *"My God will supply every need you may have, according to his riches in glory in Christ Jesus!"* (Ph 4:19).

Does he mean only *spiritual* need, as some would have it? Hardly! Paul himself had just been the beneficiary of a generous and continuing financial gift from the people at Philippi (vs. 10, 14-18). Indeed, they were on occasion the *only* church that did stand by Paul. And now, he says, just as they had met *his* needs, so God would even more richly meet *their* needs, whatever they might be – financial, social, mental, physical, spiritual, collectively and individually.

Furthermore, God's generosity would come, not just *out of* his riches in glory, but *according to* his riches in glory that is, in proportion to his wealth. There is no parsimony in the giving of God! As measureless as his riches, so is the measure of his giving.

However, we cannot take the promise to mean that we can demand anything we please, whenever we please, or for whatever reason we please. As in all things, the promise has to be tempered by the will of God, which sometimes calls us to renounce worldly goods, forsake everything, and follow Christ even to Golgotha. Hence Paul says (vs. 11-13) that he was ready to have everything or to have nothing – depending on where he was, and what the purpose of God required of him.

One thing Paul never doubted, was this – if he truly needed it, God would supply it. He took it as an absolute certainty that God would provide whatever was required to do his will, and since Paul's only desire was to do the will of God, he was rightly confident that the Lord would provide for his every need. How will God do this? If necessary, he will do it supernaturally, as he sent food to Elijah by a flock of ravens (1 Kg 17:6). Or he will do it through human agency, as when he sent money to Paul in the hand of Epaphroditus (vs. 18).

So, whatever genuine need you are facing, give thanks to God and rejoice before him, for it is certain that your God is able to meet it abundantly.

IN DEFEAT

We can rest and rejoice in the triumph of Christ, for if I have been defeated I know that *he* remains the victor. And as long as Christ is triumphant, then in him I too may declare myself victorious. John tells us that simply by being born again we have already overcome the world, and whatever further victory we may need comes to us by means of our faith (1 Jn 5:4). Mark that – not by sweat, blood, toil, nor tears – but by *faith.* The key to overcoming the world is believing that you do indeed possess victory now in Christ, and declaring that victory as a fact even before you see any visible evidence of it (vs. 14-15). Victors laugh. Victors rejoice. Victors are glad. Leave weeping to those who have lost. We are God's winners, because we believe, and because we rejoice in the sure knowledge of our triumph. We sing with the poet a song of light overcoming darkness and blessing stronger than the curse –

> *My own hope is, a sun will pierce*
> *The thickest cloud earth ever stretched;*
> *That, after Last, returns the First,*
> *Though a wide compass round be fetched;*
> *That what began best, can't end worst,*
> *Nor what God blessed once, prove accurst.* [118]

---

118) Robert Browning, *Apparent Failure*, last six lines.

IN PERSECUTION

Can there be any cause for joy when one is suffering fierce persecution? Yes, for Paul himself was suffering in prison when he wrote his laughing letter to the Philippians. Yet he rejoiced, and bade us too to be glad, because suffering gives us the privilege of sharing in the pain of Christ – *"God has doubly blessed you, by allowing you not only to believe in Christ but also to suffer for him"* (Ph 1:29). How wrong that sounds to the unbelieving world. How right it sounds to the church. What greater joy can we have than to endure affliction for the glory of Christ? How can we not delight to go "outside the camp" with him and share his reproach? (He 13:13) How can we regret losing the crumbling ruins of the doomed cities of this world, when in Christ we have become citizens of the indestructible City of God? (vs. 14; 11:15-16). When are we more like the Saviour than when we share his pain?

But why would the Lord want his people to suffer? Can he find any pleasure in our pain? Is he needlessly harsh, indifferent to injustice, callous of cruelty? Hardly! Would you reach maturity in Christ? Are you willing to be made fit to inherit the heavens? Do you want to reach the highest and best that can be gained in the Kingdom of God? Then pain is the unfortunate but unavoidable price of the prize. Any Olympic athlete will tell you that no one gains a medal without huge sacrifice. They must press past the barriers of pain, going almost beyond the limits of endurance. They struggle and agonise, yet gain only a perishable reward. We are striving for an imperishable crown of glory (1 Co 9:24-27).

Hence, when Paul tells the Philippians that suffering is part of believing, he uses a striking word that means "given to you as a privilege" or "granted as a favour" (Ph 1:29). Far from being pitiless, then, the Lord was showing kindness to them when he allowed their enemies to persecute them. The rewards that would follow their grief were so stupendous that they reduced the worst anguish to insignificance (Ro 8:18).

Of course, persecution is unpleasant. The rack is torment. The lash is agony. The flames scorch and sear. Chains chafe, and cramp, and exhaust. Death is black with grief. Tears of distress may flow, cries of anguish may rise from the most courageous saint. Jesus himself found no joy when he agonised in the garden, and his sweat fell mingled with blood to the dust at his feet (Lu 22:44). [119] Three times he struggled, until peace finally fixed itself in his spirit, and he was able, *"for the joy that was set before him"* to press on toward the cross (He 12:2). One cannot rejoice *because* of the suffering. But a Christian can rejoice *despite* it, and rejoice *in* it, finding comfort in Christ, and joy in the fellowship of his suffering, and in the promised Paradise. The grace of Christ is always sufficient.

Persecution, of course, does not always take the form of physical violence. For most people, it is more subtle – an incessant pressure to conform to the way of the world, to follow the pathway of hate rather than love, to be ruled by self-interest rather than the interests of others, to abandon the cross and seek the easy way of conformity, to give up the fight for holiness, justice, and truth in all things, to please men rather than God. Indeed –

> *The Martyr worthiest of the bleeding name*
> *Is he whose life a bloodless part fulfils;*
> *Whom racks nor tortures tear, nor poniard kills,*
> *Nor heat of bigot's sacrificial flame:*
> *But whose great soul can to herself proclaim*
> *The fulness of the everlasting ills*
> *With which all pained Creation writhes and thrills,*
> *And yet pursue unblenched her solemn aim;*
> *Who works, all-knowing work's futility;*

---

119) The condition is called *hematidrosis*. It can happen when someone is undergoing extreme stress of mind or body.

> *Creates, all conscious of ubiquitous death;*
> *And, hopes, believes, adores, while Destiny*
> *Points from life's steep to all her graves beneath;*
> *Whose thought 'mid scorching woes is found apart –*
> *Perfect amid the flames, like Cranmer's heart!* [120]

But whatever form or measure of suffering we may face as servants of Christ, our defining characteristic should be "Cranmer's heart" – that is, courage, joy, and steadfastness, in sure knowledge of the resurrection and of eternal life.

IN DEATH

Christians can look upon the grave and in the midst of tears rejoice, because the sting of death is taken away, and the resurrection is sure, and an inheritance is waiting. So much is this true that unlike those whose mind is on earthly things, we declare that

> *our citizenship is in heaven, and we are eagerly waiting for our Saviour the Lord Jesus Christ to come from there. He will change our low mortal bodies and make them like his own glorious body, using the power that enables him to subdue everything under his own control! (Ph 3:20-21).*

---

[120] Thomas Wade (1805-1875), English poet and dramatist, *The True Martyr.* "Cranmer" is Archbishop Thomas Cranmer (1489-1556), who died bravely as a martyr, being burnt at the stake by the command of Queen Mary. Because he had once written a recantation of his faith, he vowed that the offending member would first be burnt. John Foxe describes it thus – "Then it was, that stretching out his right hand, he held it unshrinkingly in the fire till it was burnt to a cinder, even before his body was injured, frequently exclaiming, 'This unworthy right hand!' Apparently insensible of pain, with a countenance of venerable resignation, and eyes directed to Him for whose cause he suffered, he continued, like St. Stephen, to say, 'Lord Jesus receive my spirit!' till the fury of the flames terminated his powers of utterance and existence." Fox's Book of Martyrs, *Chapter XIII, An Account of Archbishop Thomas Cranmer,* 2007 edition, produced by Project Gutenberg.

This is no small act! To call all the dead of all time from their graves, and to rapture the living church, will take the omnipotence of Deity, the very power by which everything in the universe must submit to the will of God, the power by which he raised Christ from the dead, and the power by which on that breathtaking day we too will be raptured and transformed!

So in every situation there is always some cause for a Christian to rejoice. Only as we do this can our lives be fully redeemed, and every situation sanctified and made into a stairway to paradise.

SIXTEEN

THE KISS OF PEACE

> *Whoever loves, if he do not propose*
> *The right true end of love, he's one that goes*
> *To sea for nothing but to make him sick.* [121]

What kind of love should we Christians express toward each other? What is its "right true end"? We can find an answer in the injunction to

> *Greet each other with a holy kiss (Ro 16:16; 1 Co 16:20; 2 Co 13:12) . . .* **Greet every saint in Christ Jesus with a kiss** *(Ph 4:21) . . . Greet all the brethren with a holy kiss (1 Th 5:26) . . . "Greet all the believers with the kiss of love" (1 Pe 5:14).*

What shall we do with those six injunctions?

The early church took them very seriously, so that from the beginning they were brought into the liturgy under the name, **"the kiss of peace."** –

Justin Martyr (c. 150)

> On the day which is called the day of the sun there is an assembly of all who live in the towns or in the country; and the memoirs of the apostles or the writings of the prophets are read, for as long as time permits. Then the reader ceases, and the president speaks, admonishing us and exhorting us to imitate these excellent examples. Then we arise all

---

121) John Donne – The Complete English Poems, ed. AJ Smith; Penguin Books, London, 1982; *Elegy 18*, *"Love's Progress"*; pg.122.

together and offer prayers ... both for ourselves and for ... all men everywhere, with all our hearts ... (Then) we salute each other with a kiss when we have ended the prayers ... We hold our common assembly on the day of the sun, because it is the same day (on which) Jesus Christ our Saviour rose from the dead. (122)

Tertullian (c. 200)

Another custom has now become prevalent. Such as are fasting withhold the kiss of peace, which is the seal of prayer, after prayer made with brethren ... (But what) prayer is complete if divorced from the "holy kiss"? (123)

But that early innocence was soon debased, and various restraints began to be imposed upon its use. Tertullian alludes to a growing scandal about the use of the kiss. He discusses the difficulties that a Christian woman faces when she is married to an unbelieving husband, and mentions in particular her spouse's suspicions about what she is doing when she goes off to church –

> For who would suffer his wife, for the sake of visiting the brethren, to go around from street to street to other men's ... cottages? Who will willingly bear her being taken from his side by nocturnal convocations, if need so be? Who, finally, will without anxiety endure her absence all the night long at the paschal solemnities? Who will, without some suspicion of his own,

---

122) *Apology*, Bk I, ch 65-67. This quotation, and those following, are all taken from The Anti-Nicene Fathers, *Vol. 1-10*; and from The Nicene and Post-Nicene Fathers, *First & Second Series*, 28 Volumes; all 1979 reprints by Eerdmans Pub. Co, Grand Rapids.

123) On Prayer, ch 18.

dismiss her to attend the Lord's Supper, which they defame? Who will suffer her ... to meet any one of the brethren to exchange the kiss? [124]

Clement of Alexandria (c. 200)

Clement shows how deeply he was scandalised by the misuse of the kiss –

> If we are called to the kingdom of God, let us walk worthy of that kingdom, loving God and our neighbour. But love is not proved by a kiss, but by kindly feeling. But there are those that do nothing but make the churches resound with the noise of their kissing, not having love itself within. Because of this shameless use of the kiss, which ought to be mystic, foul suspicion and evil report are raised against the church ... The apostle calls the kiss holy ... But there is another unholy kiss, full of poison ... (You should remember that scripture says,) "This is the love of God, that we keep his commandments," not that we caress each other on the mouth. [125]

Origen (c. 200)

In his commentary on Ro 16:16 (*"Greet one another with a holy kiss"*), Origen said it was the custom of the churches to share the kiss after prayers, but felt it necessary to insist that the kiss must be holy, chaste, sincere, an expression of peace and simplicity.

---

124) *To His Wife* II.4; written c. 207.
125) *The Instructor*, Bk III, ch 11,12.

Athenagoras (c. 180)

Athenagoras quoted some writings now lost, but which he apparently read as scripture, and warned against allowing even the tiniest corruption to creep into the holy kiss –

> On behalf of those, then, to whom we apply the names of brothers and sisters ... we exercise the greatest care that their bodies should remain undefiled and uncorrupted; for the word again says to us, "If anyone should kiss a second time because the first gave him pleasure, he will be guilty of sin;" and again, "Therefore the kiss, or rather the salutation, should be given with the greatest care, since, if there be mixed with it even the least defilement of thought, it will exclude you from eternal life." (126)

Similar scruples were expressed by

Cyril of Jerusalem (c. 370)

Cyril was anxious lest the believers should find themselves walking in the footsteps of Judas. He tells how at the appointed time in the liturgy the clergy all wash their hands ceremonially in water, (127) following which, he says,

> (The) Deacon cries aloud, "Receive ye one another; and let us kiss one another." Think not that this kiss is of the same character with those given in public by common friends. It is not such: but this kiss blends souls one with another, and courts entire forgiveness for

---

126) A Plea For Christians, ch 32
127) Many of the early churches copied a pagan practice of placing vessels of water outside the church, for the people to wash themselves before they entered; this was later brought into the church, incorporated into the liturgy, and restricted to the clergy.

them. The kiss therefore is ... reconciliation, and for this reason holy. (128)

By the beginning of the fifth century, men and women were obliged to sit in different parts of the church, and only those of the same sex were permitted to share the kiss. The clergy were forbidden to kiss the laity altogether, and were allowed only to greet the bishop –

The Apostolic Constitutions (c. 325) –

... and after (the prayer) let the deacon say, "Let us attend." And let the bishop salute the church, and say, "The peace of God be with you all." And let the people answer, "And with thy spirit." Then let the deacons say to all, "Salute ye one another with the holy kiss." Then let the clergy salute (kiss) the bishop, the men of the laity salute the men, the women the women. And let the children stand at the reading-desk, and let another deacon stand by them, that they may not be disorderly. (129)

Augustine (c. 400)

(The ungodly) resent the streams of people who gather in the church in a modest assembly, where there is a decent separation of the sexes, where they can hear how to live a good life on earth for a space, so that they may deserve hereafter to live a life of bliss for ever, and where the words of holy scripture and of the teaching of righteousness are read aloud from a raised platform in the sight of all. (130)

---

128) Catechetical Lectures, # 23.3.
129) Bk VIII, Sec 2, ch 11.
130) City of God, Bk II, ch 28.

However, Augustine still stressed the importance of the "holy kiss" by pointing out that Christ himself set us an example "when, before the passion of his body, he so bore with his disciple Judas, that ere he pointed him out as the traitor, (he did not deny) to those lips so full of guile ... the kiss of peace." (131)

The Synod of Laodicea (c. 375)

This 4th century Synod established a formal liturgy for the churches, which included the following –

> ... there should then be offered the three prayers for the faithful, the first to be said entirely in silence, the second and third aloud, and then the kiss of peace is to be given. And after the presbyters have given the kiss of peace to the bishop, then the laity are to give it to one another ... (132)

Well before the 10th century, the kiss was restricted to the clergy; a tendency that is already apparent in a letter of Jerome to Theophilus, bishop of Alexandria –

Jerome (c. 400)

Jerome wrote in praise of the worthy bishop –

> Does any turn his face away when you hold out your hand? Does any at the holy banquet offer you the kiss of Judas? At your approach the monks ... race to meet you ... You offer them a kiss; therefore they bow the neck. (133

---

131) On Patience, Sec. 8.

132) *Canon 19.-* The laity at this time were separated, men on one side of the church and women on the other; thus the Canon presumes that the kiss of peace will be given only to a person of the same sex.

133) *Letter LXXXII*, written 399 A.D.—Jerome is commending the bishop's gracious and loving rule over his monks.

Finally, in the 13th century, the use of the holy kiss was abolished altogether in the Western churches.

But now, in our time, one of the exciting aspects of the present revival is a restoration by the Holy Spirit of the *"kiss of peace"*. People are again sharing *"a holy kiss of love and peace"*. What does it mean? What is the Holy Spirit saying? Must we actually embrace? Well, there is no reason why not, so long as each kiss remains chaste, fraternal, and causes no scandal. But surely the importance of the kiss lies not so much in the act itself, but rather in the quality of love it represents, for it shows that –

OUR LOVE FOR EACH OTHER MUST BE WARM

Intimacy cannot be separated from the kiss. It represents the most vulnerable form of greeting, especially when it is compared with other forms that have been practised in diverse places, such as –

- **_prostration_**: as petitioners had to do when they approached an oriental despot.
- **_bowing_**: which is still practised in Japan; a greeting that is courteous indeed, but is also distant and safe.
- **_embracing_**: as people have done in many cultures both ancient and modern; a warmer and more involved style of greeting, but still allows emotional distance.
- **_smelling_**: which is the significance of what we call "rubbing noses together" (still practised in some European cultures); it implies the courtesy of greeting someone by catching their unique odour (note that in many cultures odour is an important part of personal identity – cp. the biblical story of Isaac and his sons).
- **_tasting_**: that is, kissing, which is the most vulnerable greeting of all, for its origin is actually that of showing someone the courtesy of catching their unique *taste*!

Many cultures are offended by the practice of kissing, because it involves an unacceptable (to them) degree both of intimacy and of vulnerability. But those very factors are what enable the holy kiss powerfully to exemplify Christian love.

Thus Peter uses two different words (in 1 Pe 5:14), *agape* and *philema* –

Agape is often presented as the kind of love God expresses, which is defined as being more a love of universal benevolence (Mt 5:45) than of warm intimacy. There is of course some truth in that idea (cp. 1 Co 13:4-7), but Peter refuses to allow Christians to hide behind a cold "spiritual" love, which they then excuse by calling it God's own *agape*. Rather, he forces us to bring intimacy, warmth, feeling, into our Christian love by associating with it the command, "Greet each other with the <u>kiss</u> (philema) *of* <u>love</u> (agape)," for indeed it is true that

> "Kisses are the messengers of love" (Danish Proverb).

Hence **Ambrose** wrote –

> (When Judas) wished to show to the Jews that kiss which he had promised as the sign of betrayal, the Lord said to him: "Judas, betrayest thou the Son of Man with a kiss?" – that is, you, who have not the love marked by the kiss, offer a kiss. You offer a kiss who know not the mystery of the kiss. It is not the kiss of the lips which is sought for, but that of the heart and soul ... So then, he who has not faith and charity has not the kiss, for by a kiss the strength of love is impressed. When love is not, faith is not, and affection is not, what sweetness can there be in kisses? [134]

---

134) Ambrose, bishop of Milan (c. 350), *Letters # 41.16, 17.*

Likewise **<u>Chrysostom</u>**, in a comment on *"Greet all the brethren with a holy kiss"* (1 Th 5:26), said –

> Oh! what fervour! Oh! what mad passion is here! Because being absent Paul could not greet them himself with the kiss, he greets them through others, as when we say, "Kiss him for me." So also do ye yourselves retain the fire of love. For it does not admit of distances, but even through long intervening ways it extends itself, and is everywhere present. [135]

Thus it should never be true of us, as an old English proverb says, that "a kiss of the mouth often touches not the heart." There should always be an element of genuine warmth, of true feeling, in the love that we have for each other in Christ. And if it is impossible to sense that love in connection with a person you don't like (and we can't be fond of everybody, for some people, even Christians, are simply obnoxious), then love the Christ who is in him or her.

OUR LOVE FOR EACH OTHER MUST BE FORGIVING

Across the centuries, although the phrase cannot be found in scripture, this has been called *"the kiss of <u>peace</u>"*. This kiss cannot be offered as a cerebral act of duty. Those who truly kiss must forgive; it is difficult to remain unforgiving while kissing!

What is the first act of two reconciling lovers? And will not a kiss a day keep anger away?

We dare not withhold from each other the welcome signified by the kiss –

---

[135] John of Antioch, known as Chrysostom ("The Golden-Tongued"), c. 347-407, Archbishop of Constantinople (398-407). The above passage is from a sermon he preached on *1 Thessalonians 5:19-27*.

As to the deacons, after the prayer is over, let some of them attend upon the oblation of the eucharist, ministering to the Lord's body with fear. Let others of them watch the multitude, and keep them silent. But let the deacon who is at the high priest's hand say to the people, "Let no one have any quarrel against another; let no one come in hypocrisy." Then let the men give the men, and the women give the women, the Lord's kiss. But let no one do it with deceit, as Judas betrayed the Lord with a kiss. (136)

OUR LOVE FOR EACH OTHER MUST BE EXPRESSED

A kiss cannot be given secretly, in the heart alone. It is a visible, physical, display of affection (cp. Lu 7:45). But that brings us to a difference between the English and Greek words –

- **_The English word_** for *kiss* has its origins in an ancient Hittite echoic (or onomatopoeic) word "*kuwass*".

So it is simply a description of the act, and lacks the love-content of the Greek word. Hence, we can speak of a breeze kissing the cheek; of sunshine kissing the grass; of justice kissing mercy; of the kiss of death; and the like.

- **_But the Greek word_** means specifically "an act of love".

And that is especially true of the word used in our texts (*philema*), in distinction from other Greek words for "kiss"; indeed, the only time *philema* is *not* used in the NT in a context of love is *Luke 22:48*, where its use is a literary device to give an added horror to Judas' act of treachery.

---

136) Constitutions of the Holy Apostles, Bk II.7.57 (c. 325).

So our love must not be merely a thing of *words*, but also of *feelings* and *actions*. <u>Demonstrate</u> it! <u>Do</u> something! <u>Show</u> that the love of Christ infuses your whole being and is the motivating force of your whole life.

OUR LOVE FOR EACH OTHER MUST BE GRACIOUS

In the ancient world, one kissed a <u>superior</u> on the foot, the knee, the hand, or the chest (depending upon social rank); one did not kiss an <u>inferior</u> at all.

> *Civility, we see, refined the kiss*
> *Which at the face begun, transplanted is*
> *Since to the hand, since to the imperial knee,*
> *Now at the papal foot delights to be.* (137)

An <u>equal</u>, (138) however, was kissed on the forehead, or more affectionately, the cheek.

Imagine, then, how radical was the command: *"kiss <u>all</u> the saints,"* which required the high- and low-born, the rich and the poor, slaves and free people, friends and strangers, <u>all</u> who were in the church, to share this warmth and equality of love!

Perhaps some idea of the effect this had on the ancient world can be gained from the disgusted reaction that many heterosexuals have when they see homosexuals (especially men) embracing in public; or how would you respond to an injunction to go down and kiss a group of drunken, unwashed derelicts?

So the church was hated, because its behaviour was an affront to the manners and social taboos of the time –

> It is mainly the deeds of a love so noble that lead many to put a brand upon us. *"See,"* they

---

137) John Donne, op. cit., Elegy 18, *Love's Progress*.
138) Mouth to mouth kissing was reserved for erotic use.

say, *"how they love one another!"* (139) for themselves are animated by mutual hatred; *"how they are ready even to die for one another,"* for they themselves will sooner put to death. And they are wrath with us too, because we call each other brethren; for no other reason, as I think, than because among themselves the names of consanguinity are assumed in mere pretence of affection ... (Thus they) cry out against innocent blood, offering as the justification of their baseless plea, that they think the Christians the cause of every public disaster ... If the Tiber rises as high as the city walls, if the Nile does not send its waters up over the fields, if the heavens give no rain, if there is an earthquake, if there is a famine or pestilence, straightway the cry is, *"Away with the Christians to the lion!"* What! shall you give such multitudes to a single beast? (140)

In Christ, we are equals <u>with</u> each other, and we should be equal in love <u>for</u> each other, excluding none from our fellowship and joy.

(To) prevent any jealousy arising (among them) ... he again mingles them in the equality of charity, and in the holy kiss, saying, "Salute one another with an holy kiss. (They are to do this, in order to) cast out of them, by this

---

139) I refer to this quote also in *Chapter Seven* and *Chapter Eleven*.

140) Tertullian, *Apology ch. 39, 40.–* The phrase "to the lion" had apparently become the common, or standardised, cry of the mobs. It suggests (along with "multitudes") the frequency of the persecutions. Note also that, common to what is often thought, the pagan cry, "How these Christians love each other!" was not a cry of praise, but of scorn. –The heathen saw it as a sign of weakness, of effeminacy, of at least corrupt manners, if not decadent morals.

salutation, all arguing that confused them, and all grounds for little pride; that neither the great might despise the little, nor the little grudge at the greater, but that haughtiness and envy might be more driven away, when this kiss soothed down and levelled every one. (141)

OUR LOVE FOR EACH OTHER MUST BE COVENANTED

The kiss arose in the ancient world from a belief that the soul flows out of the nose or throat with the breath: cp. *2 Kings 4:34*; and God breathing into Adam's nostrils.

So the kiss was the sign of communion of soul with soul; it signified the bonding of a covenant (*"sealed with a kiss"*); it conveyed the idea of giving life for life.

Chrysostom held this high view of the "kiss of peace" –

> What may the reason be (for Paul's command, "Salute one another with an holy kiss")? The Corinthians had been widely at variance with one another on account of their saying, "I am of Paul, and I of Apollos, and I of Cephas, and I of Christ;" on account of "one being hungry, and another drunken;" on account of their having contentions and jealousies and suits. And from the gifts there was much envying and great pride. Having then knit them together by his exhortation, he naturally bids them use the holy kiss also as a means of union: for this unites, and produces one body. This is holy, when free from deceit and hypocrisy. (142)

---

141) Chrysostom, commenting on the holy kiss in a sermon on *Romans 16:5-16*.

142) In a sermon on 1 Corinthians 16:10 ff, in which Chrysostom comments on verse 20 ("All the brethren salute you. Salute one another with a holy kiss.")

This was the original purpose of the kiss at the altar of marriage – it was not the beginning of conjugal love-play, rather, in early times, a bridal couple exchanged a kiss with great solemnity, as an act of committal, swearing eternal fealty as each breathed their soul into the other.

Among the "mystery" cults that flourished in the pagan world in apostolic times, those who reached full initiation were permitted to kiss the *mystagogue,* and they were then admitted to the inner circle of "those within the kiss", bound together by the most solemn oaths and covenants. But scripture declares that we are all "priests" before God, and our high office and eternal union are expressed by the free sharing of the kiss of peace. (143)

It used to be said that an Englishman's handshake was his bond, stronger than his life. So should the kiss be in the church. Auden's cynical words should never be true of Christian conduct –

> *For the clear voice suddenly singing,*
> *high up in the convent wall,*
> *The scent of elder bushes, the sporting prints in the hall,*
> *The croquet matches in summer,*
> *the handshake, the cough, the kiss,*
> *There is always a wicked secret,*
> *a private reason for this.* (144)

For us the kiss of peace must never have any reason save that we are constrained by the love of Christ (2 Co 5:14, KJV), and that by the kiss we declare the unbreakable bonds of the covenant we have made with each other and with Christ.

---

143) Based on a comment on *2 Corinthians 13:12*, in II Corintians, by Victor Paul Furnish, Anchor Bible *Vol 32A*; Doubleday & Co; 1984.

144) W. H. Auden (1907-1973), English poet; *Under Which Lyre*, second stanza.

OUR LOVE FOR EACH OTHER MUST BE HOLY

Remember the pagan culture out of which those early Christians had come – licentiousness abounded and was encouraged; every kind of sexual vice was not only tolerated but practised in public; child brothels could be found in every major community; rape and bestiality were provided for the entertainment of the crowds in the great arenas; and even worship rituals in their lovely temples were rife with fornication and prostitution. Those early Christians had grown up in an environment where in theatres, arenas, public parks, all manner of sexual depravity had been on constant display, and reckoned natural and normal. (145)

How incredible, then, was the command to share a *"holy"* kiss; how great was the apparent potential for corruption! Yet without hesitation the apostles enjoined this shared love upon the saints. They trusted the people would not misuse their injunctions, because they knew how great was the miracle of grace that had been wrought in them by Christ, how radically they had been changed by the gospel, and how splendidly they had mastered the flesh.

So then, let us too allow the grace of God in Christ to keep us holy, remembering that there are always three parties involved in the sharing of Christian love: two people, and the Holy Spirit!

CONCLUSION

Whether or not we actually *kiss* is hardly important, nor is it the point of this study. The use of an actual kiss is a matter of culture, of social custom, of personal preference. But although we may feel under no necessity to *kiss* our fellow Christians, we dare not evade the demand for the kind of

---

145) Many people with finer scruples and nobler standards, including some of the chief Greek and Roman secular thinkers and writers, protested strongly against this awful decay of public morals. But their voices were overwhelmed by the clamour of the majority of the populace.

love expressed in the kiss. The kiss is the symbol of that love. We can dispense with it if we please. But let us make sure that we *love* in the way required by the command: *"Greet every saint in Christ Jesus with the holy kiss of love."*

SEVENTEEN

ANXIOUS ABOUT NOTHING

You should never be anxious about anything. Rather, in everything by prayer and supplication with thanksgiving make your requests known to God. And the peace of God, which surpasses all understanding, will guard your hearts and your minds in Christ Jesus. (Ph 4:6-7)

In the late 5th cent. B.C., the Persian emperor Xerxes led two million troops and 1200 warships into battle against the Greeks. But in order to invade Greece, he had first to build a bridge across the Hellespont. Herodotus tells us what happened -

> The (bridge) was successfully completed, but a subsequent storm of great violence smashed it up and carried everything away. Xerxes was very angry when he learned about the disaster, and gave orders that the Hellespont should receive three hundred lashes and have a pair of fetters thrown into it. I have heard before now that he also sent people to brand it with hot irons. He certainly instructed the men with the whips to utter, as they wielded them, the barbarous and presumptuous words: 'You salt and bitter stream, your master lays this punishment upon you for injuring him, who never injured you. But Xerxes the King will cross you, with or without your permission. No man sacrifices to you, and you deserve the

> neglect by your acid and muddy waters.' (146) In addition to punishing the Hellespont, Xerxes gave orders that the men responsible for building the bridges should have their heads cut off. The men who received these invidious orders duly carried them out, and other engineers completed the work. (147)

Before you laugh at the petulant and savage monarch, ask yourself how *you* handle an unexpected crisis or set-back in life? The question is important, for one of the distinguishing marks of the man or woman of faith is an ability to remain cool under pressure, to behave wisely, and with controlled strength.

Xerxes (who is called Ahasuerus in Esther) crossed the Hellespont, but was deservedly thrashed by a tiny Greek army, and hastened back to Persia, humiliated but not much wiser. Any leader who collapses under pressure will probably suffer the same kind of humiliation and defeat.

Paul's method of handling a crisis consists of four words –

CONFIDENCE

"Be anxious about nothing"

We are prone to be anxious about many things – money, reputation, success, family, church, yesterday, today, tomorrow, and a thousand other matters, some trivial, some important. But Paul is emphatic – we should be anxious

---

146) The ancients often deified natural phenomena, such as the sun, moon, storms, ocean, thunder, etc. But apparently there was no recognised god of the waters of the Hellespont.

147) Herodotus, The Histories, *Book VII, sec. 34-36.* Tr. by Aubrey de Sélincourt; Penguin Classics, 1983; pg. 457. Herodotus (Greek writer, 5th cent B.C.), is often called "the father of history", because he is the first known systematic historian.

about *"nothing"*; which means exactly what it says – "NOTHING!"

Was that command spoken by a man at ease, who actually had nothing himself to worry about? No, for when he wrote this letter, Paul was in prison in Rome, facing execution. The church too, including the Christians at Philippi, was facing persecution and violent, cruel, death. One could easily find a multitude of things to make one frantic. But Paul would have none of it. He looked out at what was happening to him and around him, and could nowhere find any cause for anxiety.

But surely it is irrational and unnatural to demand quietness and confidence in the face of torture, enslavement, or imminent slaughter? Perhaps, if you no longer believe that your affairs are in God's hand, and that he works in all things for good (Ro 8:28), and that nothing can touch you outside of his will (Jn 19:11a). But if you do believe all those things, then what is there to worry about?

See also *Mark 4:40* (along with its stormy context), and note this – if Jesus did not agree that those near-drowning men had any right to be anxious, then he is unlikely to accept any excuse that you or I can offer!

PRAYER

"In everything pray"

This second admonition refutes the idea of some that Paul (when he said, *"don't be anxious"*) was encouraging some kind of fatalistic passivity. They think we are helpless victims, who must quiescently accept without protest whatever life thrusts upon us. Quite the contrary, Paul's emphasis is on the power of prayer, either enabling us to sustain joyful victory in every situation, or changing some present reality into another that conforms to the purpose of God. Notice the contrast –

- "in _nothing_ anxiety;"
- "in _everything_ prayer."

Worry and prayer are as incompatible as fire and water – whichever waxes stronger will destroy the other; so make sure that prayer remains the stronghold of your soul. But what kind of prayer banishes anxiety? Paul defines the nature of this prayer in three words –

- **_Prayer_** – this is prayer expressed through constant fellowship with God.

- **_Supplication_** – this is prayer for the needs of others.

- **_Requests_** – this is prayer for one's own needs

Note that the first word refers to prayer that is continual, always under the surface of your life, but sometimes coming to the forefront; it is what Paul means when he says that we should pray continually (1 Th 5:17). The second two words refer to prayer offered at specific times. And prayer should be strong, forceful, and vigorous, not merely an ephemeral murmuring, mixed with wandering attention, vague understanding, and ill-focussed faith. The expression *"made known to God"* is emphatic in Greek, and has the idea, *"boldly, in the very presence of God"*; upon which the best commentary is *Hebrews 10:19-23*. Think, too, about the words of Jesus – *"The kingdom of heaven has been forcefully advancing, and forceful people have been seizing it!"* (Mt 11:12, GW)

So let us pray. Let us pray without ceasing. Let us pray emphatically. And above all, let us pray with confidence, knowing what we are asking, and, if we know we are asking in agreement with God's will, confident of receiving an affirmative answer (1 Jn 5:14-15).

Sadly, many people have scant appreciation for the magnificence of what the Father has given us in Christ. But it becomes stunningly apparent when one compares our privileges with the wretched superstitions of the past –

> Every five years the Thracians send a messenger to their god Zalmoxis. The messenger is chosen by lot from the whole

nation, and he is commissioned to carry to the god their various requests. The way they send him to Zalmoxis is this – several soldiers stand in a group, holding their spears upright. Other soldiers take hold of the messenger by his hands and feet, swing him a few times, and then toss him into the air, to fall upon the spear points. If he is pierced and dies, they think that the god is propitious to them; but if not, they blame the messenger, accuse him of being a wicked man, and send him away. Then they choose another messenger. The messages, of course, are given to the man while he is still alive. This same people, when there is thunder and lightning, shoot arrows into the sky, shouting threats against the god, for they refuse to honour any god but their own. (148)

Many such horrific stories could be quoted, showing the almost unbelievable ignorance and brutality of ancient superstitions. How different is the gospel! What simplicity and beauty surrounds the promise of answered prayer that we have received. Yet those ancient Thracians did at least perceive the need for someone to go before them into the heavens, someone to represent the entire nation, whom the gods would receive, and there to make intercession for them. That need has been for ever met in Christ, who is even now in the Father's presence, pleading on our behalf, having offered himself as our ransom, and being welcomed back into heaven to take his seat at the right hand of the majesty on high (He 1:3), there to intercede continually on our behalf (He 7:25).

---

148) Herodotus, op. cit., *Book Four*. Adapted from the Internet Classics Archive.

THANKSGIVING

Paul says that we must make our requests to God with *"thanksgiving"*. In other words, worship and prayer belong together, they are not incompatible, as some think. Worship without request, or request without worship, are both a fault to be avoided by true believers.

In particular, *thanksgiving* is prayer and worship expressed through spoken and unspoken, but unbroken, gratitude and praise. Without praise, prayer is like a bird with only one wing, it cannot rise into heaven. The apostle says that we should *"offer a sacrifice of praise continually"* (He 13:15), giving thanks for

- ***past favours*** – all that God has done for us in days gone by, in granting us redemption, in meeting our needs, in guiding and keeping us..

- ***present access*** – all that God is doing for us today, in keeping open heaven's door so that we come boldly into his presence at any time, in the name of Jesus.

- ***expected answers*** – all that God will do for us tomorrow, in answering our prayers, keeping us to the pilgrim pathway, carrying us from earth to heaven, enthroning us for ever with Christ.

He calls this a *"sacrifice"*. When is praise a sacrifice? Praise becomes sacrificial when it is offered –

- ***Continually*** – from a heart that finds in every circumstance some cause for giving thanks to the Lord, and especially when every urge presses one to complain, to get angry, to lament, to do almost anything except raise one's hands in joyful thanksgiving!

It is when you least feel like praising God, yet still do so, that praise becomes a sacrifice of sweet savour to the Lord.

- **_Brokenly_** – echoing the cry of Malachi, *"But as for me, I will keep on trusting God. I will wait for my salvation to come from God, for my God will surely hear me. So do not rejoice yet, O my enemy, for though I have fallen I shall stand up again; though I am sitting in darkness, the Lord will be a light to me. I will submit to the anger of the Lord, because I know that I have sinned against him. But I know also that he will plead my cause and make everything right again. He will bring me out into the light, and I will see his victory!"* (Mi 7:7-9)

So too we, when the enemy has thrown us face down into the mire, should turn our gaze upward once more, and praise the Lord, sure that he will pick us up, wash us, welcome us back into the light of his love and fellowship, and keep us in his service.

Or we could echo the determination of the poet, who vowed always to regather his hope out of the darkest night, to stand up again no matter how often he might fall, and always to put aside tears for laughter –

> *Though I do my best I shall scarce succeed.*
> *But what if I fail of my purpose here?*
> *It is but to keep the nerves at strain.*
> *To dry one's eyes and laugh at a fall,*
> *And, baffled, get up and begin again –*
> *So the chase takes up one's life, that's all.*
> *While, look but once from your furthest bound*
> *At me so deep in the dust and dark,*
> *No sooner the old hope drops to ground*
> *Than a new one, straight to the self-same mark,*
> *I shape me.* (149)

---

149) Robert Browning, *Life in a Love*, lines 10-20.

Yes, in the presence of your own defeat it is hard to praise God; but that is just when praise becomes a sacrifice, well-pleasing to the Lord.

- **_Confidently_** – that is, praising God when it seems that *God* is the one who has failed, when good things you were sure of do not arrive, when promised blessings are withheld, when despite tear-drenched pleas heaven remains like brass, seemingly indifferent, unheeding, impotent.

But you are not alone in your pain. Jesus himself was driven to cry, *"Why have you forsaken me?"* – yet was soon saying, *"Father, into your hands I commend my spirit."* (Mt 27:46; Lu 23:46). Likewise, Jeremiah raised an angry fist at God, crying,

> *Lord, why do you tell such terrible lies! You have failed me when I most needed you. You are like a desert mirage, like a brook that promises abundant water but then turns dry!* (150)

Yet he too stifled his complaint, turned anger into praise, and continued as a powerful prophet of God.

PEACE

"The peace of God will guard you" (Ph 4:7)

A sense of inner peace is one of the marks of successful prayer. Its absence is usually a sign that prayer has not yet prevailed. This peace cannot be willed into existence; it is either present as a gift of God, a sign of the Father's approval, or it is not.

---

150) That passage is a paraphrase drawn from *Jeremiah 4:10; 12:1-2; 14:19; 15:18; 20:7*. If you read those verses carefully, you will realise that they do indeed voice a complaint as awful as the paraphrase suggests.

Yet here is a paradox. We are talking about peace, but Paul introduces a metaphor of war! He says that the peace of God stands *"guard"*, like a sentry. Why do we need such a guard? To protect two vital areas in our prayer life –

• *It protects our MINDS against skeptics*

How mysterious to an unbelieving world is the deep peace displayed by Christians in the midst of disaster. When Lindy Chamberlain's baby Azaria was killed by a dingo, and she was falsely accused of ritually slaughtering the infant, one reason for the charge was the calmness and peace she had displayed despite the child's death. Her accusers could not understand her seeming lack of the shattering grief that an ungodly mother usually suffers when her infant meets an untimely and savage death. The secular authorities had no apprehension of that Christian reaction, and took it as a sign of guilt. (151)

So this peace of ours is **enigmatic to the ungodly**; like colour to the blind, or music to the deaf, or life to the dead! It is also **invincible against the ungodly**; for it enables us to stand firm despite all their doubts, arguments, and vitriolic attacks.

• *It protects our SOULS against remorse*

We are easily troubled by guilt and self-loathing, but the peace of God brings us assurance in Christ.

• *It guards our HEARTS against fears*

No dreads or terrors can finally overwhelm, or even deter, people who are firm in their trust in Christ, and who refuse to be separated from him, or from the grace of the gospel.

---

151) She actually spent three years in prison, but was later released and fully exonerated (in 1988) of all and any charges of murdering her baby. A fourth inquest was held in 2012, and the coroner ruled that a dingo had indeed taken baby Azaria and killed her.

No fear is so great, I suppose, as the fear of death. What panic people fall into if death confronts them! How quickly ordinary people can turn into a howling, desperate mob when death suddenly looms. None of us, I suppose, is indifferent to death's threat. We all strive strenuously to preserve our lives. If we can possibly avoid death, we do. Yet even death's grim threat cannot truly overwhelm the man, the woman, whose heart is guarded by the peace of God in Christ!

I have already said something about the victory over death Christ has wrought for every believer; but let me add this –

DEATH

Harun al Raschid was an immensely wealthy and powerful Caliph in the Muslim world of the 8th century. Because of his association with Scheherazade and the fables of the *Thousand and One Nights*, he is often thought to be fictitious. But he was a real monarch, and reigned from 786-809. During his time, the Arab world enjoyed great cultural and religious prosperity, and much scientific progress was made. Indeed, the caliphate was a place of glittering wealth, sophistication, and learning, while Europe was still largely wallowing in dark ignorance and brutal tyranny.

Many anecdotes are told about Harun's life, including one that just prior to his death, and knowing that he would soon join his fathers in the grave, the caliph found morbid consolation in reading poems about the brevity of life, the fragility of existence, and how even the mightiest empires eventually crumble to dust.

The American poet Henry Wadsworth Longfellow read about Harun and his gloomy death-bed meditations, and he was inspired to write –

> *One day, Haroun Al Raschid read*
> *A book wherein the poet said –*

"Where are the kings, and where the rest

> *Of those who once the world possessed?*
>
> *"They're gone with all their pomp and show,*
> *They're gone the way that thou shalt go.*
>
> *"O thou who choosest for thy share*
> *The world, and what the world calls fair,*
>
> *"Take all that it can give or lend,*
> *But know that death is at the end!"*
>
> *Haroun Al Raschid bowed his head:*
> *Tears fell upon the page he read.* (152)

Both the prince and the poet had to accept that death mocks all human pretensions. From dust we all come. To dust we all return. For the poorest pauper or the most powerful potentate their destiny is the same – the grave and the all-consuming worm. For anyone without the hope of the gospel, how can death be anything except a bleak and dismal prospect? Add to that a fear of the Judgment of God, and death becomes a thing of terror. But not for us who believe, who see death as the Portal of Paradise.

Yet, although in a sense, because of the living Saviour, we Christians can mock death, we should not treat it lightly. The Bible itself calls death *the last enemy* (1 Co 15:26), and implies that it is not yet fully conquered, nor will be until all other of God's enemies have been crushed beneath his feet (vs. 25). Hence even we Christians still die, even we have to bid loved forms farewell, and weep as they vanish into the darkness. Ah! what a mystery is this? I am alive, and I cannot truly visualise or feel what it means to be dead. Life seems so vital, so *alive*, so inevitable. How can I die? Yet I know that die I must. But it is hard to think about, difficult to contemplate one's end, repulsive to look at the coming grave

---

152) Longfellow (1807-1882), *Haroun al Raschid*.

and its awful corruption. We cannot help but hope fervently that the Second Coming of Christ will prevent death from overtaking us!

Among all living creatures on this planet, we alone know that we must die, and have to live under that chill shadow all the days of our lives. Philosophers and poets have railed against it. Scholars and scientists have tried to solve the mystery, asking what is the spark of life, and how can it be so easily snuffed, and they are no wiser now than when they began.

Harun reflected on the pomp and splendour of his palace and reign, of how many he had sent to their own deaths, and how empty and worthless it now was as he lay on his bed, dying. He saw that he would walk naked and alone into the void. None could go with him. None could support him. Alone and naked he came into the world and naked and alone he would go out of it. Where now all his riches? Where now all his power? Where now all his fawning courtiers and his mighty empire? Like all others who have ever lived, whether in squalor or in a palace, he had to depart this life empty handed – sans wealth, sans friends, sans glory. He bowed his head, and wept.

We too would have to weep, except we have the incredible words of scripture, which answers every question in one simple statement –

> *Christ means everything to me in this life, and when I die I'll have even more! (Ph 1:21, GW)*

Hence Paul was able to add –

> *I find it hard to choose between the two. I would like to leave this life and be with Christ. That's by far the better choice. But for your sake it's better that I remain in this life. (vs. 23-24, GW)*

So even when we turn our eye to the grave, and contemplate all that has horrified the sages old and new, we finally laugh, and rejoice in the Lord. Death has lost its sting. The grave has been robbed of its victory (1 Co 15:55; Ho 13:14). Our times are in the Lord's hands (Ps 31:15). If he appoints that we should live, then we shall live. If he appoints that we should die, then we shall die. But alive or dead, we are the Lord's, and we know that those songs of praise filling our hearts today, will still be on our lips throughout the eternal ages.

EIGHTEEN

SELF-SUFFICIENT

> *In whatever circumstances I find myself, I have learned to be self-sufficient"* (Ph 4:11)

Self-sufficient! That is a strange word to find a man using who everywhere else proclaims his dependency upon Christ! But hold on, you say, surely the correct word is *"contented"*? Well, that depends upon how the text is translated. Paul uses a Greek word, *autarkeia*, which occurs also in two other places, where both meanings ("contented" or "self-sufficient") may be properly chosen –

> You have <u>all-sufficiency</u> in Christ (2 Co 9:8).

> Godliness with <u>contentment</u> is great gain (1 Ti 6:6).

So which one is correct for our text? There are two sets of opinions –

AMONG TRANSLATORS

Translators differ little in their rendering of the other two passages, but vary greatly in their renderings of our text. They are uncertain about whether they should give *autarkeia* an <u>*active*</u> sense (as in 2 Co 9:8), or a <u>*passive*</u> sense (as in 1 Ti 6:6). Here are some examples -

PASSIVE RENDERINGS

> *I have learned, in whatever state I am, therewith to be content (KJV, ESV, GW, NRSV, NASB, AmpB, etc.)*

> *I have learned the secret of contentment in every situation (LB, NIV, Phillips, etc.)*

> *I have learned to be satisfied with whatever I have (CEV, GNB, etc.)*

I have learned to manage on whatever money I have (JB).

ACTIVE RENDERINGS

I have learned to find resources in myself, whatever my circumstances ... Whatever situation I find myself in, I have learned to be self-sufficient (NEB, NAB, etc.)

AMONG COMMENTATORS

Commentators also differ in their understanding of the way Paul used *autarkeia* in our text. Here are some examples –

- This commentator gives both ideas, but seems to prefer the passive sense –

  Paul had learned to be content, to be satisfied with what he was and had, to be inwardly independent of the varying outward circumstances. (NIC)

- This commentator prefers the active sense –

  Autarkeia was used to describe the person who ... had become independent of external circumstances, and who discovered within himself resources that were more than adequate for any situation that might arise. (WBC)

- This commentator prefers the passive sense –

  He quotes Socrates' reply to the question, "Who is wealthiest?" and says: "He that is content with the least, for *autarkeia* is nature's wealth." (Lightfoot)

Thus, while some commentators and translators prefer the active sense, the majority of them choose the passive meaning of *autarkeia*. Let us explore the matter –

THE CONTEMPORARY MEANING

In the Greek world of the New Testament *autarkeia* was used in two ways –

- It was a common term in daily conversation, where it implied nothing more than a sufficient quantity of something; hence, a rather passive state of contentment.
- But it was also used by philosophers as a central concept in learned discussions, where it defined a person who was content, not so much with his external circumstances as with his own inner possibilities – an independent person, sufficient within himself, having need of no other, inwardly secure and indestructible, unmoved by circumstances, and possessing all that he needed to achieve his destiny. (153)

In which of those senses did Paul use *autarkeia* in our text? Surely Paul himself defines his meaning in the two following verses, which I think show that he must intend us to read *autarkeia* in its ***active*** sense –

> *I know how to live in poverty or prosperity. No matter what the situation, I've learned the secret of how to live when I'm full or when I'm hungry, when I have too much or when I have too little. I can do everything through Christ who strengthens me. (Ph 4:12-13, GW)*

If that is so (and it is certainly my choice), then the text should be translated something like this -

> *I do not talk about what I lack; for I have learned, no matter what my circumstances are, to be **self-sufficient** (autarkeia) ... I have learned how to surmount every problem. In*

---

153) See The Complete Word Study Dictionary; Vine's Expository Dictionary of New Testament Words; Thayer's Greek Definitions; all in *e-Sword* at www.e-sword.net . Also, *The Letters to the Philippians, Colossians, Thessalonians*, by William Barclay; The Daily Study Bible; The Saint Andrew Press, Edinburgh; 1960; pg. 103-105.

Christ who is the source of my strength, I am more than equal to every challenge that faces me!

A FAITH STATEMENT

So our text is not, as many translations, commentaries, and sermons suggest, a statement of resigned acceptance of unchangeable fate. Rather, it is a powerful **faith-confession**. Outwardly, Paul might lack (or seem to lack) victory, healing, money, liberty (he was in prison in Philippi), and so on, but he was resolved never to allow such circumstances to undermine his unshakable confidence in the promise of God. It is as though he had said: *"I do not use the language of want; rather, I will speak only words that express my inner resources in Christ."*

If that is so, why do so many interpreters give *autarkeia* a passive meaning? Probably because the modern concept of piety often differs from the biblical one. In our culture, inside and outside the church, submissiveness rather than achievement is equated with piety. For example, what image does the word "saint" call into your mind? Almost certainly it will be a picture of a flagellante, a hermit, a person enduring bitter suffering with patient sweetness, portrayed in art as emaciated, ethereal, unworldly, barely human, more in heaven than on earth.

No doubt such persons *may be* saints; but they represent the abnormal, not the normal; not a majority, but a minority. The biblical notion of a saint is more akin to someone who is active, confident, outgoing, bold, vigorously obeying God. Saints in the Bible are very much alive. They are on earth, busy serving both God and his covenant people. Yet that picture (if removed from the Bible) remains offensive to many pious souls. They prefer a modern view of piety. They embrace a false sense of humility. They think of themselves as worthless sinners, weak and helpless. They see goodness in Christ, but never in themselves.

Why is that? I suppose, because they are not integrated with Christ, and they always view him as being "over there", distant and separated from themselves. Often the worship style of their church inculcates that view, always focussed on Christ in his transcendent majesty, far removed from the worshippers. Sometimes, because Jesus is seen as so far elevated above daily life, people replace him with the Virgin, or with one of the Saints, who seem much more human and accessible. All such notions are thoroughly unbiblical. Scripture is emphatic –

> *There is one God, and there is only one mediator between God and man, and that is the man Christ Jesus. He sacrificed himself as a ransom for everyone, which is an unchanging message for all time. (1 Ti 2:5-6)*

One God, one Man, one Mediator, one Message for everyone for all time! Perhaps Paul had a sense that Jesus was going to be etherealised and made distant from the people, so he stressed the humanity of Christ (one "Man"), and that he alone is an all-sufficient Mediator between God and man. With Christ interceding for me, representing me before the Father, why on earth would I ever want or need some saint or even angel to take over the role of mediator? I would want it or need it only if somehow Jesus had been moved far from me, and made inaccessible. Or perhaps, if I felt so undeserving of grace that I needed to call upon the merits of a saint, I might avoid turning to Christ. God forbid! The merits of the Saviour are ten thousand times enough to cover all my sins, and his intercession before the Father on my behalf ten thousand times more effective than that of any other! (He 7:25)

So, by contrast with that spurious piety, *autarkeia* shows the image I should have of myself – a man <u>self-sufficient</u> in Christ. It is the confession of the *"new man"* in Christ. It is the bold affirmation of those who are determined to see themselves only as God sees them, and to say about themselves only what God says.

A CONFIDENCE LEARNED

Twice Paul says that he had *"learned"* this great secret, and he uses two different words that express two different ideas—

HE LEARNED IT BY REVELATION

> *I have **learned**, in whatever condition I am, to be self-sufficient.*

The verb translated *"learned"* is in the aorist tense, which implies knowledge that broke upon him in a moment of time. It stands in contrast with knowledge gained by patient discipline and study. A full Christian life needs both kinds of learning. Obviously, as the next heading stresses, we do learn many things just by living and working day by day. But there is a kind of learning that comes immediately from the hand of God, usually in response to prayer –

> *I continually remember you in my prayers, asking that the God of our Lord Jesus Christ, the Father of glory, may give you **a spirit of wisdom and of revelation** in the knowledge of him, having **the eyes of your hearts enlightened**, that you may know what is the hope to which he has called you ... and the immeasurable greatness of his power that is at work in you. (Ep 1:16-19)*

> *We are constantly asking God to fill you with the knowledge of his will by giving you **every kind of spiritual wisdom and insight**. ... You will then be able to live the kind of lives that prove you belong to the Lord. (Cl 9-10)*

Do you want to please God, to live well, to serve him well, to enjoy his strength and enabling power, and to reach all your potential in Christ? Then you will need to apply yourself to obtaining a *revelation* of the word of God – that is, a deep inner spiritual insight into all that belongs to you in Christ; a profound awakening to the limitless greatness of his power in you, and to all the resources that are yours as a believer.

Sometimes that revelation comes while reading the Bible, sometimes it arises out of a sermon, sometimes it results from prayer – or it may come in some other way. But however it happens, without an inner *revelation* of **who** you are in Christ (the very righteousness of God), and **where** you are in Christ (enthroned in the heavenlies), and **what** you have in Christ (every spiritual blessing, Ep 1:3), and **how** you have all these treasures (by grace alone through faith), you will never be fully alive as a Christian.

HE LEARNED IT BY EXPERIENCE

*I know how to be abased, and I know how to abound ... I have **learned** the secret.*

The Greek word for *"learned"* here has the sense of gaining discipline and maturity from the ongoing experiences of life. Gaining spiritual revelation in the gospel is wonderful and necessary; but by itself, it is inadequate. Revelation-knowledge must be buttressed by practical knowledge; that is, the kind of knowledge that comes only by *experience*. The truth *discovered* (by inner revelation) must be the truth *done* (in daily action). No doctrine is truly possessed until it is practised. Only after Paul had established both forms of "learning" was he then able to say of himself, with simple truth, *"I am able! I am self-sufficient!"*

CHRIST THE SOURCE

As we have seen, *autarkeia* carries the sense of a person who is complete in himself, or herself, and able to cope with every exigency without any outside help. Here indeed is "a man for all seasons". [154] Here truly is a person who remains serene under all pressures. Here are people who see no reason to

---

154) The phrase was coined by Robert Whittinton, 16th century grammarian and school master. It was part of a piece he wrote for schoolboys to translate into Latin, in praise of Sir Thomas More, who was Lord Chancellor of England prior to his execution by order of King Henry VIII in 1535.

fear any day. A complete man. A complete woman. In Christ they are *self-sufficient*.

In the Greek world this concept of self-sufficiency did not have the pejorative sense it has gained in our society. On the contrary, it was a highly admired ideal, yet it remained an aspiration rather than a reality. Indeed, it was an impossible ideal for any fallen man or woman to achieve.

Yet Paul makes the daring claim that he had in fact done so!

Of course, he does not claim to have achieved self-sufficiency unaided. On the contrary, he freely declares that only because Christ is the source of his strength does he have strength for anything.

Why then does he claim "self-sufficiency", rather than "Christ-sufficiency"? Simply because Paul saw himself as so fully united with Christ that distance between them was no longer possible. What was true of Christ, was equally true of him.

People search for completeness in many things, and usually the wrong thing. As Sirach once said –

> Do not give yourself to money, or say, "With this I am self-sufficient." (5:1)

The Greek word is again *autarkeia*, and the verse shows both the true meaning of *autarkeia* (self-sufficiency), and the folly of locating it in the wrong place. For we who call Christ Saviour, no other source is thinkable; but in union with him, and taking him as the source of all strength, we do indeed boldly proclaim ourselves *self-sufficient* in every way.

FOR EVERY BELIEVER

Some will argue that because Paul was an apostle this kind of language may have been appropriate for him, but it cannot be so for us. But consider the following, addressed to ordinary Christians, and to every Christian –

God is able to cause to ABOUND toward you ALL grace, in order that in ALL things, ALWAYS having ALL-sufficiency (autarkeia), you may ABOUND in ALL good works!" (2 Co 9:8).

Was that written to ALL believers? Then it was written to you and to me! Our all-sufficiency may come from God through Christ, but it nonetheless enables us to claim it for ourselves!

CONCLUSION

There is an English word based on *autarkeia*, namely *autarchy*, which describes a nation that has no need to import any goods from outside its borders. All that it requires to sustain national prosperity, health, and happiness, lies within its own territory. That is how God wants us to see ourselves in Christ. So do not allow your language to be conditioned by want, but resolve to possess all the riches that are yours in Christ. We should be able to sing with Paul –

> *Wherever I find myself, and in whatever circumstances, I have learned to be self-sufficient! I can do all that God wants, through Christ who strengthens me! (Ph 4:12-13)*

NINETEEN

STRONG IN CHRIST

*In union with Christ, who continually fills me
with his own strength, I can do anything!*
(Ph 4:13)

Oliver Cromwell, the unfairly maligned Lord Protector of England in the early 17th century, reckoned the above text had saved his life after he had been devastated by the untimely death of his eldest child, the 18-year-old Robert. He spoke about it many years later, in the final year of his own life (1658) –

> At Hampton Court Palace, sitting in his bed chamber, he would have some scriptures read to him; and ... he asked to hear once more St. Paul's words in his epistle to the Philippians: – *"I have learned in whatever state I am to be content. I know both how to be abased and how to abound. ... I can do all things through Christ, which strengtheneth me."* ... When silence followed the reading, he said, "This scripture once saved my life, when my eldest son died, which went as a dagger to my heart – indeed it did." ... And then he said, "Surely He that was Paul's Christ is my Christ too!! With this reflection he seemed to gain the "faith that comes of self-control," and with it, peace. [155]

Strangely, the story has been incorrectly linked with the later death in infancy of his seventh child and fifth son, James,

---

155) Oliver Cromwell – *The Man and His Mission*, by James Allanson Picton; Cassell, Petter, Galpin & Co, London; 1883; pg. 497.

and with an unconnected saying taken from a letter Cromwell wrote to a cousin, Mrs St John, 13th October, 1638. He wrote in part –

> The Lord accept me in His Son, and give me to walk in the light, as He is the light! He it is that enlighteneth our blackness, our darkness; I dare not say He hideth His face from me. He giveth me to see light in His light. One beam in a dark place has much refreshment in it:– blessed be His name for shining upon so dark a heart as mine! ... O the riches of His mercy! Praise Him for me, pray for me that He who hath begun a good work would perfect it in the day of Christ. (156)

Like most of his other letters, those lines show a man whose faith was deeply embedded in the gospel, and whose heart was the Lord's. The poor opinion many have of Cromwell is scarcely warranted. He was by any measure a great man, and in general, a great Christian too, although tainted by the inescapable horrors of a civil war. However, I have quoted the letter, not only because it shows a true Christian spirit, but also because it contains that expression which is often incorrectly linked with our text and with the death of little James – "one beam in a dark place."

So the true story is this — Cromwell's baby son died. Six years later he wrote a letter to a cousin, in which he makes no mention of little James, but does say how the light of Christ is more refreshing to the soul than a ray of light is to a

---

156) Ibid. pg. 74, footnote. Picton cites the letter in the footnote simply to illustrate Cromwell's strong faith, which enabled him to cope well with the death of his infant son. But despite the claims of some commentators, the letter had no actual connection with the child's death, nor with *Philippians 4:13*! I mention it, because the mistaken attribution cost me two or three hours of tiresome research before I was able to sort it out and get it right in the passages above!

lost traveller on a dark night. Many years later, as his life was ending, Cromwell testified that Paul's words in *Philippians 4:13* (our text) had saved his life when he was ravaged by the death of his eldest son.

Somehow, in the minds of several commentators, those facts became conflated into a charming scene, that when his son died Cromwell said that *Philippians 4:13* shone like a radiant beam for him, and saved his life! It is an illustration of how one needs to be cautious about accepting all that one reads! Do I exclude my own books? Regretfully, no. As careful as I try to be, no doubt a sharp eye can find an occasional error! Do tell me if you do!

Still, it remains true that our text can indeed be to any troubled person as refreshing as a beam of light on a dark night, and it may even be a life-saver! Both before and after Cromwell, countless Christians have found in Paul's bold words an encouragement to grasp the strength of Christ, and to prevail over insuperable odds. They discovered that in the strength of Christ they truly were

ABLE TO DO ANYTHING

The expression *"anything"* or *"all things"* or *"everything"* in the text cannot be understood as *"anything I want to do"*, or even, *"anything I am asked to do"*, or even what *other people* think I can do (or not do). It refers rather to anything, and everything, the *Father* has called us to do, or be, or receive. It refers to the fulfilling of *God's* will, to the realisation of his promise, to reaching full maturity in Christ. Here, I want to apply the statement to four aspects of Christian life –

THROUGH THE STRENGTH OF CHRIST, YOU CAN WALK IN PURITY

Why are you saved? Certainly not just so that you might be **pardoned** from sin, but rather that you might **overcome** sin, learning to live in holiness, and to reflect in your attitudes, actions, accomplishments, the beauty of Christ.

In practice, that means putting an end to such things as ungodly sex (whether pre- or post-marital), cheating, lying, greed, violent anger, envy, drug addictions, and anything else that may be seen as a violation of Christian standards. It includes obedience to the law of God as exemplified in the *Ten Commandments* (Ex 20:1-20) [157] and as written by the apostles.

Why do so many Christians fall short of this? Some reasons can be found in –

THE POPULARITY SYNDROME

The common excuse used to justify sin is that everyone else is doing it. Thus one often hears an argument like the following –

> "Since these other people are apparently getting away with their sin, and not suffering any ill consequences; why can't I do the same? These things can't be too wrong; or at least they must be excusable, and so should be tolerated. Surely, if God were really opposed to this behaviour he would punish the wrongdoers?"

There are two answers to those conceits –

- in many cases, divine vengeance *is* exacted, for sin often *is* followed by inevitable consequences (AIDS, herpes, divorce, sickness, etc); and

- the day of Judgment has not yet come; the hour of divine Reckoning has not yet arrived; it is not yet time

---

157) Not that we Christians have any duty to the *Ten Commandments* as they stand. We have been freed from them in Christ (2 Co 3:6-12), and we keep them now only insofar as they have been brought into the New Covenant that God has struck with us in Christ. Thus, the 4th command, to observe the Sabbath, finds its fulfilment in the Sabbath-rest God gives us *every* day of the week in Christ (He 4:1-9).

for God to make up his final accounts – but one day he will!

THE PLEASURE SYNDROME

The peculiar idea has arisen that everyone has a "right" to enjoy the same range of pleasures; so people feel cheated if some popular indulgence, or some delightful experience, is denied them. Yet the Christian's goal should not be *pleasure* but **holiness.** Thus, for us the important thing in, say, marriage, is not to reach some pinnacle of delight, but rather to achieve the goal of genuine faithfulness, true love, and of giving rather than receiving pleasure.

THE PATHETIC SYNDROME

These are people who excuse sin because they reckon they are too weak to overcome it; their sin seems too powerful, their passions are too insistent, the temptations that press on them are too strong to resist. But all such pathetic excuses are demolished by passages like these – *1 Corinthians 10:13; Romans 6:11-14; Colossians 3:1-5.*

Here is where we show the wondrous strength of Christ, that in an impure world we remain a holy people.

THROUGH THE STRENGTH OF CHRIST, YOU CAN WALK IN PROSPERITY

Many people face the future with anxiety, fearful about unemployment, worried about the national economy, in despair because of the diminishing value of their savings/insurances, anxious about the political state of the world, and so on. A lady once showed me a chain-letter, which threatened dire perils if she failed to mail it to several friends within a certain time. She didn't want to send it, but feared the consequences if she did not. I showed her *Romans 8:38-39.* It contains the expression *"neither height nor depth",* which is a reference to astrology, and to those who superstitiously fear the influence of the stars. Then I bade her trust the love of God. She heeded me, burnt the letter, and suffered no ill consequences!

There are two things you can be sure of in Christ —-

YOU WILL NOT BE FOUND BEGGING

See *Psalm 37:23-28*, then believe God's promise, and affirm that even if your affairs look bleak for the present, you will not fall into despair, but will fix your trust in the goodness and unfailing love of the Father. In his own time, and in response to unwavering faith, God will turn things around for you, and all will be well again; your prosperity will be restored. And even if it is not restored in this world, it will certainly be heaped up, pressed down, and running over in the next!

YOU WILL SUCCEED IN DOING THE WILL OF GOD

I mean, that if you keep your hand in the hand of God, you can absolutely trust him to bring you safely to the fulfilment of all that he has ordained for your life. You don't need to know the details, and the pathway may take unexpected twists, but the Lord knows the way; just be content to walk one step at a time with him. Nor should you forget that when Paul wrote to the Philippians he was himself in prison! (1:12-14; but then see vs. 19-20).

So these two certainties ought constantly to be on each believer's lips as a bold faith-confession –

- We should resolve to prosper under the hand of God.
- We should resolve to succeed in all that God has given us to do.

We should maintain that double confidence even if, from time to time, life deals with us differently, and we find ourselves temporarily impoverished, or defeated, or denied the answer to our prayers. Indeed, here is a law that God has built into nature itself – if the tide goes out, no matter how far, it does so only to return again. Every valley must eventually end with a mountain whose peak basks in the sunshine of God; every midnight will assuredly be followed by a glowing dawn; and the trees that look so dead in winter will begin to bud and blossom and flourish again in spring!

THROUGH THE STRENGTH OF CHRIST, YOU CAN WALK IN VICTORY

What kind of person can speak the words of our text with confidence? Surely, only one who is resolved to be a slave of no one or no thing except God. These are people who know that the Christ who is in them is mightier than any bondage. Paul may have been in Caesar's prison, wearing Caesar's chains, but he knew that no iron bars could hold him for a moment longer than the will of God allowed. In the meantime, no one could put a chain on Paul's mind, spirit, or heart; he reckoned himself a free man, and saw himself as prospering in the will of God.

What then should you and I do if some manacle of sin, or of the flesh, hangs upon us, and we can't seem to shake it off?

RESOLVE TO BE FREE

Simply refuse to be a slave to any work born in hell (Ga 5:1).

CHANGE YOUR CONFESSION

The devil may say you are weak; but God says you are strong (Cl 1:11). The devil may cast you down; but the Lord lifts you up (Mic 7:8). The devil says you will never change; but the Spirit carries you from glory to glory (2 Co 3:17-18). The devil puts you in chains; but Jesus breaks every bond (Re 5:5). The devil says you can't; but God says that in Christ you *can*! (Ph 4:13). As I once heard Robert Schuller preach in his Crystal Cathedral, "I am whom God says I am. I can do what God says I can do. I will be what God says I can be. I will have what God says I can have. Because I am a man in Christ!"

THROUGH THE STRENGTH OF CHRIST, YOU CAN WALK IN SECURITY

Sometimes life seems long and the Golden Gates far distant. By contrast, the world, the flesh, the devil, can seem so near, so urgent, so insistent, so strong, and we may feel so alone. But we are not alone! Christ is in you! Christ is with you! In him every believer is united with the Strength of God, the Rock of Ages, the Resurrection and the Life, the King of kings and the Lord of lords!

So let it be settled in your mind and spirit once and for all – you *can* do all that the Lord has called you to do; you can be all that he has called you to be; you can possess all that he has given you to possess; you can go the full distance; you can complete the race; you can win the prize. And in the end, if you are truly a person who is irrevocably united with Christ by faith, it is certain that you will take up your inheritance in the kingdom and be triumphantly enthroned with him in Paradise! (2 Ti 4:6-8).

Index to Texts from "Philippians"

Reference	Page
1:1	17
1:12-14	270
1:14-18	134
1:15; 3:2, 18; 4:2	14
1:19	204
1:19-20	270
1:2, 7; 4:23	115
1:20	32, 41
1:20; 2:19	73
1:21	14, 252
1:23-24	252
1:27; 4:23	25
1:28	204
1:29	54, 220
1:29; 1:6	43
1:29-30; 2:17-18	58
1:3-5	164
1:4, 25	13
1:6	54
1:7,12-14	58
1:8; 4:1	14
2:12	204
2:1-2	164
2:12, 13	197
2:13-15	87, 101
2:15	199
2:16	131
2:19	78, 200
2:2, 29	13
2:25-27	14
2:3-4, 14	199
2:5	197
2:6-7	21
2:6-8	183
2:7	15
2:8	103
2:9	200
2:9-11	192
3:10	52
3:10, 14-18	218
3:12	162
3:12-13	143
3:12-15	141
3:12-16	160
3:13-14	41, 173, 182
3:14	145
3:14-15	139
3:15	147, 162

3:15b 147	4:11-13 218
3:17-19 147	4:12-13 .... 257, 263
3:1a; 4:4 215	*4:13* 265
3:20 .... 152, 204	4:15 164
3:20-21 .... 84, 145, 151, 222	4:18 219
3:21 154	4:19 218
3:7-11 44	*4:21* 168, 225
3:8-10 164	4:4 13
3:8-9 .... 22, 26	4:5 142
3:9 .... 122, 123	4:6 216
4:1 13	4:7 .... 22, 248
4:10, 14-18 14	4:6-7 241
4:11 255	

BIBLIOGRAPHY

Adventure of the Cardboard Box, The; by Sir Arthur Conan Doyle; 1892.

Aesop's Fables, *The Book of Anecdotes*; ed. Clifton Fadiman; Little, Brown and Co; Boston, 1985.

Anabasis of Alexander; tr. M. M. Austin.

Anchor Bible; *Second Corinthians*; by Victor Paul Furnish, *Vol 32A*; Doubleday & Co; 1984.

Anti-Nicene Fathers,The; Vol. 1-10.

Athenian Popular Religion; by Jon D. Mikalson; University of North Carolina Press, London; 1983.

Attributes of Splendour; by Ken Chant; Vision Publishing; Ramona, Califorrnia.

Believer's Bible Commentary; William Macdonald; Thomas Nelson Publishers; 1989.

Bible Background Commentary; Intervarsity Press, Nottingham UK; 1993.

Bible Believer's Commentary, ed. Arthur Farstad; Thomas Nelson Publishers, Nashville; 1995.

Bible Knowledge Commentary, The; by John Walvoord and Roy Zuck; Cook Communications, Colorado Springs, Colorado; 1989.

Life of Samuel Johnson; James Boswell.

Bullfinch's Mythology; by Thomas Bullfinch; The Modern Library

Calvin's Commentaries; John Calvin (1509-1564).

Cambridge Declaration of the Alliance of Confessing Evangelicals, The; (April 20, 1996.

Christian Life; by Ken Chant; Vision Publishing; Ramona, California.

City of God; Augustine; tr. By Henry Bettenson; ed.by David Knowles; Penguin Books; London, 1972.

College Press NIV Commentary, The; Joplin, Missouri; 1996.

Commentary on Ephesians, A; Charles Hodge (1797-1878).

Commentary on the Bible; Adam Clarke (1715-1832).

Commentary On The Old And New Testaments, A; John Trapp (1601-1669).

Commentary on the Old and New Testaments, A; Robert Jamieson, A. R. Fausset, David Brown; 1871.

Complete Word Study Dictionary, The.

Constitutions of the Holy Apostles; *Book ll.*

Daily Study Bible, The; by William Barclay; The Saint Andrew Press, Edinburgh; 1960.

Epigrams 1:12; Decimus Magnus Ausonius (*circa* 310-395).

Description of Greece; *Book X.* tr. by WHS Jones; William Heinemann Ltd., London, 1918.

Ecclesiastical History; Eusebius (A.D. 263-339) Baker Book House; Grand Rapids; 1977.

Emmanuel, The Man Who Is God; *Part One & Part Two*; by Ken Chant; Vision Publishing; Ramona California.

Explanatory Notes on the Whole Bible; John Wesley (1703-1791).

Exposition of the Entire Bible; John Gill (1690-1771).

Expositor's Bible Commentary, The; ed. Frank E. Gaebelein; Zondervan Publishers, Grand Rapids, Michigan.

Expository Commentary; H.A. Ironside (1876-1951).

Fox's Book of Martyrs; *An Account of Archbishop Thomas Cranmer;* 2007 edition, produced by Project Gutenberg.

Gods of the Greeks, The; by C. Kerenyi, tr. by Norman Cameron; Thames and Hudson; 1988.

Greek Myths, The; *Volume One*, by Robert Graves; Penguin Books Ltd; 1975.

Great Sea Battles; *Battle of Lepanto*; by Oliver Warner; Hamlyn Publishing Group Ltd, London U.K., 1972.

Greek Anthology, The; ed. Peter Jay; Penguin Classics, 1986.

Holman New Testament Commentary; ed. Max Anders; B & H Publishing Group, Nashville, Tennessee; 2004.

Illustrated Dictionary of Greek and Roman Mythology, The; by Michael Stapleton; Peter Bedrick Books, New York, 1986.

Interpreter's Bible, The; Abingdon Press, New York; 1952.

IVP New Testament Commentary Series, The; Intervarsity Press, Nottingham, UK.

Jewish New Testament Commentary; David H. Stern; Jewish New Testament Publications, Inc., Clarksville, Maryland; 1982.

Lives and Opinions of Eminent Philosophers; by Diogenes Laërtius, circa 250 B.C.

Man Who Was Thursday, The; by G. K. Chesterton.

Matthew Henry's Commentary; Marshall, Morgan, and Scott, London; 1953.

Matthew Poole's Commentary; 1685

Mountain Movers; by Ken Chant; Vision Publishing, Ramona California.

Nelson's New Illustrated Bible Commentary; Thomas Nelson Inc., New York; 1999.

New Testament Commentary; Baker's Publishing House, Grand Rapids, Michigan; 1987.

Nicene and Post-Nicene Fathers, The; *First & Second Series*, 28 Volumes; all 1979 reprints by Eerdmans Pub. Co, Grand Rapids.

Notes on the Bible; by Albert Barnes (1798-1870).

Notes on the New Testament; Kregel Publications; Grand Rapids, Michigan, 1966.

Oliver Cromwell; The Man and His Mission; by James Allanson Picton; Cassell, Petter, Galpin & Co, London; 1883.

Oxford Classical Dictionary, The; ed. N.G.L. Hammond & H.H. Scullard; Clarendon Press, 1969.

Oxford Dictionary of Saints, The; ed. D. H. Farmer; Oxford University Press, 1987.

Passover Haggadah, The; by Rabbi Shlomo Riskin; Ktav Pub. House, New York; 1983.

People's New Testament Commentary, The; by B. W. Johnson; Word Search Corporation, Nashville, Tennessee; 2010.

People's New Testament, The; by B. W. Johnson; 1891.

Pilgrim's Progress, The; by John Bunyan.

Poor Man's Commentary On The Whole Bible, The; Robert Hawker; 1850.

Preacher's Commentary, The; Word Inc., Nashville, Tennessee; 1992.

Preacher's Outline and Sermon Bible; Word Search Corporation, Nashville, Tennessee; 2010.

Pulpit Commentary, The; ed. Joseph S. Exell, Henry Donald Maurice Spence-Jones; 1881.

Ruba'iyat of Omar Khayyam, The; tr. Peter Avery & John Heath-Stubbs; Penguin Classics, 1983.

Rubaiyat of Omar Khayyam,The; tr. by Edward FitzGerald (1809-1883).

Sands Of Time, The; by Walter Sichel; 1923.

Sirach; Apocrypha; *circa* 185 B.C.

Smaller Classical Dictionary, A; by William Smith; John Murray, 1882.

Strong Reasons; by Ken Chant; Vision Publishing; Ramona, California.

Superstitions of Nature; by J. B. Redmond.

Thayer's Greek Definitions; *e-Sword* at www.e-sword.net .

Vincent's Word Studies; by Marvin R. Vincent; 1886

Expository Dictionary of New Testament Words; by W. E. Vine; Oliphamts, Blundell House, London 1969.

What the Rabbis Said, by Ronald L. Eisenberg; pub. ABC-Clio, Santa Barbara Ca.; 2010.

Wiersbe's Expository Outlines; by Warren W. Wiersbe; Publisher, David C. Cook, Colorado Springs, Colorado.

Word Pictures In The New Testament; by A. T. Robertson; 1933.

World's Greatest Story, The; by Ken Chant; Vision Publishing; Ramona, California.

POEMS, PLAYS and HYMNS

Albert E. Brumley (1905-1977) Wikipedia.

Alfred, Lord Tennyson; Poem; *The Voice and the Peak*.

Algernon Swinburne; Poem; *Tristram of Lyonesse*/Joyous Guard

Art of Expression, The; Poem; *In a Hundred Years;* Grace A. Burt; Heath & Co., Boston, USA, 1905.

Ben King's Verse; Poem; *The Pessimist.*, Benjamin King (1857-94) ed. Nixon Waterman; Pub. The Press Club of Chicago, USA, 1894.

Best of Robert Service, The; Robert Service; Pub. Dodd, Mead & Co., New York, 1953.

Church Hymn Book, The; Hymn; *Rock of Ages Cleft for Me;* AM Toplady; 1872.

Hymns Ancient and Modern; John B. Dykes; 1861.

Hymns and Sacred Poems; Charles Wesley; 1742.

Hymns of Praise; Edward Mote, Pub. circa 1834.

Isaac Watts; Hymn; When I Survey The Wondrous Cross.

John Donne; Poem; *Love's Progress.*

Longfellow (1807-1882),Poem; *Haroun al Raschid.*

Longfellow; Poem; *The Rainy Day*

Lyman W. Allen, Poem *The Coming of His Feet;* 1914.

Matthew Arnold; Poem; *Empedecles on Etna*, by (1822-1888).

Percy Bysshe Shelley; Poem based on Euripedes Play *Cyclops*; (1792-1822).

Robert Browning; Poem; *Apparent Failure.*

Robert Service; Poem; It is Later Than You Think

Septimus Winner (1827-1902); Song: *Listen to the Mocking Bird.*

Thomas Heywood; Play; A Woman Killed With Kindness

Thomas Wade (1805-1875), Poem; *The True Martyr.*

W. H. Auden (1907-1973), Poem; *Under Which Lyre.*

William Shakespeare; Plays; Richard II; McBeth; and Hamlet.

GLOSSARY

Agnostic – One who believes God is unknown or unknowable.

Amalgam – A mixture of different elements.

Aorist – An inflectional form of a verb denoting a simple occurrence of an action.

Aphorism – A concise statement of a principle.

Apollo – A mythical god of ancient Greece

Apotheosis – Elevation to divine status.

Arbitrary – Depending on choice or discretion.

Avocation – a subordinate occupation pursued in addition to one's vocation.

Conundrum – A riddle or puzzle.

Cyclops – A giant in ancient Greek mythology, with only one eye in its forehead.

Disenamel – To remove the enamel, take away the shine or sparkle.

Disparate – Markedly distinct in quality or character.

Echoic – Relating to an echo.

Efficacy – The power to produce an effect.

Endemic – Belonging or native to a particular people or country.

Enigmatic – Puzzling.

Ephemeral – Transient, lasting a very short time.

Eponymous – Relating to the same.

Ethereal – Heavenly, intangible, insubstantial..

Eucharist – Communion

Exigency – A state of affairs that makes urgent demands.

Expunged – Obliterate, blot out.

Fortuna – A mythical goddess of the ancient Romans.

Heavenlies – A term relating to heaven.

Immutable – Not capable of, or susceptible to, change.

Incarnadine – To make red.

Indulgences – Remission sold by Catholic priests for all or part of sins committed.

Infrangible – Not capable of being broken or separated into parts.

Injunction – Order, admonition.

Insipid – Tasteless.

Irrefragably – Impossible to deny or refute.

Judicial – Relating to a judgment.

Jupiter - The mythical supreme god of the ancient Romans.

Manacles - Chains

Mars – The mythical god of war of the ancient Romans.

Metamorphosis – Change of physical form, structure or substance, especially by supernatural means.

Midrash – Exposition, explanation of the underlying significance of a Bible text.

Millennia – Thousands of years.

Minerva – mythical goddess of ancient Rome.

Moribund – Approaching death.

Obnoxious – Repugnant, hateful.

Onomatopoeic – The use of words where the sound suggests the sense, such as "buzz" or "hiss"

Paraclete – Advocate, intercessor, the Holy Spirit.

Paradox – A statement that is seemingly contradictory or opposed to common sense but is perhaps true.

Perennial – Continuous.

Polity – Political organisation.

Precept – A command or principle intended as a general rule of action.

Quiescent – At rest, inactive.

Redolent – Exuding fragrance.

Regicide – Murder of a king.

Renovative – Restoring to life, vigour or activity.

Requitement – To make return for, to repay.

Resile – To withdraw, to recoil.

Salvific – Having the intent or power to save and redeem.

Supernal – Ethereal, heavenly.

Synod – An ecclesiastical governing or advisory body.

The laurel crown – The crown given to ancient Greek athletes who won a race.

Vicissitude – Change, difficulty.

Zeus – The mythical supreme god of the ancient Greeks.

www.ingramcontent.com/pod-product-compliance
Lightning Source LLC
Chambersburg PA
CBHW062011180426
43199CB00034B/2330